Organizational Behaviour in Healthcare

Published in co-operation with the Society for Studies in Organizing Healthcare (SHOC), this series has two strands, the first of which consists of specially selected papers taken from the biennial conferences held by SHOC that present a cohesive and focused insight into issues within the field of organizational behavior in healthcare.

The series also encourages proposals for monographs and edited collections to address the additional and emergent topics in the field of health policy, organization and management. Books within the series aim to advance scholarship on the application of social science theories, methods and concepts to the study of organizing and managing healthcare services and systems.

Providing a new platform for advanced and engaged scholarship, books in the series will advance the academic community by fostering a deep analysis on the challenges for healthcare organizations and management with an explicitly international and comparative focus.

More information about this series at
http://www.palgrave.com/gp/series/14724

Marie-Pascale Pomey
Jean-Louis Denis • Vincent Dumez
Editors

Patient Engagement

How Patient-provider Partnerships Transform Healthcare Organizations

palgrave
macmillan

Editors
Marie-Pascale Pomey
School of Public Health
University of Montreal
Montreal, QC, Canada

Jean-Louis Denis
School of Public Health
University of Montreal
Montreal, QC, Canada

Vincent Dumez
Faculty of Medicine
University of Montreal
Montreal, QC, Canada

ISSN 2662-1045 ISSN 2662-1053 (electronic)
Organizational Behaviour in Healthcare
ISBN 978-3-030-14100-4 ISBN 978-3-030-14101-1 (eBook)
https://doi.org/10.1007/978-3-030-14101-1

This Palgrave Macmillan imprint is published by the registered company Springer Nature Switzerland AG.
The registered company address is: Gewerbestrasse 11, 6330 Cham, Switzerland

Foreword

Our grandchildren will be astonished to learn that there was a time not so long ago when it was widely assumed that patients had no knowledge of anything of relevance to their healthcare. All medical knowledge rested with doctors, it was believed, and patients were expected to listen politely and follow the doctor's instructions unquestioningly. Those assumptions of medical superiority and passive obedience are largely behind us now, thank goodness, though pockets of resistance remain.

Meanwhile those of us who care about these things have set our sights higher, aiming for a world in which the knowledge and capabilities of patients, their families and communities are recognized as essential underpinnings of a high-quality health service. We start from the firm belief that patients are uniquely knowledgeable about their values and preferences, their social circumstances and milieu, and their own experiences of health and illness. This tacit knowledge is hugely valuable. It is, or should be, the basis for selecting appropriate treatments, for effective management of long-term conditions, for preventing ill-health and avoiding recurrence, for designing and redeveloping health services, and for shaping health policy. Those with ambitions to improve population health should value and build on these assets, not ignore them.

Self-care is the most prevalent form of healthcare. As children we learn from our parents how to monitor our health and cope with minor illnesses and we often manage to do this without recourse to professional help. Indeed, we spend far more time looking after ourselves and our families than in direct contact with health professionals. With no formal training or preparation for this role, we may need to seek advice and support, but the popularity of media reports on diseases and treatments is evidence of how keen we are to learn more. Nowadays patients expect to be told about their treatment options and be involved in decisions about their care. They hope clinicians will recognize their strengths and capabilities, not just their vulnerabilities. Treat us like intelligent individuals, not just collections of body parts, is a common refrain. The chapters in this book underscore the importance of this—evidence is mounting that personalizing care and giving patients greater control leads to more effective self-care, improved professional practice and better health outcomes.

While patients' knowledge and activation can make a real difference to health experiences and outcomes at the individual level, it is just as powerful when mobilized collectively. We are fortunate that large numbers of people are motivated to share their healthcare experiences and use this knowledge to press for changes that will benefit all. Many examples of collective action are described in this book, some of which were generated and led by health professionals, while others emerged from patient-led organizations. These groups have played a major role in changing attitudes and behaviour both at the point of care and at more strategic levels. They have campaigned for better, safer, more humane healthcare and for improvements in the quality of care delivery. They are motivated by a conviction that we have a better chance of transforming health systems if we work together, combining all our assets to ensure they are responsive and sustainable into the future.

This ambition unites the authors of this book. Here you will find examples of patient involvement at all levels of healthcare and health policy—in individual care, in healthcare facilities, in regulatory processes, in education and research, and in policy developments. The chapters describe innovative approaches to building and strengthening collaborative partnerships between patients and professionals, showing how these are helping to transform healthcare. Inspiring case studies provide practical illustrations of what it means to work in a different way and the benefits that can ensue. And the editors have ensured that the professional and academic authors practise what they preach, encouraging them to work with patient representatives to craft their chapters.

Each of the accounts reminds us how far we have come in the last 20 years or so. Patient and public involvement is now well embedded in the health policies of leading countries, while others are at an earlier stage but moving in the same direction. Progress is still patchy and fragile in places, but there is clear evidence of cross-fertilization that is helping these ideas to spread. Concepts such as shared decision making, personalized care planning, experts-by-experience, co-production, patient leaders, experience-based co-design and asset-based community development are becoming more widely understood. Anyone still flummoxed by these terms will find clear descriptions here, together with practical examples showing why they are relevant and important.

Yet this is no Panglossian account. The authors are realistic in their assessments of the many challenges still to be faced. How to build health literacy is one such challenge. While starting from the premise that everyone can make an important contribution to their health and that of their families and communities, it is nevertheless obvious that some people need more help than others to play an active role. Lack of basic literacy, numeracy and health knowledge skills has a detrimental effect, so development of these skills is key to building a healthier society. Even people with good basic literacy and numeracy skills may struggle to understand and interpret health information in a way that prompts them to act appropriately to protect and enhance their health. Tackling low levels of health literacy requires well-designed, carefully targeted approaches, but it is also important to address the health information needs of the whole population. Health literacy ought to be accorded higher priority than is the case.

A related problem is how to ensure that improvement efforts take account of the diversity of needs and views, especially those in less advantaged groups. Many patient activists come from relatively privileged sections of society. People from more vulnerable groups may not have the time or inclination to join committees engaged in what may seem like endless meetings to plan improvements. What can be done to ensure that the needs and preferences of these "seldom heard" groups are placed at the forefront of improvement efforts? Several chapters touch on this—readers may find some useful ideas here on how to tackle this conundrum.

Another problem lies in the common tendency to overestimate the efficacy of medical care and underplay its limitations. If we are overly-dependent on technical solutions to health problems, it's largely because various vested interests—professional and commercial organizations, media, politicians and others—have encouraged an over-optimistic view of what can be achieved through medical intervention. The risk is that we waste time and resources searching for medical solutions to problems that are essentially socio-economic in nature. The demand for costly technical solutions masks the need for more humane care for those whose health problems cannot be fixed and distracts attention from tackling the wider determinants of health. Somehow we have to find a way to encourage a more sceptical and balanced approach without undermining trust in valued institutions.

Finally, what are the priority issues we'll be grappling with now and into the future? Digital technologies and genomics are already beginning to make a difference to the way we access medical advice and manage our care. Many of these technologies depend on accessing, linking and sharing personal data. Data-driven systems have the potential to improve individual care and build knowledge on better ways to prevent and treat illness, but there are legitimate concerns about privacy and how to safeguard personal information. How can we encourage innovation that benefits people's health while maintaining trustworthiness? I don't know what the right answer is, but I'm sure the best way to find out is to involve patients right from the outset of these developments.

Oxford, UK Angela Coulter

Contents

Notes on Contributors

Paula Arro is the consumer and carer participation coordinator—Mental Health, Suicide Prevention, Alcohol and other Drugs (MHAOD) Program at Brisbane North Primary Health Network (PHN). Paula has a lived experience with MHAOD both as a consumer and as a carer. She is employed by the PHN to develop the capacity and support opportunities for people with a lived experience to actively participate in MHAOD reforms. Her role was also established to build the capacity of the PHN to embed lived experience engagement in all aspects of the PHN's commissioning process, including working with funded services to ensure this occurs. Along with establishing a regional framework for engagement with people with a lived experience and the Peer Participation in Mental Health Services (PPIMS) network, her role has also been expanded to Chair and provide secretariat support to the National PHN Mental Health Lived Experience Engagement Network (MHLEEN). Paula has been an active leader in the development of the Lived Experience Workforce, both in Queensland and Australia. She has been invited to present at a range of state, national and international conferences and forums in relation to strategies for ensuring authentic and "nothing about us without us" engagement. Paula has worked in the social and community services sector for over 30 years across a range of areas including child protection, disability, young people, volunteerism and community development, and has been an active advocate for ensuring social justice principals are applied to all. She has a BA, a postgraduate diploma in Psychology and Training and Assessment qualifications. Her life and work goal is "to make it better than what it was before".

Cherelle Augustine is the engagement co-ordinator at Collaboration for Leadership in Applied Health Research and Care, National Institute for Health Research, London, UK. She is a founding member of the Exchange Network and a CLAHRC NWL Improvement Leader Fellow. Diagnosed with sickle cell at six weeks old, Cherelle, at 19, co-founded the charitable organization Broken Silence, with the ambition to gain equality for those living with sickle cell. Broken Silence was founded by young people; it champions young people and targets awareness towards young people. After a decade of campaigning, she hopes to challenge health stereotypes and break the stigma associated with sickle cell disease.

Justin Baker is a volunteer at Central and North West London NHS Foundation Trust, London, UK. He experienced multiple hospital admissions related to alcohol misuse, leading to the removal of his spleen and part of his pancreas in April 2011. He was warned that if he carried on drinking, it would lead to early death. He stayed free from alcohol for just over a year, although he continued to use drugs, mainly cannabis and crack cocaine. He started drinking alcohol again in May 2012. At first, it was restricted to weekends, before, inevitably, it became every day. Justin stopped using crack but carried on using cannabis. In January 2014, Justin attended Addaction services. It was there that he met Sean Hendry. Sean proved a massive influence in supporting people on the road to recovery. Justin was "fast-tracked" to receive a three-month residential rehabilitation, but fell seriously ill and yet again ended up in hospital. His parents were both warned to prepare for the worst. He went straight from hospital to rehabilitation where he completed the full stay and left three months later in 2014. Justin has not touched alcohol since then and continues in recovery contributing his experience to improve care for others with addiction.

Richard M Ballerand is a tri-national policy advisor and managing partner of Axolotl Associates. He is a Public Governor at the Chelsea and Westminster Hospital NHS Foundation Trust, London, UK. With a background in the financial and defence sectors, Richard has degrees in economics, strategy and psychology. In earlier years, he served as charity trustee (Royal Institution, Royal United Services Institute, Chelsea Society), London University senator and Zoological Society London vice president. He is a lay member of NHS England's London Clinical Senate, National Institute of Health Research (NIHR's) Health Technology Assessment (HTA) prioritization committee and the National Institute for Health and Care Excellence (NICE) Technology Appraisal Committee. A Central Commissioning Facility (CCF) public reviewer and *British Medical Journal* patient reviewer, he also serves on several NHS trust advisory bodies.

Susan Barber is a social scientist with research interests relating to patient and carer engagement and involvement in and co-production of health service improvement, evaluation and the changing roles of services and infrastructure to support patient self-management. She has extensive experience of working for the NHS and in Third Sector organizations on health-related initiatives including policy development, policy analysis, applied research and piloting of innovations, including how to spread good practice and the application of it in new and often complex settings.

Alexandre Berkesse is a management consultant, social responsibility researcher and PhD candidate in philosophy. He has been contributing to the patient partnership cultural and organizational transformation since 2010 through medical education, as project manager of the reform of the MD programme at the Université de Montréal and now as scientific advisor at the Collaboration and Patient Partnership Unit of the Faculty of Medicine. He led the integration of patient partnerships within major healthcare continuous improvement projects in 19 health institutions across Quebec and he has accompanied five Canadian research networks in the elaboration and the implementation of their patient partnership strategies. He also co-teaches with a patient the first masters degree seminar on patient partnership at the University of Montreal, Canada.

Howard Bluston is an independent investment adviser with expertise in Local Authority Pension Funds. He was a city investment manager for nearly forty years and a local councillor for eight years and still chairs and is a trustee of various charities. Howard is a service user with many interests in improving care and advocating for people with inflammatory bowel disease (IBD). He was integral to a quality improvement project at St Mark's Hospital in London to improve the experience of people using hospital and community services, for example introducing telephone consultation instead of hospital appointments for people in remission with IBD. He is a founder member and Acting Chair of the St Mark's Hospital Patient Panel.

Antoine Boivin, MD, PhD, is a practising family physician and holds the Canada Research Chair on Patient and Public Partnership at CHUM Research Centre, University of Montreal, Montreal, QC, Canada. His research programme focuses on patient and citizen engagement in community health, end-of-life and research. He is the co-director of the Centre of Excellence for Partnership with Patients and the Public and the Strategy for research in partnership with patients and the public for the Quebec SPOR-SUPPORT Unit.

Matthew Bolz-Johnson has worked for EURORDIS since 2014 and has led on advocating for the rare disease community by shaping the development and delivery of European Reference Networks (ERNs). Matt has worked under two Joint Action for Rare Diseases to structure patient involvement in the ERNs and the PACE-ERN consortium that develops technical proposals for the ERN accreditation framework. Prior to joining EURORDIS, Matt worked for 14 years in the National Health Service in England in hospitals and commissioning organizations, specializing in highly specialized healthcare services.

Jeffrey Braithwaite is founding director, Australian Institute of Health Innovation; director, Centre for Healthcare Resilience and Implementation Science; and Professor of Health Systems Research, Faculty of Medicine and Health Sciences, Macquarie University, Australia. His research examines the changing nature of complex health systems, having attracted funding of more than AUD$111 million. These projects have a strong patient focus, with Jeffrey leading multiple research teams that are reconceptualizing how we engage with consumers and communities in healthcare. He has contributed over 450 peer-reviewed publications including 12 edited books and 69 book chapters, and presented at international and national conferences on more than 930 occasions, including over 90 keynote addresses. His research appears in journals such as *JAMA, BMC Medicine, The BMJ, The Lancet, Social Science & Medicine, BMJ Quality & Safety, Cancer Medicine* and *International Journal for Quality in Health Care*. He has received 45 different national and international awards for his teaching and research, including the prestigious Health Services Research Award by Research Australia (2015).

Adrian Brown is the Alcohol Nurse Specialist, Addiction Services, Central and North West London NHS Foundation Trust, London, UK. He has worked in acute hospital trusts as an alcohol nurse specialist since 1994. At St Mary's Paddington, he was part of the clinical research team which developed the Paddington Alcohol Test. This work fed into national studies on alcohol brief interventions. Since 2014, Adrian has worked with the liaison psychiatry teams at Northwick Park and Central Middlesex, in Harrow and Brent. He provides training for medical and nursing staff, and support for managing complex cases—such as substance use and mental health—and he has begun work with head and neck cancer nurses, to help pre-surgery screening. He has been project lead for the alcohol care bundle supported by NIHR CLAHRC NWL and is now back in the deep end of daily alcohol withdrawal management.

Yann Le Cam was one of the founders of EURORDIS-Rare Diseases Europe in 1997. He has been the organization's Chief Executive Officer since 2001. Yann initiated Rare Diseases International (RDI) in 2009. He is an elected member of the RDI Council and Chair of the RDI Advocacy Committee. He is a founding member of the NGO Committee for Rare Diseases (United Nations, New York), in 2014, and a member of its Executive Committee. Since 2016, Yann Le Cam is a member of the Management Board of the European Medicines Agency (EMA). Recent past positions include: Chair of the Therapies Scientific Committee of the International Rare Diseases Research Consortium (IRDiRC), 2013–2017; Vice Chairman of the EU Committee of Experts on Rare Diseases (EUCERD), 2011–2013; and a member of the Commission Expert Group on Rare Diseases, 2014–2017. He was also one of the first patient representatives appointed to the Committee for Orphan

Medicinal Products (COMP) at the EMA, where he served for nine years and was its elected vice chair for six years. Yann holds an MBA from HEC Paris. He has three daughters, the eldest of whom is living with cystic fibrosis.

Carolyn Canfield works as a citizen-patient across Canada and internationally to expand opportunities for patients, carers and communities to partner with healthcare professionals. Arising from personal tragedy in 2008, Carolyn's full-time volunteering has earned her recognition as Canada's first Patient Safety Champion in 2014, appointment at the University of British Columbia as Adjunct Professor in the Department of Family Practice, and Admissions Subcommittee member with the Faculty of Medicine. She co-founded "Patients In Education" in British Columbia and the Patient Advisors Network to develop capacity and leadership in citizen-patients across Canada.

Kate Churruca is a health services researcher with a PhD in psychology. Her research focuses on the application of complexity science to healthcare and using social-psychological theories to understand organizational culture. She has been involved in projects understanding how mental health professionals collaborate during uncertainty, and men's perceptions of risk in prostate cancer and its impact on their treatment decisions. As part of her doctoral thesis, she previously conducted research with women about their experiences of eating disorders, including their interactions with the healthcare system and the potential benefits of taking a recovery-oriented approach. She uses both quantitative and qualitative research methods, including surveys, social network analysis, observations and interview. Kate is involved in the supervision of multiple Master of Research and PhD students, and is a postdoctoral research fellow at the Centre for Healthcare Resilience and Implementation Science, Australian Institute of Health Innovation at Macquarie University, Australia.

Nathalie Clavel is a PhD candidate in public health, University of Montreal, School of Public Health and Research Centre of the University of Montreal Health Centre (CHUM). She is also a member of the research chair in Technology Assessment, and Advanced Practices at the CHUM, which centres on Citizen and Patient Engagement in Organizational and Health System Transformation. Since 2013, she has been working on several research projects on patient and family partnership in direct care, continuous quality improvement and patient safety. Her thesis focuses on the practices of healthcare organizations' managers in the implementation of patient and family engagement in quality improvement and direct care.

Angela Coulter is a UK-based health policy analyst and researcher, with special interests in patient and public involvement. A social scientist by training, she has higher degrees in health services research from the University of London and the University of Oxford. Now freelance and still involved in research, her previous roles include Chief Executive of Picker Institute Europe, Director of Policy and Development at the King's Fund, Director of the Health Services Research Unit at the University of Oxford and Director of Global Initiatives at the Informed Medical Decisions Foundation. She is an associate member of the Health Services Research Unit at the University of Oxford, honorary professor at the University of Southern Denmark, an honorary fellow of the Royal College of General Practitioners and a non-executive director of the National Institute for Health and Care Excellence (NICE). Angela has published more than 350 research papers, articles and reports and several books including *The Autonomous Patient*, *The European Patient of the Future* (winner of the 2004 Baxter Award), *The Global Challenge of Healthcare Rationing*, *Hospital Referrals*, *Engaging Patients in Healthcare* and *Understanding and Using Health Experiences*. She was the founding editor of *Health Expectations*, an international peer-reviewed journal on patient and public involvement in healthcare and health policy. She has won awards for her work from the Donabedian Foundation of Barcelona in 2012 and the International Shared Decision Making Conference in 2013.

Pam Dardess is Vice President of Strategic Initiatives and Operations at the Institute for Patient- and Family-Centered Care (IPFCC), where her work focuses on providing training and technical assistance to healthcare organizations, helping them improve quality, safety and experiences of care through the development of meaningful partnerships with patients and families. Pam is also responsible for strategic planning to develop evidence for and scale up the practice of patient- and family-centred care nationally and internationally. Prior to joining IPFCC, Pam was a principal researcher at the American Institutes for Research (AIR), where her work concentrated on stakeholder engagement; patient-centred measurement; and the development, evaluation, and dissemination of strategies and interventions to promote patient and family engagement (PFE). While at AIR, Pam served as Director for the virtual Center for Patient and Consumer Engagement (AIR CPCE). Pam's contributions to the field include the development of resources to guide the conceptualization and implementation of PFE across multiple settings and stakeholders, including an influential framework for patient and family engagement that has been cited in over 600 articles since its 2013 publication. Pam has also led work to develop and evaluate practical training and educational resources to promote PFE, including the Agency for Healthcare Research and Quality-funded Guide to Patient and Family Engagement in Hospital Quality and Safety—strategies from which have been implemented in hospitals across the United States and internationally. Pam holds an MPH in Maternal and Child Health from the University of North Carolina—Chapel Hill, Gillings School of Global Public Health.

Eskil Degsell is a Patient or Informal caregiver Representative at Malignant Brain Tumour Pathway at Karolinska University Hospital, Department of Quality and Safety at Karolinska University Hospital. He is associated with Regional Cancer Centre Stockholm-Gotland and co-investigator at Co-care research programme at LIME, MMC, AIM at Karolinska Institute.

Jean-Louis Denis is Full Professor of Health Policy and Management at the School of Public Health, Université de Montréal, researcher at the CHUM Research Center (CRCHUM) and holds the Canada research chair (tier I) on health system design and adaptation. He is a visiting professor at the Department of Management, King's College London. His research looks at healthcare reforms and health system transformation, roles of the medical profession in health systems, professional leadership and clinical governance. In recognition of his academic contribution to the field of health policy and management, he was nominated member of the Academy of Social Sciences of the Royal Society of Canada in 2002 and fellow of the Canadian Academy of Health Sciences in 2009. Recent papers have been published in *Journal of Health Politics, Policy and Law*, *Organization Science*, *Academy of Management Annals*, *Milbank Quarterly*, *Administration and Society*, *Implementation Science* and *Journal of Public Administration Research and Theory*. Since 2016, he has been co-editor of the new Palgrave series of research monographs on healthcare organizing.

Annie Descoteaux learned self-management and the importance of taking part in medical decisions after kidney disease severely hit her newborn daughter. She has developed a specific interest in the skills and expertise that patients develop in living with chronic disease on a daily basis. Annie has a background in Economics and holds a masters degree in Education. She has been a project manager at the Collaborative Partnership and Patient Partnership (DCPP) at the Faculty of Medicine of the University of Montréal since 2014 and a strategic advisor at the Center of Excellence on Patient and Public Partnership. Among other things, she is responsible for managing the expertise of the patient partners who collaborate with the DCPP and the CEPPP.

Vincent Dumez holds a finance degree and a master in science of management from Montreal's international business school, Hautes Études Commerciales (HEC). Up until 2010, Vincent was an associate in one of Montreal's most influential consulting firms, where he acted as a senior strategic consultant. Suffering from severe chronic diseases for more than three decades, Vincent has been actively involved in the development of the "patient partner" concept at Montreal University. This involvement has come forward through the completion of his masters dissertation on the patient—doctor relationship, his contribution to the training of patients, his work on boards of healthcare organizations and his involvement as a speaker at international healthcare conferences. Since 2010, Vincent has founded and developed the patient partnership programme at the Faculty of Medicine. He now co-leads the Centre of Excellence on Partnership with Patients and the Public with Philippe Karazivan, Antoine Boivin and Marie-Pascale Pomey.

Laura Fischer is an interdisciplinary practitioner who blends scientific methods with creative approaches, and vice versa. She is an artist, activist, researcher, speaker, and author. Her work is woven around mental health, with a particular focus on trauma and the socio-cultural context of violence and abuse. She aims to challenge societal constructs, raise awareness, create space for the voices of trauma survivors and others with lived experience of mental health issues, reframe survivors or 'patients' as active leaders of change, and improve our approach to treatment. Her main projects seeks to understand the neuropsychological and neurophysiological underpinnings of trauma and develop a creative body-based practice for the expression and processing of traumatic memories. As a CLAHRC Improvement Leader Fellow (National Institute for Health Research, London, UK), she draws from this work to improve current trauma treatments. Laura is also a consultant on several other projects in healthcare and in research, and she has spoken, exhibited and published internationally.

Luigi Flora is a patient researcher with a PhD in education sciences. A specialist in experiential knowledge resulting from living with disease and the interactions disease generates with health systems and their actors, he is co-author of a summary note published on the subject in 2010 as part of a book coordinated with Emmanuelle Jouet on how the patients' share of knowledge in the health system. In 2012, as part of his doctoral thesis, he identified the "patient" competency framework that has since been developed with the Patient Partnership Collaboration Department to stabilize the concepts and methodologies of the Montreal model. Collaborating since 2011 with Vincent Dumez, he is the main pedagogical advisor in Quebec to organizations proving the Montreal model, co-initiator of the first university of patients in a medical school in France from 2009 and co-designer of the UniverCité du Soin in Nice, a module of which was awarded by the French Ministry of Higher Education and Research as a pedagogical innovation for lifelong learning in 2018. Luigi is also an associate researcher at the EXPERICE laboratory of the

University of Paris 8/Paris Lumière in the area of lifelong learning and in the RETINES interdisciplinary team at the University of Côte d'Azur, Nice, France.

Catherine French is a health service manager and researcher specializing in developing organizational approaches and capacity building to translate research into practice. Catherine's research background is in social science and her interests include knowledge mobilization, academic healthcare organizations, and qualitative methodology. Catherine was awarded an NIHR Doctoral Research Fellowship to undertake her PhD at UCL (researching boundary spanning processes in Academic Health Science Centres) which she completed in November 2016. Catherine has over 15 years' experience in operational management, programme management, capacity building, and service improvement roles in the NHS across acute care, commissioning, and mental health, including from 2104 to 2018 as Collaborative Learning and Partnerships lead at CLAHRC North West London where she was responsible for developing a quality–improvement, capacity-building programme informed by an action research approach. Since 2018 Catherine has been leading a programme of transformation to integrate clinical care and research across a large university and NHS partnership.

Véronique Ghadi is a sociologist and conducted many research projects on patient engagement and user representation for ten years before joining the Haute Autorité de Santé (HAS) to develop the issue of well-treatment, patient rights and the participation of representatives of users in the certification of health facilities. She is director of the social and medico-social sector of the HAS, aiming to produce recommendations for social and medico-social structures and build the evaluation system of these same structures. Today, Véronique participates in the work of the network "combine our knowledge" to promote the commitment of care-receivers and to accompany the training of professionals.

Ron Grant became passionate about prevention following a massive heart attack and triple bypass and was inspired to give something back. In 2003, he pioneered Lifestyle road shows going into the community to do blood pressure, BMI and blood cholesterol testing. He is an accredited tutor on the LDX cholesterol testing machine. He became an active member of the Upbeat Heart Prevention & Patient Support Group and is now the CEO, a role for which he was awarded the British Heart Foundation's "Heart Hero" award in 2013. In 2012, he was awarded the West Middlesex University Hospital "Inspirational Volunteers" award as well as Barclay's "Let's Do It" award for community spirit. Ron is a Royal Institute of Public Health-accredited health trainer and regularly holds screening events for cardiovascular diseases and diabetes in the community. Ron has contributed to a number of NIHR CLAHRC NWL projects including the Hounslow Community Atrial Fibrillation Screening project, and is an NIHR CLAHRC NWL Improvement Leader Fellow.

Stuart Green is a public health research fellow at Imperial College London within the NIHR CLAHRC, London, UK. Over the last ten years he has been involved in a range of quality improvement projects in Northwest London, working in a range of specialities from acute medicine, to primary care and mental health. Since 2013, he has been undertaking a part-time Doctor of Public Health course at the London School of Hygiene and Tropical Medicine (LSHTM), which explores the implementation of evidence-based guidelines in clinical services. His research particularly focuses on participatory approaches to engaging clinicians and patients in improving "knowledge to practice". Stuart has published over 25 peer-reviewed papers and contributes to teaching and supervision on the Masters of Public Health at Imperial College London, University of Liverpool and LSHTM.

Maurice Hoffman is a member of the NIHR CLAHRC Northwest London Early Years steering group. Maurice joined the NIHR Imperial Biomedical Research Centre because he believes that through his knowledge of the research process, together with an understanding of service improvement, he can provide valuable input into patient safety research projects. He is a lay member of National Research Ethics Service (NRES) Brent Research Ethics Committee, reviews grant applications for the NIHR and provides input as a patient member of the Imperial Biomedical Research Centre. He is also an independent member of the Statinwise Trial Steering Committee. Within the NHS, he is a lay member of the

Advisory Committee for Clinical Excellence Awards, London North West, patient representative on the NHS Digital E-Referrals Advisory Board and lay partner of Imperial College Healthcare NHS Trust.

Fran Husson is a Patient Adviser at Collaboration for Leadership in Applied Health Research and Care, National Institute for Health Research, London, UK. She has extensive experience in championing the views of patients with a background in journalism. She was instrumental in the development of "My Medication Passport" and has contributed to many initiatives across Imperial College, Imperial College NHS Trust and in the UK. Fran is particularly interested in the ownership, accuracy and access to electronic patient records, digital innovations, health literacy and antimicrobial resistance.

Mathieu Jackson has Haemophilia B moderate. He is vice president of the Canadian Hemophilia Society (CHS). He is also Patient Coordinator of the School of Partnership at the Centre of Excellence on Partnership with Patients and the Public (CEPPP) at the University of Montreal Health Centre (CR-CHUM), where he participates in training patients, caregivers, health professionals and researchers to work together in a partnership healthcare model. Mathieu completed the 2017–2018 International AFFIRM fellowship.

Pascal Jarno is a medical doctor. On the one hand, he coordinates the evaluation unit in the public health department of CHU de Rennes, Rennes, France, and on the other hand, the regional structure supporting quality of care and patient safety in Brittany (CAPPS Bretagne). In this context, since the beginning of the 2000s, he has been developing activities to promote the involvement of patients in the health system at the local, regional and national levels, whether in the field of care, evaluation of practices or organizations, teaching or research.

Sandra Jayacodi is a qualified solicitor, with a law degree from the University of Westminster and a postgraduate diploma from Bournemouth University. Since 2014 Sandra has been involved in the SHINE project at Central and North West London NHS Foundation Trust, which aims to improve the physical health of people with severe mental illness. Sandra has been involved in the co-design of a patient-held physical healthcare record, with healthcare professionals. She has also contributed to developing the project aims and deliverables, process mapping and designing health education materials. She was awarded a CLAHRC Improvement Leader Fellowship (National Institute for Health Research, London, UK) in 2016. Throughout the project Sandra has demonstrated growing confidence as a presenter and speaker, and has presented amongst others, at the Trust board, to senior members of the NIHR, and taught on the Masters in Public Health at Imperial College London.

Philippe Karazivan is a family physician, a teacher and a researcher at Université de Montréal. He is the co-director of the Office of Collaboration and Patient Partnership (DCPP) within the Faculty of Medicine and co-director of the Center of Excellence on Partnership with Patients and the Public (CEPPP). The DCPP is co-directed by a patient (Vincent Dumez) and a physician (Philippe Karazivan), and it brings patients and their specific expertise into the medical school where they can mobilize their competencies to help students develop theirs. They coordinate over 250 patients who are not only active members of their own healthcare team but are also involved in research and provide valuable training to health science students. Philippe is also the lead author of the first academic paper on the Patient as Partner approach in 2015.

Tony Lawson is Chair of the Consumers Health Forum (CHF) of Australia, elected to this role in 2015 and recently re-elected for a further three years. In total, Tony has been a board director of Consumers Health Forum for 12 years. He is a member of the Minister of Health Advisory Committee on Private Health Insurance and a former member of the Australian Commission on Safety and Quality in Health Care's Australian Atlas of Healthcare Variation Advisory Group. Tony is also a board director of the Australian Council on HealthCare Standards. He has over 30 years' expertise in public policy-making, including the introduction of mutual recognition and the establishment of national health and social programmes (e.g. Home and Community Care Program (HACC)). As a CEO, he has been responsible for multi-million dollar budgets and significant employees and undertaken large-scale organizational change programmes. As Director of Tony Lawson Consulting, he has undertaken many health policy projects in conjunction with the University of South Australia, Baker IDI Heart and Diabetes Research Institute and SA Medical and Health Research Institute, particularly in Aboriginal and Torres Strait Islander health. Through this work Tony is the co-author of a number of published articles, including "Essential service standards for equitable national cardiovascular care for Aboriginal and Torres Strait Islander people" (Brown et al., 2015) and "A strategy for translating evidence into policy and practice to close the gap - developing essential service standards for Aboriginal and Torres Strait Islander cardiovascular care" (Brown et al., 2015).

Paule Lebel is a specialist in public health and preventive medicine and medical advisor at the Regional Director of Public Health in Montreal (CIUSSS du Centre-Sud-de-l'Ile-de-Montréal). She is a Clinical Associate Professor in the Department of Family Medicine and Emergency Medicine (DMFMU) at the Université de Montréal. Since 2018, she has been working to develop and evaluate collaborative practices in partnership with patients, families and communities in the clinical aspects, continuous quality improvement and management of care and services, and partnerships with the public health population.

Hélyette Lelievre is a representative of users at the CHU de Rennes, Rennes, France, and the Beaulieu Centre of medicine and pedagogy in RENNES, administrator of the Maison Associative de la Santé, and member of the "users-professionals" group of the Coordination Group for Improving Practices of Health Professionals in Brittany (CAPPS Bretagne).

Dionne Matthew is the Improvement Science Manager for CLAHRC (National Institute for Health Research, London, UK) NWL's Breathlessness Theme and currently supports improvements in heart failure and community atrial fibrillation screening services across Northwest London. Her research interests include improvement science, exercise and health promotion, and the use of technology to enhance patient care. Dionne obtained her PhD in cardiovascular health in

November 2013. Her PhD research assessed the benefits of using a mobile application for heart rate variability in patients with heart failure. She holds an MSc in sport and exercise science, along with a Bachelor of Arts in psychology and kinesiology.

Rachel Matthews supports research improvement teams to involve patients and carers across a range of clinical and community settings. She is a registered nurse with clinical experience in cardiorespiratory care. She completed postgraduate studies in Health Education and Health Promotion at King's College London and completed the King's Fund Top Manager Programme in 2014 and NIHR Leaders Programme in 2018. Rachel is a member of the Health Foundation Q Community.

Maureen Maurer is a principal researcher at the American Institutes for Research, where she directs health services research projects focused on patient and family engagement and communicating about medical evidence. In her work to conceptualize and implement patient and family engagement practices, Maureen was a co-author on a framework and roadmap for patient and family engagement, led an environmental scan that catalogued engagement interventions, and has developed strategies and materials to engage patient and families in hospital quality and safety. She is the project director for the Patient-Centred Outcomes Research Translation Center that creates plain language summaries of research findings for the public within a legislatively mandated 90-day time frame. Recently, she led the development and evaluation of an intervention that helped pregnant women more effectively use maternity care quality information. As an experienced qualitative researcher, Maureen designed large-scale qualitative research studies exploring the influence of patient and other stakeholder engagement in research and getting public input into policy decisions about the use of medical evidence in healthcare. Maureen is passionate about working to achieve health equity. She is a founding member of a non-profit, community-based organization that hosts racial equity workshops, trains community organizers and works to confront overt and subtle forms of racism. Previously, Maureen was a Peace Corp volunteer in Mali, West Africa. She holds an MPH in health behaviour and health education from the University of North Carolina at Chapel Hill.

Rowan Myron is a healthcare researcher with expertise in psychology and improvement science. Rowan graduated from Dundee University in 1995 with an MA (Hons) first class in Psychology. She then studied for her PhD at Goldsmiths. Rowan first lectured on Psychology at the University of Hull, and then Rowan moved out of academia to the Mental Health Foundation where she became Associate Head of Research and began working with service user researchers on a range of projects. In 2009, Rowan joined the NIHR CLAHRC NWL programme. Rowans holds a joint role between the University of West London, as Associate Professor for Healthcare Management, and the role of Education Lead at CLAHRC NWL. Rowan leads doctoral, masters and fellowship programmes which aim to build capacity in improvement methodologies. She works with multi-disciplinary front-line clinical staff and patients to improve services and implement evidence-based change.

John Øvretveit is Director of Research and Professor of Health Care Improvement Implementation and Evaluation at the Medical Management Centre, The Karolinska Institute, Stockholm, Sweden. His research examines implementation of management and organization improvements, and clinical care coordination for safety and lower costs. His recent work concerns adaptive implementation and evaluation and combining quality improvement and implementation science. Projects include co-care, integration and coordination of services. His work is based on the belief that organization and management can bring out the best and worst in people, and that the right organization design is critical for effective healthcare. A theme underlying his work is how practical research can contribute both to better care for patients and to "healthy work organization". John has pioneered action evaluation methods for giving rapid feedback for service providers and policy-makers to improve their services, and for assessing the role of context on implementation. He was awarded the 2014 Avedis Donabedian international quality award for his work on quality economics and has served for 12 years as a board member of the USA joint commission international, and is chair of their healthcare quality and safety standards committee. He is founder and chair of the Quality Improvement Research Network; a board member of the Global Implementation Initiative and chair of the Global Implementation Society. He chairs the

UK selection panel for the future programme of applied collaborative research University—NHS partnerships.

Marie-Pascale Pomey is a public health doctor with a doctorate in public health from the University of Montreal and the University of Paris 7. She is a professor in the Department of Health Management, Evaluation and Policy at the University of Montreal's School of Public Health, and a researcher at the Research Center of the University of Montreal Health Centre (CR-CHUM) in the Crossroads of Innovation and Health Assessment. She is also a medical advisor to the National Institute of Excellence in Health and Social Services (INESSS) where she is responsible for the CoMPAS programme to improve front-line services and integrate patients and families in all the work of INESSS. She has led the International Masters Degree, the DESS diploma and the Quality Management and Care Security programme, QUÉOPS-I, from 2005 to date. Since March 2017, she has led a research chair in Technology Assessment and Advanced Practices at the CHUM. Her research programme, which centres on Citizen and Patient Engagement in Organisational and Health System Transformation, focuses on three areas: (1) the contribution of new e- and m-health technologies that change the relationship between health professionals and patients and the organization of care; (2) assessing the contribution of patient and relative involvement at all levels of the health system (policy, organizational and care); and (3) the development of tools to measure the commitment of patients and their families at all levels of the health system. She is also co-director of the Centre of Excellence on Partnership with Patients and the Public.

Frances Rapport is Professor of Health Implementation Science and Academic Lead MD Research at the Australian Institute of Health Innovation (AIHI), Macquarie University, Australia. She retains an Honorary Professorship in Qualitative Health Research at Swansea University, UK and has visiting professorships in Norway, Bournemouth and Riyadh (previously Harvard and Texas). Before moving to Australia (2015), Frances was Professor of Qualitative Health Research and Founding Director of both the Qualitative Research Unit (QUARU) and the Qualitative Enquiry Supporting Trials (QUEST) Unit at Swansea University's Medical School. Her research examines the use of Implementation Science in patient-reported determinants of health and wellbeing, hearing loss and listening effort, cancer genomics and melanoma. She has contributed over 340 publications and refereed outputs in journals such as *The Lancet GH, The BMJ*, *Clinical Epidemiology*, and *Epilepsy and Behaviour* and is the top-cited Qualitative Health Researcher worldwide. She has won prizes for publication excellence, a Julian Tudor Hart Senior Research Fellowship (2003–2006) and an award from the American Anthropology Association for use of poetic ethnographic methods with survivor testimonials.

Ghislaine Rouly was born with two rare genetic diseases and has been a patient partner for most of her life. She has been accompanying patients in their end of life care for the last 45 years and she is on two committees on Aid in Dying. She is also the primary patient in two research studies at CHUM Research Centre, University of Montreal, Montreal, QC, Canada: "Caregiving Community" and "Compassionate Community". For the last six years she has taught along with clinicians and medical students, especially on the topic of clinical ethics.

Tara Bristol Rouse is a Patient and Family Engagement (PFE) Project Consultant for the American Hospital Association (AHA), where she supports PFE strategy and provides technical assistance and subject matter expertise to the Health Research & Educational Trust (HRET) Hospital Improvement Innovation Network (HIIN). Inspired by her experience as a patient and caregiver, Tara's work focuses on building partnerships among healthcare professionals, patients and families. In 2006, she became a founding member of the Newborn Critical Care Center Family Advisory Board at NC Children's Hospital, developing Family Faculty and Family Support Programs and integrating family partners into localized quality improvement efforts. Tara is the former director of Patient and Family Partnerships for the Perinatal Quality Collaborative of North Carolina (PQCNC) and has served as a patient family partner on numerous hospital, state and national committees over the past 13 years, including faculty appointments with the Institute for

Healthcare Improvement (IHI), the National Institute for Children's Healthcare Quality (NICHQ) and Patient and Family Centered Care Partners (PFCCpartners). In 2014, Tara's work was recognized by the Caregiver Action Network (CAN) as one of the Nation's top 25 for Best Practices in Patient and Family Engagement. Tara holds an MA in Psychology from Wake Forest University.

Jean Straus is an Improvement Leader Fellow at Collaboration for Leadership in Applied Health Research and Care, National Institute for Health Research, London, UK, who draws on her professional background in education and her experience of sudden hearing loss to raise awareness of this condition in the healthcare system. She promotes the use of visual formats and innovative participatory approaches, for example hackathons, to generate better insight and empathy between people and to foster improvement.

Jenny Trite is a service improvement project assistant at Central and North West London NHS Foundation Trust. Through this role she has been involved with the SHINE project since 2014, which aims to improve the physical health of people with serious mental illness. She has contributed to the co-design of an innovative patient-held physical health record that supports people with mental illness to take control of their physical health and supported ward nurses to use Plan-Do-Study-Act cycles to share learning. She has presented at national conferences and co-authored a number of reports and academic papers. Prior to this, Jenny worked with the NIHR Mental Health Research Network North London Hub.

Jo Watson is the inaugural deputy chair of the Pharmaceutical Benefits Advisory Committee (PBAC), and has been a consumer nominee on the Committee since 2013. She is the deputy chair of the Consumers Health Forum, the peak national health consumer organization in Australia, and the chair of the Consumer Consultative Committee within the Office of Health Technology Assessment in the Department of Health. Jo has been a community representative and patient advocate for the Australian HIV response since the early 1990s, including as the executive director of the

National Association of People living with HIV Australia (NAPWHA) from 1998 to 2014. She was also the consumer nominee on the Pharmaceutical Benefits Pricing Authority (PBPA) from 2002 to 2012. Her areas of interest include developing model pathways for patient engagement in health technology assessment, public health issues in population health, and capacity building for patient representatives at the national level. She has contributed to health policy reform and analysis in the areas of communicable diseases, the National Medicines Policy and Pharmaceutical Benefits Scheme (PBS) programmes over the past two decades, including contributions to peer-reviewed publications and both national and international research projects.

Leanne Wells is the chief executive officer of the Consumers Health Forum of Australia. She is a health advocate and service executive with over 30 years' experience in health and social policy, programme and service development. Leanne has held executive positions within federal government and in national and state non-government organizations. Leanne is Board Director of Coordinare South East New South Wales' Primary Health Network, the Ozhelp Foundation, PainAustralia and the Australian Pharmacy Council. She is the independent chair of Coordinare's Community Advisory Committee. She has several advisory appointments including the Commonwealth's Primary Health Care Advisory Group, NSW Agency for Clinical Innovation's International Expert Advisory Committee and the Primary Care Committee of the Australian Commission on Safety and Quality in Health Care's Board. Leanne has tertiary qualifications in communications and business. She is a member of both the Australian Institute of Company Directors and the Australian Institute of Management.

Abbreviations

AFD	Association Française des diabétiques (French Association of Diabetics)
AFDET	Association Française de développement et d'éducation thérapeutique (French Association for Therapeutic Education and Development)
AFM	Association française de Myopathie (French Association of Myopathy)
AIDES	Association française de lutte contre le VIH et les hépatites virales
APF	Association Française des Familles (French Association for Families)
ARS	Agence Régionale de Santé (Regional Health Agency)
CAB	Community advisory board
CAPPS	Coordination pour l'Amélioration des Pratiques des Professionnels de Santé en Bretagne (Coordination for Improving Practices of Health Professionals in Brittany)
CISS	Collectif Inter-associatif Sur la Santé (Inter-Associative Health Collective)
CDU	Commission des usagers (Users Commission)
CEG RD	Commission Expert Group on Rare Diseases
CHF	Consumers Health Forum
CLIAS	Comité de Lutte contre les Infections Associées aux Soins (Committee Against Healthcare-Associated Infections)

CLAHRC	Collaborations for Leadership in Applied Health Research and Care
CLAN	Comité de Liaison Alimentation Nutrition (Food-Nutrition Liaison Committee)
CLUD	Comité de Lutte contre la Douleur (Pain Control Committee)
CHMP	Committee for Human Medicinal Products
CRO	Contract research organizations
UD	University Diploma
TEP	Therapeutic Education for Patients
EATG	European Aids Treatment Group
EC	European Commission
EU	European Union
EUCERD	European Union Committee of Experts on Rare Diseases
EURORDIS	European Organisation for Rare Diseases
EMA	European Medicines Agency
ePAGS	European Patient Advisory Groups
ERN	European Reference Networks
ESMO	European Society for Medical Oncology
FDA	Food and Drug Administration
FAS	France Asso Santé
FORAP	Fédération des Organismes Régionaux et territoriaux pour l'Amélioration des Pratiques et organisations en santé (Federation of Regional and Territorial Bodies for the Improvement of Health Practices and Organisations)
GEM	Groupes d'entraide mutuelle (Mutual Help Groups)
GRAM	Groupe de Réflexion Avec les Associations de Malades (Patient Group Think Tank)
HAS	Haute Autorité de Santé (French National Authority for Health)
HTA	Health Technology Assessment
HPHT	Hôpital, Patients, Santé, Territoire (Hospital, Patients, Health, Territory)
INSERM	Institut National de la Santé et de la Recherche Médicale (National Institute of Health and Medical Research)
IPDS	Institut Pour la Démocratie en Santé (Institute for Health Democracy)
JARC	Joint Action Rare Cancers
JARD	Joint Action on Rare Diseases

MDT	Multidisciplinary team
NIH	National Institutes of Health
NIHR	National Institute of Health Research
NGO	Non-Governmental Organizations
OMP	Orphan Medicinal Products
PACE	The Parliamentary Assembly of the Council of Europe
PACE-ERN	Partnership for the Assessment of Clinical Excellence in European Reference Networks
PACTEM	Patients ACTeurs de l'Enseignement en Médecine (Patient ACTors in Medicine Education)
PNSP	Programme National Sécurité Patient - National Programme for Patient Safety
PREPS	Programme de Recherche en Evaluation et Performance en Santé (Research Program on Health Evaluation and Performance)
RD	Research and Development
TRT-5	Traitement Recherche Thérapeutique 5 (Therapeutic Research and Treatment 5)
UNAPEI	Union Nationale des Associations de parents et amis de personnes déficientes intellectuelles (National Association of Groups representing Parents and Friends of People with Intellectual Disabilities Groups)
UN	United Nations
WHO	World Health Organization

List of Figures

List of Tables

1

Introduction

Marie-Pascale Pomey, Nathalie Clavel, and Jean-Louis Denis

Built between 1940 and 1970, healthcare systems were structured around acute and highly specialized care provided by health facilities. Now, and over the last 30 years, needs have considerably changed due to the significantly increased prevalence of chronic diseases, which are currently the leading cause of morbidity and mortality in western countries (Jeon et al. 2009; Beaglehole et al. 2011). Patients, in the vast majority of cases, do not recover from their illness and face a number of chronic health conditions that coexist with acute events. This trend is expected to worsen in the coming years in all countries of the Organisation for Economic Co-operation and Development (OECD 2013). In addition, these epidemiological mutations result from changes in lifestyles, enhanced self-management

M.-P. Pomey (✉) • N. Clavel • J.-L. Denis
School of Public Health, University of Montreal, Montreal, QC, Canada
e-mail: marie-pascale.pomey@umontreal.ca; nathalie.clavel@umontreal.ca; jean-louis.denis@umontreal.ca

M.-P. Pomey et al. (eds.), *Patient Engagement*, Organizational Behaviour in Healthcare,
https://doi.org/10.1007/978-3-030-14101-1_1

from patients, increased accessibility to healthcare professionals and better continuity and coordination of care and services (Tinetti et al. 2012; Grady and Gough 2014; Clarke et al. 2017). In order to respond to emerging challenges, one promising avenue for improving population health and the quality of health care and services is to engage patients and their relatives at all levels of the health system (clinical, organizational and strategic) (Coulter 2012; Carman et al. 2013; Richards et al. 2013; Pomey et al. 2015b).

Moreover, in 2013, a few months apart from each other, an editorial in *Health Affairs* mentioned "The Blockbuster Drug' Of Patient Engagement" (Dentzer 2013), followed by one in the *BMJ* which stated: "Let the patient revolution begin" (Richards et al. 2013). In the first editorial, reference was made to the fact that "the emerging evidence is that patients who are actively involved in their health and health care achieve better health outcomes, and have lower health costs, than those who aren't" (Dentzer 2013). It was also written that patient participation could better meet the triple AIM goal proposed by the Institute of Health Improvement in the USA (IHI 2018), offering to simultaneously improve "the patient experience of care (including quality and satisfaction); [...] the health of populations; and [...] the per capita cost of health care" as well as "the conditions for the healthcare workforce to find joy and meaning in their work and in doing so, improving the experience of providing care" (Sikka et al. 2015). As for the *BMJ*, the editorial highlighted: "[The] corruption in the mission of healthcare requires urgent correction. How better to do this than to enlist the help of those whom the system is supposed to serve—patients? Far more than clinicians, patients understand the realities of their condition, the impact of disease and its treatment on their lives, and how services could be better designed to help them" (Richards et al. 2013).

In fact, over the last 20 years, paternalistic approaches of health care have gradually given way to patient-oriented approaches that consider differences, values and experiences of patients (Stewart et al. 2000; Karazivan et al. 2015). Around the world, healthcare organizations, institutions and universities are doubling their efforts to involve patients and make their participation increasingly active, using different modalities of engagement (Karazivan et al. 2015) and various means of motivation (Flora 2008). However, recent initiatives such as shared decision-making

(Legare and Witteman 2013) and some therapeutic education approaches (Foster et al. 2007) maintain the healthcare provider's monopoly when determining the course and outcomes of treatment. The prospect of care partnership goes one step further by considering the patient as a full member of the care team, whose status is based on care expertise (Karazivan et al. 2015). This generates a rupture and emancipates the "oriented approach". The Patient Partnership perspective suggests considering the patient as a healthcare provider, an equally valued member, a partner of the healthcare team (Karazivan et al. 2015; Pomey et al. 2015b). When dealing with a chronic disease, which generally cannot be completely cured, the patient's life experience with the disease becomes a rich source of knowledge, essential for decision-making (Pomey et al. 2015b). Current models, such as that of Carman et al., suggest a continuum of patient engagement going from informing the patient to partnering with the patient (Carman et al. 2013). Patient engagement can also happen at different levels of healthcare systems: policy or systemic level, healthcare organizations level and clinical care/direct patient care level (Carman et al. 2013; Pomey et al. 2015b).

In this context, the objectives of this monograph are to show if the ongoing patient revolution (Richards et al. 2013), based on patient knowledge, has contributed to transform, improve or innovate the ways in which care services are organized and delivered as well as the culture and practices of healthcare professionals regarding direct patient care.

The monograph will illustrate—through six countries, a Canadian province, and a European patient organization (EURORDIS)—the different forms of patient engagement that have been put in place at different levels of the healthcare system by way of specific experiences. In particular, it will highlight the methods behind successful patient engagement and ways to measure the impact of patient engagement in various dimensions and at different levels of the healthcare system, including challenges that are encountered and possible improvements to strengthen patient engagement in the future. Each chapter takes into consideration the patients' point of view and was co-signed by patients. The first country explored is one of Canada province, **Québec**, where, in 2010, thanks to the leadership of a patient hired by a medical school, the "Montréal Model" enabled the simultaneous roll out of patient engagement within the health system, training, research and communities. This movement spread across the entire Canadian province through the care and services partnership feature in the Health Minister's 2015–2020 Strategic Plan (Ministry of Health and Social Services 2017) and the promulgation of a reference framework for the partnership approach between users, their families and health and social services stakeholders (Ministry of Health and Social Services 2018).

The **French** model illustrates the strategic role of patient organizations, which, starting in 2015, began organizing to counterbalance different players in the health system. On the one hand, what started as the defence of patients' rights and therapeutic education for patients, patient involvement is now progressively evolving towards a greater share of partnerships between professionals and patients and, on the other hand, a greater share of voice for patients and patient partners. Over the years, this model has gradually imposed the presence of users at almost all levels of the system: national, regional and within health facilities. However, the movement still suffers from weak clinical presence and low visibility among the general public. In the **United Kingdom**, there is a substantial history of user movements in both service and research. Moreover, initially, the movement of patient engagement is mainly structured around research and this chapter presents how, in Northwest London, the Collaboration for Applied Health Research and Care (CLAHRC NWL), started in 2009, helped structure patient engagement in care. Thanks to this programme, which focused on patients' needs and benefits to patient outcomes, it was possible to involve patients, carers and service users at all levels of governance. Through testimonials, it is possible to realize the impact that these initiatives have had on people and on how to design the health system. In **Sweden**, the notions of co-care and self-care have a long history and substantial investment in the context of health promotion and wellness programmes. However, in the context of care, the widening gaps between needs and supply as well as between cost and affordability need to engage and support citizens, patients and health workers to carry out more effective self-care and co-care. This chapter presents examples on how the health system translates self-care and co-care concepts and calls for experimentation pilot schemes to investigate how self-care and co-care are best developed, especially for the most disadvantaged members of the Swedish community. Under the impetus of many organizations such as the Patient-Centered Outcomes Research Institute (PCORI), The Robert Wood Johnson Foundation, The Gordon and Betty Moore Foundation, The Institute of Health Improvement and The California HealthCare Foundation, progress was made in shifting the paradigm from patients solely as care recipients to patients as partners in care in the **United States.** To illustrate this situation, several initiatives show the shift towards a vision of shared leadership, with patients as active partners in their care and in the organizations and structures that provide care to improve the quality of care and population health. As for **Australia**, multiple promising initiatives at different levels of health system governance have been conducted considering the patients as partners. Whether in the context of institutional accreditation, healthcare organization governance, research or on how professionals should work at the point of care delivery, patient and consumer involvement is recognized for its added value in health care. This chapter highlights the importance of a more systematic approach to patient involvement, in terms of: (1) health and medical policy initiatives, (2) drug developments, (3) technology adoption, (4) service delivery; (5) medical and health services research design and (6) outcome translation.

The final example is **EURORDIS**, an organization created in 1997 to gather all rare diseases at the European level to gain visibility and create a new social space, and emerge as a civil society community able to voice the needs and expectations of 30 million people living with such conditions in 48 European countries. The objectives of the organization are achieved by connecting patients, families and patient groups, as well as by bringing together all stakeholders and mobilizing the rare disease community. In those years, thanks to a very structured strategy, based on the (1) Patient Empowerment; (2) Patient Engagement; (3) Patient Advocacy tryptic, EURORDIS established partnerships through Consortiums (e.g. Accreditation Canada for PACE-ERN, DOLON for Rare Impact on gene & cell therapy, university biomedical or social research academic teams for projects funded by Innovative Medicines Initiatives or EC Horizon 2020 Research programme); projects (e.g. ministries, hospitals, universities, research institutions); conferences (e.g. EMA, FDA, NIH, ministries and national institutions, learned societies) and membership (e.g. Round Table of Companies for pharmaceutical companies, CRO, specialists in rare disease therapy development). Recognizing the importance of networking to be able to capitalize on the strengths of everyone in Europe and the world, EURORDIS promotes the European Reference Networks (ERN) working model that currently connect 900 experts and 300 hospitals across the 26 Member States in the EU with the aim of having representation of all EU Member States in all 24 ERNs.

Thus, after reading these examples, the reader will be able to judge whether patient engagement is in fact a transitory mode or a true breakthrough innovation, a revolution, which induces new practices and leads to a cultural change in the health system and among stakeholders to better meet the evolving needs of the population.

Indeed, patients' ability to be agents of change also depends on other factors such as the place of technology, as well as the culture and value system in which engagement is embedded. Technology seems to be a powerful contributor which enables patients to be increasingly involved not only in their health but also in the way the health system is organized. As the health system gradually engages with big data (i.e. patient data), becoming a powerful change agent occurs in a context where legislation, legal and ethical frameworks can either promote or inhibit change capabilities. In a sea of internet giants (GAFAM) and social networks which too often bypass existing regulatory paths, patient organizations must learn how to swim to defend patient rights and interests. What about disadvantaged people or people unaware of current issues? Despite the above, at least one thing remains for sure: the recognition of patients' experiential knowledge, combined with access to precise physiological and behavioural data, will lead to a new way of conceiving medicine, health professions, the organization of our health systems and probably their funding mechanisms.

In the discussion and conclusion, the role of new technologies (e-and m-technologies) and artificial intelligence will be discussed, and their potential impact on the way healthcare systems will change in a near future. In the next few years, the world will probably witness a new revolution that places patient engagement at the centre of the digital realm and the integration of artificial intelligence.

References

Beaglehole, R., R. Bonita, R. Horton, C. Adams, G. Alleyne, P. Asaria, V. Baugh, H. Bekedam, N. Billo, S. Casswell, M. Cecchini, R. Colagiuri, S. Colagiuri, T. Collins, S. Ebrahim, M. Engelgau, G. Galea, T. Gaziano, R. Geneau, A. Haines, J. Hospedales, P. Jha, A. Keeling, S. Leeder, P. Lincoln, M. McKee, J. Mackay, R. Magnusson, R. Moodie, M. Mwatsama, S. Nishtar, B. Norrving, D. Patterson, P. Piot, J. Ralston, M. Rani, K.S. Reddy, F. Sassi, N. Sheron, D. Stuckler, I. Suh, J. Torode, C. Varghese, and J. Watt. 2011. Priority actions for the non-communicable disease crisis. *Lancet* 377 (9775): 1438–1144.

Carman, K.L., P. Dardess, M. Maurer, S. Sofaer, K. Adams, C. Bechtel, and J. Sweeney. 2013. Patient and family engagement: A framework for understanding the elements and developing interventions and policies. *Health Affairs* 32 (2): 223–231.

Clarke, J.L., S. Bourn, A. Skoufalos, E.H. Beck, and D.J. Castillo. 2017. An innovative approach to health care delivery for patients with chronic conditions. *Population Health Management* 20 (1): 23–30.

Coulter, A. 2012. Patient engagement—What works? *The Journal of Ambulatory Care Management* 35 (2): 80–89.

Dentzer, S. 2013. Rx for the 'blockbuster drug' of patient engagement. *Health Affairs (Millwood)* 32 (2): 202.

Flora, L. 2008. *Le patient formateur auprès des étudiants en médecine: De l'approche historique, la contextualisation, à l'intervention socioéducative.* Master Université Vincennes Saint-Denis Paris 8.

Foster, G., S.J. Taylor, S.E. Eldridge, J. Ramsay, and C.J. Griffiths. 2007. Self-management education programmes by lay leaders for people with chronic conditions. *Cochrane Database of Systematic Reviews* 4: Cd005108.

Grady, P.A., and L.L. Gough. 2014. Self-management: A comprehensive approach to management of chronic conditions. *American Journal of Public Health* 104 (8): e25–e31.

IHI. 2018. The IHI Triple Aim. http://www.ihi.org/Engage/Initiatives/TripleAim/Pages/default.aspx. Accessed 23 Nov 2018.

Jeon, Y.H., B. Essue, S. Jan, R. Wells, and J.A. Whitworth. 2009. Economic hardship associated with managing chronic illness: A qualitative inquiry. *BMC Health Services Research* 9: 182.

Karazivan, P., V. Dumez, L. Flora, M.-P. Pomey, C. Del Grande, D.P. Ghadiri, N. Fernandez, E. Jouet, O. Las Vergnas, and P. Lebel. 2015. The patient-as-partner approach in health care: A conceptual framework for a necessary transition. *Academic Medicine* 90 (4): 437–441.

Legare, F., and H.O. Witteman. 2013. Shared decision making: Examining key elements and barriers to adoption into routine clinical practice. *Health Affairs (Millwood)* 32 (2): 276–284.

Ministère de la santé et des services sociaux. 2017. *Plan stratégique du ministère de la Santé et des Services sociaux 2015–2020*. Québec MSSS, Gouvernement du Québec 33p.

———. 2018. *Cadre de référence relatif aux comités des usagers et aux comités de résidents*. Québec MSSS, Gouvernement du Québec.

OECD. 2013. *Panorama de la santé 2013. Les indicateurs de l'OCDE*. Paris: OECD.

Pomey, M., L. Flora, P. Karazivan, V. Dumez, P. Lebel, M. Vanier, B. Debarges, N. Clavel, and E. Jouet. 2015b. The Montreal model: The challenges of a partnership relationship between patients and healthcare professionals. *Santé Publique* 27 (1 Suppl): S41–S50.

Richards, T., V.M. Montori, F. Godlee, P. Lapsley, and D. Paul. 2013. Let the patient revolution begin. *BMJ* 346: f2614.

Sikka, R., J.M. Morath, and L. Leape. 2015. The quadruple aim: Care, health, cost and meaning in work. *BMJ Quality & Safety* 24 (10): 608–610.

Stewart, M., J.B. Brown, A. Donner, I.R. McWhinney, J. Oates, W.W. Weston, and J. Jordan. 2000. The impact of patient-centered care on outcomes. *The Journal of Family Practice* 49 (9): 796–804.

Tinetti, M.E., T.R. Fried, and C.M. Boyd. 2012. Designing health care for the most common chronic condition—Multimorbidity. *JAMA* 307 (23): 2493–2494.

2

From Medical Paternalism to Care Partnerships: A Logical Evolution Over Several Decades

Vincent Dumez and Marie-Pascale Pomey

Introduction

This book focuses on the Partnership in Care and Services movement that has progressively emerged in health care since the beginning of the 2000s. In order to fully understand the foundations of this movement, this following will explore the way that this movement has come about within healthcare delivery systems, in health education, research, and community work, in comparison and continuity with a variety of medical models that have evolved over time and led to this significant paradigm shift.

Over the past 50 years, healthcare systems throughout the developed countries have gone through three major models of care that, still today, coexist together: medical paternalism, Patient and Family Centered Care

V. Dumez
Faculty of Medicine, University of Montreal, Montreal, QC, Canada
e-mail: vincent.dumez@umontreal.ca

M.-P. Pomey (✉)
School of Public Health, University of Montreal, Montreal, QC, Canada
e-mail: marie-pascale.pomey@umontreal.ca

M.-P. Pomey et al. (eds.), *Patient Engagement*, Organizational Behaviour in Healthcare,
https://doi.org/10.1007/978-3-030-14101-1_2

(PFCC), and now Partnership in Care (PC). In order to fully understand the current emergence of the Partnership in Care model, it is important to analyse how it came to be and how it emerged in continuity yet at times in parallel with the other two, while also drawing from other less institutionalized but equally important approaches, such as Shared Decision-Making (SDM), Self-Management (SM), or Therapeutic Patient Education (TPE).

The Rise and Limitations of Medical Paternalism

The 1950s, 60s, and 70s were marked by unprecedented scientific discoveries at all levels of the medical field (drugs, surgery, biology, etc.). The steady increase of human life expectancy led us to imagine the possibility of disease-free existence fueled by expert medicine that would ultimately have the answers to address all ailments and lead to optimal health. The model of care that emerged from this period has often been described as 'medical paternalism', a one-way relationship between a sick person and an expert physician who manages the sick person and solves their health condition through science (Emanuel and Emanuel 1992).

In such a paternalistic approach, the doctor's role is central: he makes the diagnosis and decides on the care plan, he manages the care team according to the objectives that he alone sets, and he delivers this care towards the patient. His communication style is mostly unilateral, not only with his patients but also with the other health professionals in his team. It is he who is at the centre of care and this is legitimized by the expertise he has acquired through many years of training. This phenomenon has been abundantly described in the scientific literature, in particular by Michel Foucault (France) (Foucault 1988).

Medical paternalism reached its peak in the early 1980s, at which time several societal phenomena led to the questioning of this model, thus serving as the basis for the emergence of Patient and Family Centered Care. Criticism of the former model observed that a paternalistic style of practicing medicine did not provide an adequate framework by which to manage the psychosocial dimensions of individual health. Rather, interventions remained primarily focused on the physiological and biological aspects of health, which were disproportionately fueled by contemporary scientific discoveries of the time. As early as the 1970s, this model began to show its limitations in addressing the growing challenges of caring for certain populations of patients including addictive/illegal drug users and mental health patients which demanded more humane approaches to care and, in the 1980s, in responding to the systemic repercussions of the AIDS crisis (Jouet et al. 2010). In addition, the steady rise of chronic diseases has further undermined medical paternalism by challenging its very foundations, highlighting the inadequacy of prioritizing the curing of disease over caring for a sick person, as well as the primacy of acute curative care over primary care, rehabilitation and integrated long-term care.

The realities of patients made it evident that a philosophical and structural transformation of healthcare systems was needed. However, shifting an entire system away from a model focusing on acute and curative care towards a model focusing on chronic disease management and prevention is structurally very complex and therefore difficult to achieve in terms of human capacity, organizational and governance practices.

The Rise and Limitations of Patient and Family Centered Care

As medical paternalism reached its limits, PFCC emerged as a model that would offer a more holistic and less unilateral approach to care, giving more legitimacy and independence to other health professionals. This would allow for professionals to gain a better understanding of the ever-increasing needs of patients and enable them to offer better responses for patients who, for the most part, would have to deal with the long-term consequences of chronic diseases.

PFCC is defined as an alternative to the medical paternalism of previous decades as it is anchored in the basic premise that the person must take precedence over the disease, and that a more interdisciplinary approach to care is needed to ensure effective care. In contrast to the dominant biomedical model which underlies medical paternalism, it is a movement that is rooted in the social sciences and humanities. Its leadership is mainly provided by non-medical health disciplines, in particular nursing. PFCC is inspired by the functional principles of the Nurse Caring Model (Held 2006), which advocates for better coordination of care and services, as well as the decompartmentalization of physician interventions, in favour of a more multidisciplinary and humane approach (Rathert et al. 2013).

It is for these specific reasons that PFCC has historically focused on the functioning and interactions between health professionals to meet patients' needs, rather than on the relationship or partnership with patients themselves. As an example, PFCC will recognize the complexity and holistic nature of the patient's situation, the need to consider the specificities of their context in the treatment plan, as well as the importance of involving their family, friends, or informal caregivers, without explicitly addressing the patients' role and action in the care process (Karazivan et al. 2015). Thus, PFCC is more interested in the effectiveness and quality of services provided to patients, access to and coordination of care, and interprofessional collaboration, rather than the concrete engagement of patients in their own care, their specific role as actors in their care, and the means by which they can fulfil this role.

For this reason, we can see that although PFCC is certainly moving away from a logic of 'care *to* patients' towards one of 'care *for* patients', it has not yet entered the realm of 'care *with* patients', which can give the impression that medical paternalism has been replaced by a form of 'maternalism'. It should also be noted that maternalism is at the root of Nurse Caring Model, even though the model has done everything possible to emancipate itself from it (Held 2006).

The Three Founding Approaches of Partnership in Care

Since the 1990s, at least three other important approaches based on engaging patients and a 'care with the patients' logic has developed in parallel to PFCC, each without formally integrating with one other nor with PFCC in particular. These approaches include Shared Decision-Making (SDM), Self-Management (SM), and its European counterpart, Therapeutic Patient Education (TPE). SDM opens the door to a negotiated decision-making process based on the evidence of available scientific data and consequently raises the fundamental question of power-sharing with the patient in the decision-making process, particularly with regards to treatment options (Legare et al. 2012).

Knowing that it is difficult to develop individual capacity for action without having a minimum of decision-making power helps us to understand the importance of the SDM approach in strengthening patients' involvement in their own care. In recent decades, the tools to support SDM have multiplied, yet its application by clinical teams is not yet widespread, likely due to the same type of professional resistance as the one currently experienced by the Partnership in Care approach that will be described later.

SM (Lorig and Holman 2003) in the USA, or TPE (De La Tribonnière 2016) in Europe, brought to the forefront the recognition of patients' knowledge and the development of their own care skills as part of the care process. The appreciation of these two major points lay the epistemological foundations of the 'care *with* patients' logic by recognizing that patients develop knowledge and skills through their experiences of living with disease and through using health services; that this knowledge holds value for themselves; that it can be strengthened with the help of more experienced peers and/or health professionals and can be mobilized to improve health status.

Therefore, as much as the SDM approach raises the fundamental question of shared decision-making as a lever for patient action, SM or TPE raises the question of strengthening patients' knowledge and developing their skills to increase autonomy and one's ability to manage oneself. In a world where medical knowledge is being democratized through the Internet, social networks, and electronic clinical records that are shared and accessible by patients, this question of patient knowledge and skills is even more important and opens a new era of advocacy for the voice of the patient (Flora 2013).

A Convergence of These Approaches at the Heart of the Partnership in Care Concept

As for SDM, it must be noted that the SM and TPE models have also had difficulties in taking root in healthcare systems, perhaps because they carry notions of the Partnership in Care approach. Partnership in Care requires a culture change that is largely underestimated because it touches the very foundations of an expert health system that has defined itself for decades without its users, patients, and citizens. The PC approach was developed in 2010 at the Faculty of Medicine of the University of Montreal through a co-leadership of patients and health professionals, and is based on the three approaches above, which each carried elements of 'doing *with* patients' in contrast to the PFCC, which was more focused on 'doing *for* patients'.

From these beginnings, the foundation for Partnership in Care—now called 'The Montreal Model' (Pomey et al. 2015)—was laid as follows:

1. The need to empower patients to make free and informed decisions;
2. The need to recognize the value of the experiential knowledge that one develops through the experience of living with disease and illness (including the use of different health services);
3. The need to develop one's skills throughout the care process;
4. The need to consider oneself as an actor of care and therefore as full members of one's care team;
5. The need to focus the objective of the care process on achieving one's overall life project rather than on a single curative objective that may be reductive and often unrealistic in the context of chronic disease.

Partnership in Care is therefore very clearly in line with the logic of SDM, SM, and TPE, but also relies on a number of elements that are historically at the heart of PFCC, namely: (1) the shift from a disease-oriented perspective to a human-oriented perspective which includes the different dimensions of the patient's life; (2) the importance of medical access and the emergence of the notion of an interdisciplinary care team; and (3) considering the notion of a life project, as borrowed from rehabilitation care and strongly inspired by the Nurse Caring Model and PFCC. It is also worth mentioning that Partnership in Care was influenced by the feminist model embedded in nursing sciences, which has allowed for the notions of autonomy and emancipation to emerge (Gaucher and Racine 2015). These notions are central to the concept of the *patient as partner*, in that it accentuates the self-learning aspect of the care process, as well as the patient's will to get back to a normal life despite one's illness.

Looking back at how these approaches to care evolved over the past few decades, one can trace the complementary steps that have finally led us today to a more humanistic, integrative, and certainly more complete vision around the notion of partnership in care and services. Indeed, this implies that we recognize the importance of all care partners, especially patients and their relatives who are no longer only 'at the centre' but rather, fully integrated into the dynamics of care. This ensures that the patient, along with their family, friends, or informal caregivers, are provided the best conditions and supported to achieve one's life project. Partnership in Care pushes us to bring our focus on the quality of the *care relationship*, on the overall care experience, on the patient's necessary involvement in his or her own care, and on the ability to provide interdisciplinary support, aligned with the patient's course of life and life goals. It also implies deliberately moving away from a hospital-centric and 'per episode' perspective of care towards a longitudinal and 'lifelong trajectory' perspective. Finally, it involves embracing the reality of chronic diseases, with the patient as the expert of living with illness and the professional playing a supportive role in the patient's health trajectory.

The Partnership in Care movement is therefore based on recognizing the role and knowledge of patients and their families. In this context, healthcare systems around the world are gradually changing to work increasingly in *partnership* with patients in order to better support them throughout their lives and promote an optimal care experience, the ultimate objective being to enable them to acquire a state of health in accordance with their own life project.

References

De La Tribonnière, X. 2016. *Pratiquer l'éducation thérapeutique: L'équipe et les patients*. Paris: Elsevier Masson.

Emanuel, E.J., and L.L. Emanuel. 1992. Four models of the physician-patient relationship. *JAMA* 267 (16): 2221–2226.

Flora, L. 2013. Savoirs expérientiels des malades, pratiques collaboratives avec les professionnels de santé: état des lieux. *Education permanente* 195: 59–72.

Foucault, M. 1988. Technologies of the self. In *Technologies of the self: A seminar with Michel Foucault*, ed. L. Martin, H. Gutman, P. Hutton, and M. Foucault. Amherst, MA: University of Massachusetts Press.
Gaucher, N., and E. Racine. 2015. Théories de la justice. Dans Payot A. et Janvier A. Éthique clinique: un guide pour aborder la pratique. *Montréal; Éditions du CHU Sainte-Justine* 75–86.
Held, V. 2006. *The ethics of care: Personal, political, and global*. Oxford: Oxford University Press.
Jouet, E., L. Flora, and O. Las Vergnas. 2010. Construction et reconnaissance des savoirs expérientiels des patients. *Pratiques de Formation-Analyses* 58–59: 13–94.
Karazivan, P., V. Dumez, L. Flora, M.-P. Pomey, C. Del Grande, D.P. Ghadiri, N. Fernandez, E. Jouet, O. Las Vergnas, and P. Lebel. 2015. The patient-as-partner approach in health care: A conceptual framework for a necessary transition. *Academic Medicine* 90 (4): 437–441.
Legare, F., S. Turcotte, D. Stacey, S. Ratte, J. Kryworuchko, and I.D. Graham. 2012. Patients' perceptions of sharing in decisions: A systematic review of interventions to enhance shared decision making in routine clinical practice. *Patient* 5 (1): 1–19.
Lorig, K.R., and H. Holman. 2003. Self-management education: History, definition, outcomes, and mechanisms. *Annals of Behavioral Medicine* 26 (1): 1–7.
Pomey, M.P., L. Flora, P. Karazivan, V. Dumez, P. Lebel, M.-C. Vanier, B. Desbarges, N. Clavel, and E. Jouet. 2015. Le "Montreal Model": enjeux du partenariat relationnel entre patients et professionnels de la santé. *Santé Publique* HS (S1): 41–50.
Rathert, C., M.D. Wyrwich, and S.A. Boren. 2013. Patient-centered care and outcomes: A systematic review of the literature. *Medical Care Research and Review* 70 (4): 351–379.

3

The Participation of Patients and Relatives in Quebec's Health System: The Montréal Model

Marie-Pascale Pomey, Vincent Dumez, Antoine Boivin, Ghislaine Rouly, Paule Lebel, Alexandre Berkesse, Annie Descoteaux, Mathieu Jackson, Philippe Karazivan, and Nathalie Clavel

M.-P. Pomey (✉) • N. Clavel
School of Public Health, University of Montreal, Montreal, QC, Canada
e-mail: marie-pascale.pomey@umontreal.ca; nathalie.clavel@umontreal.ca

V. Dumez • P. Karazivan
Faculty of Medicine, University of Montreal, Montreal, QC, Canada
e-mail: vincent.dumez@umontreal.ca; philippe.karazivan@umontreal.ca

A. Boivin • G. Rouly
CHUM Research Centre, University of Montreal, Montreal, QC, Canada
e-mail: antoine.boivin@umontreal.ca; ghislaine.rouly@ceppp.ca

P. Lebel
Direction régionale de santé publique de Montréal, CIUSSS du Centre-Sud-de-l'Ile-de-Montréal, Montreal, QC, Canada

Department of Family Medicine and Emergency Medicine (DMFMU), Université de Montréal, Montreal, QC, Canada

M.-P. Pomey et al. (eds.), *Patient Engagement*, Organizational Behaviour in Healthcare,
https://doi.org/10.1007/978-3-030-14101-1_3

Introduction

As Canada's second most populous province behind Ontario, Quebec has an estimated population of more than 8,400,000, largely composed of a Francophone majority and English, Allophone and Indigenous minorities. It is the only Canadian province to hold French as its single official language, understood by 94.6 per cent of its population.

Within the Canadian Confederation, the provincial government of Quebec wields the authority to legislate in several areas of exclusive jurisdiction, including health administration. That said, despite provincial jurisdiction, to benefit from federal funding, Quebec's health and social services system must respect five basic principles which are: (1) Universality—so that all residents can benefit from services; (2) Public management by a health insurance scheme administered by a public authority; (3) Accessibility—so as to negate financial (or other) barriers which may impede satisfactory access to hospital and medical services; (4) Transferability—to be able to benefit from services from one province to another during a relocation or a trip; and finally, (5) Entirety—as in 100 per cent coverage of medical services provided by hospitals and physicians (Government of Quebec 2002).

In the Quebec province, the public health system was born in 1961 with the creation of the Hospitalisation Insurance Plan (*Régime d'assurance hospitalisation*), which was supplemented in 1970 by the Health Insurance Plan (*Régime d'assurance maladie*) to cover medical expenses and, in 1997, by the General Drug Insurance Plan (*Régime général d'assurance médicaments*) to cover drug expenditures for all Quebecers (Quebec Ministry of Health and Social Services 2009).

A. Berkesse • A. Descoteaux • M. Jackson
Centre of Excellence for Partnership with Patients and the Public (CEPPP), University of Montreal, Montreal, QC, Canada
e-mail: alexandre.berkesse@umontreal.ca; annie.descoteaux@umontreal.ca; mathieu.jackson@ceppp.ca

Compared to others health systems in Canada, a unique feature of Quebec's system is its association of health services and social services to easily engage one or the other when needed. In addition, funding for those services is essentially based on general taxation in order to fairly distribute the financial burden to society. Revenues originate mainly from taxes levied by the Government of Quebec, employer and individual contributions, and transfers from the federal government (Quebec Ministry of Health and Social Services 2015).

In 2017, total health expenditure per capita was $6434 in Quebec (Canadian Institute for Health Information 2018), which comprises public expenditure (including direct federal government spending on clients under its responsibility) and private expenditure (private insurance claims, direct payments—such as contributions to long-term care facilities and drug purchases—made by individuals, donations, etc.). In terms of workforce, the health and social services network represents approximately 6.9 per cent of Quebec's labour force, including 8710 general practitioners and 9779 medical specialists (Quebec Ministry of Health and Social Services 2018).

From a governance perspective, Quebec's health and social services system is made up of two levels: the Ministry of Health and Social Services (*Ministère de la Santé et des Services sociaux* [MSSS]), the 22 integrated, university or non-university, health and social services centres, newly created by the merger healthcare organizations, long-term care centres (*Centres d'hébergement de soins de longue durée* [CHSLD]) and local community health centres (*Centres locaux de santé communautaire* [CLSC]), four university hospital centres (CHU) and three are healthcare institutes (IU). Five institutions are offering services to an Aboriginal and northern population.

The role of the MSSS is to: (1) regulate and coordinate the entire health and social services system; (2) determine health and well-being orientations and standards for the organization of services, as well as manage the network's human, material and financial resources while ensuring their proper application; (3) equitably distribute and control financial, human and material resources; and (4) evaluate results against set objectives with a view to improve the system's performance. To cover all healthcare needs of a population in a given geographical area, each Integrated

Health and Social Services Centre (Integrated Centre) has a shared responsibility with its partners (unmerged hospitals and university institutes, medical clinics and family medicine groups (FMGs), community pharmacies and organizations, social economy enterprises, private healthcare organizations) to provide services which meet the needs of the territory's population and aim to promote the maintenance or improvement of this population's health and well-being. To uphold this responsibility, a set of interventions and services, as complete as possible, must be made proximately available to people's living environments.

With regard to health indicators, life expectancy at birth in Quebec was 82.6 years in 2017, that is, 80.6 for men and 84.5 for women (*Institut de la Statistique du Québec* 2018), which is among the highest in the world. A very high proportion of the population reports being in good health, both physically and mentally, and population health indicators have improved since the 2000s in terms of heart disease and cancer survival. However, as in most industrialized countries, chronic diseases and disabilities exert significant pressure on the health and social services system. Half of the population aged 12 and over had at least one chronic health problem in 2010–2011, and one-quarter had at least two. Hypertension now affects 16 per cent of Quebecers, and diabetes, 6 per cent. Also, heart disease and cancer prevalence are increasing, in addition to one in 10 adults suffering from mental disorders each year (Quebec Ministry of Health and Social Services 2018).

Within this context, it is hypothesized that greater patient and public participation, both in terms of their own care and health governance, could add value in finding solutions to Quebec's health system challenges (Denis et al. 2011, p. 23). In their report, Denis et al. argue that "patient and public participation should be a hallmark of good health service governance, and that strategies to encourage them should be designed" (Denis et al. 2011, p. 23).

In Quebec, as elsewhere, engaging patients as care partners has gradually replaced the traditional paternalistic approach and is now an essential component of an adaptive system (Karazivan et al. 2015; Pomey and Lebel 2016). As a patient-focused approach, where patients are primarily informed and consulted as part of their care plans, the evolution of care partnership has led to the recognition of patients' experiential knowledge and their role as full members within care teams. In other words, decisions are made with patient oversight and according to their life plans and health goals. Since then, the patient engagement phenomenon has manifested itself at different levels of health system: at clinical, organizational and strategic levels, as well as in health research and education. (Pomey et al. 2015b).

Hence, with those elements in mind, this chapter will present the way in which citizen and patient participation in Quebec's health and social services system came about, particularly though the presentation of what is now recognized as the "Montréal Model", which refers to simultaneous integration of patients in education, research and the health system.

The History of Public Participation

In Quebec, public participation materialized out of two sources: a citizen representation model and another model based on patients' experiential knowledge.

Citizen Participation

The importance of public participation has been established ever since the creation of Quebec's public health system in 1970 (Castonguay and Nepveu 1967). Article 2 of the Act Respecting Health Services and Social Services (*Loi sur les services de santé et les services sociaux* [LSSS]) stipulates that the health system ensures "the participation of individuals—and groups they constitute—in choices regarding the orientations, establishment, improvement, development and administration of services" (Government of Quebec 2002).

That said, in the 1980s, a commission in charge of assessing the health network over a 10-year period since its establishment (Rochon 1988) noted how the network had become hostage to pressure groups, and that more space should be attributed to the public to express its needs and take part in decision-making processes. Following the publication of this report, one of the implemented reforms in 1991 was the election by universal suffrage of members of Regional Health Assemblies (*Assemblées régionales de santé*) which were abolished in 1995. In 1993, Complaint Assistance and Support Centres (*Centres d'assistance et d'accompagnement aux plaintes* [CAAP]) were created in different regions of Quebec to assist people seeking to lodge complaints (*Fédération des centres d'assistance et d'accompagnement aux plaintes* 2018).

Also in the 1980s and 1990s, healthcare organizations set up user committees on a voluntary basis in long-term care facilities and psychiatric hospitals (Godbout et al. 1987). Then, in 2005, the LSSS was amended to require the creation of user committees in all Quebec public institutions. As a result, the mandate of user committees now revolves around three main objectives: (1) to inform users of their rights and obligations; (2) defend the collective and individual rights and interests of users; and (3) promote the quality of users' living conditions and assess users' satisfaction with the services provided by the institution.

Following the merger of health institutions and the creation of Integrated Centres in 2015, user committees are currently composed of at least six members elected by user committee chairpersons (from each merged healthcare organization), and five representatives from resident committees (i.e. in integrated long-term care facilities). By direct suffrage, committee members are elected as representatives of the population served by the healthcare organization, and their operating budget represents 0.04 per cent of the organization's budget from the previous year. While user committees are not under the authority of the senior management teams, they must publish an annual activity and financial report and submit it to the Executive Board (Quebec Ministry of Health and Social Services 2018a).

Furthermore, two community organizations participate in networking user and resident committees: the Council for the Protection of the Sick (*Conseil pour la protection des malades* 2018) which follows legal aspects regarding the respect for human rights; and the Provincial Group of User Committees (*Regroupement provincial des comités des usagers* 2018), created in 2003, which seeks to promote the role and mandate of user and resident committees to help them perform their functions successfully.

Patient Participation

In Quebec, patient integration in universities accelerated in 2010, namely after a meeting between Vincent Dumez, a patient suffering from several chronic diseases, and the Dean of the University of Montreal (UofM) Faculty of Medicine, Dr. Jean-Lucien Rouleau. After acknowledging the absence of patients within his faculty, the Dean decided to create the Patient Partner Office (*Bureau du patient partenaire*) and entrust Vincent Dumez with developing initiatives related to patient engagement as part of the initial training programme for medical students.

Patient participation legitimacy is based on the recognition of patients' experiential knowledge, which can be defined as knowledge derived from life experiences with health or psychosocial disorders, experience with care and the organization of services, as well as repercussions on personal life and that of relatives (Coulter 2012; *Centre de pédagogie appliquée aux sciences de la santé* 2013, 2014). This knowledge can be mobilized to supplement scientific knowledge and educate future health professionals on how patients actually live with their diseases.

As a result, experiences acquired in university education helped progressively establish what is now recognized as the "Montréal Model". This model was initially driven by the Patient Partner Office, then migrated to the Patient Collaboration and Partnership Directorate (*Direction collaboration et partenariat patient* [DCPP]) within the Faculty of Medicine which works closely with the Centre of Excellence on Partnership with Patients and the Public (CEPPP), a centre which supports the Model's development across the province (CEPPP 2018a, b).

Additionally, the Health Minister's 2015–2020 strategic plan states that real partnership between users and health actors can lead to an improvement in the quality of care and services and healthcare-related cost control (Quebec Ministry of Health and Social Services 2017). Moreover, a reference framework for the partnership approach between users, their relatives and health and social services stakeholders (Quebec Ministry of Health and Social Services 2018b) reinforces the ministry's desire to encourage care and service partnerships with users across Quebec's health and social services network. Of note, it also specifies that patients who participate in activities of the health and social services system cannot be paid, under any circumstances.

The "Montréal Model"

The Montréal Model holds three main characteristics. First, it builds on the notion of care and service partnership where patients (and their relatives) are recognized for their experiential knowledge from living with a given disease and utilizing the health system. As such, patients are not only considered as their own caregivers and as full members of their care team but also as people empowered to make decisions for themselves, supported by care teams throughout their healthcare pathway (Karazivan et al. 2015).

The Patient Engagement Continuum

The Montréal Model sits within the patient engagement continuum (Carman et al. 2013; Pomey et al. 2015b) in terms of co-creation and co-leadership (Lebel et al. 2014). That is to say, when searching for solutions and implementing measures, patients are equally and jointly engaged in the same way as other professionals, which leads to a shared responsibility among all actors.

The Different Patient Roles

The Montréal Model also recognizes that patients acquire experience over time, leading to the development of skills which can be shared by participating in certain activities (Flora et al. 2016a, b). Indeed, patients develop knowledge about life with their disease, self-management abilities and the use of health services. Once mastered, knowledge and skills can be put to use in various training activities (as Resource Patients in Education), activities improving the health and social services system (as Resource Patients in Healthcare), research

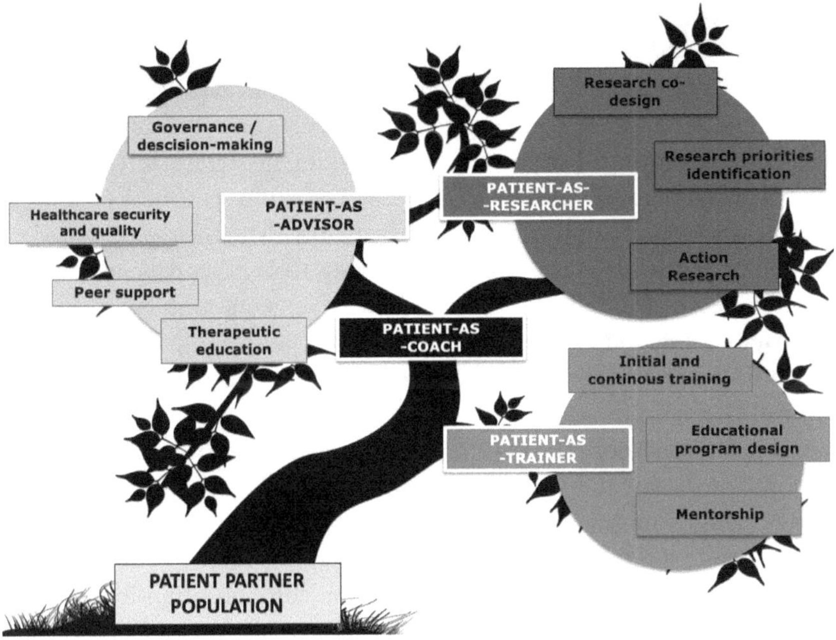

Fig. 3.1 Different expert patient types. (Source: Adapted from Flora et al. 2016a)

projects (as Resource Patients in Research) (Pomey et al. 2015b; Flora et al. 2016a, b) and so on (see Fig. 3.1). Considering this fact, the Montréal Model acknowledges distinct types of expert patients.

Patient Partners

Patient Partners can potentially be anyone dealing with a health problem. They convey their experiential knowledge as a supplement to scientific expertise. They are on the lookout for various sources of information and care options (colloquia, forums, etc.) to help facilitate informed and optimal care decision-making in accordance with their life plans. Patient Partners can align care with their preferences and life projects. For them, understanding illnesses and leveraging experiential knowledge can infuse new meaning into a life with chronic illness (Flora et al. 2016a).

Patient-as-Advisors

Patient-as-advisors in Healthcare are patients who wish to share their experience with other patients (Flora et al. 2016b). Participation can occur in care settings (empowerment), working groups (quality) or strategic planning (governance).

In terms of empowerment, Patient-as-advisors share their experiences to help other patients through their ordeals. They allow other patients in rehabilitation, or in acute disease, to identify with someone who experienced a comparable situation and managed to resume a normal life despite illness. Patient-as-advisors stories create better complicity and more active listening relative to physician advice. Moreover, these interventions not only give meaning to the life of Patient-as-advisors but also to the person going through the same predicament, which helps break isolation (Pomey et al. 2015b, d).

With regard to quality, Patient-as-advisors can participate in working groups to improve the quality of care and services (Pomey et al. 2015a). Since patients are the only ones to navigate through often-fragmented healthcare organizations, their position gives access to a vision which is not accessible to healthcare providers. More specifically, their knowledge of healthcare settings highlights coordination and integration issues in the care continuum (Flora et al. 2016b).

Patients can also intervene at the strategic level of health system and in governance (Pomey et al. 2015b). At this level, patient engagement can be individual or collective and occur in user committees or executive boards (board of directors, etc.) as well as during the design, implementation and evaluation phases of health policy and programmes (Pomey et al. 2015b).

Patient-as-Trainers

Thanks to the leadership of the DCPP (the Patient Collaboration and Partnership Directorate at the UofM Faculty of Medicine), experiential knowledge from patients is mobilized in the initial and continuing education of future and current health professionals. This materializes in several ways.

The first way—a competency-based approach to training—engages patients for their experiential knowledge to help students develop their caring abilities. This can be achieved either via co-teaching with a health professional or co-facilitating student training workshops. At the UofM, patient partners also participate in the evaluation of health sciences students.

The second way—mentoring—offers patient support to future professionals throughout their studies. This form of mentorship allows students to shadow patients through their care path and discuss practical issues encountered during internships in healthcare organizations.

The third way—training engineering—involves patients co-creating (with health professionals) pedagogical programmes and activities.

Patient-as-Researchers

In research settings, patients can be valued as "Experience Collectors", full members of the research team (action research) or contribute more broadly to reflections on the orientations of research institutions (co-design) (Cambon and Alla 2013).

First, as Experience Collectors, patients can report their own experiences or that of peers, thus contributing to data collection and processing during research projects (Flora et al. 2016a, b). Experiences "collected" by patients, backed by their expertise and knowledge, can generate a fuller picture of the studied object and may even help reveal new research topics (Instituts de recherche en santé du Canada 2018).

Furthermore, in action research, patient involvement can occur when developing research questions, writing protocols, recruiting patients, interpreting data or disseminating results (Carman and Workman 2017). By doing so, patients contribute to the structuring and management process of field research projects. Partnership between patients (as co-investigators) and researchers contributes to a culture of analysis, calling into question existing approaches to patient care (co-design) (Instituts de recherche en santé du Canada 2018) with the aim of underscoring and eliciting ideas and innovative solutions.

Additionally, patient engagement in the research community promotes accountability, data transparency, improves the credibility of results and their application to target populations, thereby improving research quality which, in turn, enhances the quality of care received by patients. From a patient perspective, patient contributions to research also increases their confidence, their mastery of new skills and provides them with a sense of accomplishment, given their participation in research that is so relevant to their needs (Instituts de recherche en santé du Canada 2018).

Patient Leaders/Coaches

Patients with significant experience from multiple care settings and who are able to support other individuals or groups can become Patient Leaders/Coaches (Flora et al. 2016a, b). As experienced Resource Patients, they can train other potential Resource Patients and inspire peers with their enthusiasm, actions, and indirectly become mentors. Specifically, Patient Leaders/Coaches guide patients or patients groups (or even health professionals) towards sharpening skills related to their functions, help individual or group members hone their partnership skills, promote learning through adapted tools and value individual or group initiatives as part of their duties (*Direction collaboration et partenariat patient* 2015). This training cycle contributes to the care partnership's deployment in clinical settings as these patients provide transformational leadership (Pomey et al. 2015b).

As demonstrated by these elements, the Montréal Model simultaneously integrates partnership activities within the health and social services system, in healthcare professional training, in research and among health jurisdictions. This section also illustrated, without being exhaustive, the way patients are integrated in Quebec, knowing that the Montréal Model has now expanded beyond UofM borders.

Patient Participation in the Health System

Patient Participation in Healthcare Organizations

There are 22 Integrated Health and Social Services Centres in Quebec, as well as four university hospitals and three health institutes. All of them host a Quality, Evaluation, Performance and Ethics Directorate known as the DQEPE (*Direction de la qualité, de l'évaluation, de la performance et de l'éthique*), whose mission includes developing care and service partnerships within the organization. The initiatives that are about to be presented below are most often supported by these directorates, whether in terms of patient selection, patient training or patient coaching (Pomey et al. 2018d).

Patient Participation in Care

In Quebec, the participation of patients in their own care takes place via two types of activities. On the one hand, empowering patients to become more proactive in self-care and develop partnership-based relationships with professionals; and on the other hand, making patient experiences available to other patients.

As patients, being in partnership requires knowing oneself and one's illness very well, which stresses the importance of remaining in a constant learning mode and seeking out information through several sources (websites, popular or scientific journals, etc.) or people (health professionals, other patients). It also requires assessment capabilities to not only determine the nature of one's relationship with health professionals but also grasp their scientific knowledge and technical know-how. From these assessments, patients should be able to adjust accordingly to situations, compensate and adapt to what can be perceived as optimal or non-optimal health or healthcare circumstances (Pomey et al. 2015c). In fact, research on this topic led to the co-creation of a questionnaire to help measure partnership levels around seven key partnership dimensions as identified by patients. These dimensions are grouped under the acronym CAD♥CEE as in "Confidence (trust), Autonomy, Decision-Making, Information, Communication, Expertise recognition and Empathy" (Pomey et al. 2018b).

The second type of patient participation occurs at a clinical level as peer support programmes, some of which have already been implemented in Quebec's health and social services system.

For example, in surgery, at the University of Montreal Hospital Centre—known as the CHUM (*Centre hospitalier de l'Université de Montréal*), a special clinic in charge of revascularization or hand replantation after traumatic injuries has introduced Support Patients as role models to help recently injured and operated patients go through rehabilitation. Introduced in 2014 as a pilot project, six support patients took part in the intervention, and preliminary results indicate that patients who received support from them: (1) were less likely to drop out of rehabilitation, especially when occurring away from the location where surgery was performed; (2) suffered less post-surgical and rehabilitation treatment pain; and (3) recovered superior fine motor skills (Pomey et al. 2016, 2018a). These very encouraging results were validated by a pragmatic randomized test of the target population. By extension, the model was also exported to burn victims with the participation of the *Association des Grands Brûlés* (Serious Burn Victims Association) who recruited support patients for direct intervention in healthcare settings along the care continuum (resuscitation and rehabilitation). Other disease areas include mental health, oncology and chronic disease management.

In mental health, the MSSS inserted the concept of recovery into its mental health plan. Among measures in support for recovery, Peer Helpers were identified to act as mentors. These mentors are part of an association and are made available to healthcare organizations willing to offer mentorship services to their patients. Officially, mentors are now trained through a programme recognized by the UofM Faculty of Medicine (see below).

In oncology, the PAROLE-Onco programme is a research project funded by the Canadian Institutes for Health Research (CIHR) which aims to introduce support patients in clinical teams for the provision of informational and emotional support to patients undergoing cancer treatment (*Centre de recherche du CHUM* 2018a). Currently, six healthcare organizations in Quebec are making support patients available within care teams.

In chronic disease management, support patients intervene to help patients with kidney failure or going through kidney transplants (Pomey et al. 2018c).

Lastly, there are three ongoing pilot projects to support patient transitions from paediatric to adult medicine. The first project concerns patients with congenital heart disease, the second one helps patients with gastrointestinal problems (Crohn's disease and haemorrhagic rectocolitis), while the third one supports liver transplant patients.

Patient Participation in the Organization of Care and Services

The Patient Collaboration and Partnership Directorate (DCPP) at the UofM Faculty of Medicine advocated for applied patient involvement in organizational settings, thus created the "Partnership in Care and Services" programme, referred to as PSS (*Partenariat de soins et de services*). The PSS programme starts with awareness at the senior management level to not only spur cultural change which will result from the approach but also obtain a formal commitment. Then, the programme trickles down to departments, which are engaged to improve collaborative practices (PSS-based practices), more tangibly by assembling a committee in charge of "continuous quality improvement in healthcare and service partnerships". What could be labelled as "PSS committees" consist of managers, key healthcare professionals (physicians, nurses, secretaries, social workers or others) and at least two patients. Participating patients are considered as Patient advisors, meaning that they are no longer in episodes of acute care and were previously treated by the service to which the committee is affiliated. During PSS committee meetings, patient advisors can assert their point of view about notable systemic malfunctions or deficiencies—knowing that they have taken a step back to reflect upon their experiences. In other words, they are recognized for their expertise with regard to patient care pathways and identification of patient needs.

The selection criteria for patient advisors centre around their wealth of experience in healthcare, their ability to speak and assert themselves within committees, and their motivation and commitment towards the improvement of services/programmes for all patients (see Table 3.1). Prior to joining PSS committees, patient advisors are initially trained by the DCPP and are mentored until autonomy. Furthermore, their roles and responsibilities are clearly defined to ensure harmonious working relationships between all committee members.

Operationally, PSS Committees usually establish one or two goals to improve the quality of care and services. Initially, these goals are to be reached within four to six months in order to quickly observe changes within practices. Then, actions designed to achieve these goals are implemented, followed by regular progress assessments, tak-

Table 3.1 Patient Selection Criteria

• Expresses him/herself clearly and simply • Expresses general health network concerns through a constructive attitude in his/her interventions • Has significant life experience with the disease • Has significant experience in healthcare and services targeted by the project • Is in a steady state of health at the time of recruitment (not in an acute or crisis situation) • Has the ability to share his/her own experience with the disease and has learned to live with it • Can generalize his/her own experience to other contexts of care	• Demonstrates a desire to help people and contribute to an objective that goes beyond his/her individual experience • Has interpersonal skills to facilitate collaboration (listening, empathy, etc.) • Has a critical mind, even within teams in which he/she has already been a patient • Understands the vision and implications of the partnership in health(care) model • Is available and motivated to commit during the duration of the project

Source: *Direction collaboration et partenariat patient* (2015)

ing advantage of support from the organization and the DCCP. Between 2011 and 2014, in Quebec, 26 teams in 16 healthcare organizations were involved in the PSS programme, which included patients from various age groups and departments such as general medicine, home care, long-term care, specialized care (mental health, oncology, diabetes, rehabilitation, etc.).

Patient Participation in Strategic Bodies

At the strategic level, each Quebec healthcare organization hosts a 17-member Executive Board. In each Board, one member is nominated by and from members of the Users Committee, while nine independent members are appointed based on their abilities, expertise and experience in several domains, including governance, ethics, finance, quality management, community organizations, youth protection, mental health and experience as users of social services.

One of the Executive Board's subcommittees is called the Vigilance and Quality Committee. It is made up of five members, including the General Manager and the Local Service Quality and Complaints Commissioner. The other three members are chosen by the Executive Board among members who are not employed by the healthcare organization or do not practise their profession in one of the facilities operated by the healthcare organization. One of the three members is most often a representative of the Users Committee or a person with experience as a user within the healthcare organization. This subcommittee is responsible for analysing all reports related to quality, ensuring the respect for users' rights and proper handling of complaints. It is also responsible for making recommendations to the Executive Board to improve the quality of care.

In addition, each healthcare organization holds a Risk Management Committee that must ensure balanced representativeness among employees, users and professionals within the organization (Government of Quebec 2015). This committee's function is to monitor the risks of incidents and accidents in order to ensure user safety, victims support and the establishment of a register to track incidents and accidents. It also makes recommendations to the Executive Board to avoid the reoccurrence of reported incidents and accidents.

Patient Participation for Sharing Practices

To support healthcare organizations in carrying out their functions and exchanging on patient engagement-related practices, a community of practice (CoP) was created in 2016 by the CHUM's Research Chair in Advanced Technology and Modality Assessment, with support from the Centre of Excellence on Patient and Public Partnership (CEPPP). This CoP consists of care partnership managers within healthcare organizations and patients, and meets four times a year to work on several issues such as: (1) implementing measures to enable patient engagement in care safety; (2) partnership indicators; (3) relations between Users Committees and patients involved in care and service partnership initiatives; (4) deploying these initiatives; (5) strengthening the role of patients in care safety (*Centre de recherche du CHUM* 2018b).

Patient Participation in Primary Care

Primary care in Quebec is largely characterized by independent private practices owned and managed by general practitioners, which, in recent years, have evolved towards interdisciplinary group practices and other elements from the Patient's Medical Home model (Katz et al. 2017). Patient engagement initiatives in primary care mostly focused on direct patient care (e.g. use of patient decision-aids for shared decision-making, implementation of a self-management support programme) (Legare et al. 2012; Chouinard et al. 2013), as well as on meso-level decision-making, such as priority-setting in primary care, quality improvement and governance within practices (Boivin et al. 2014).

Patient Participation in Care

In 2017, an initiative was born in a university family medicine group (U-FMG) in Montreal—the *GMF-U Notre Dame*—by a family physician (Dr Antoine Boivin) who "hired" a resource patient (Ghislaine Rouly) to supplement his consultations. For certain patients facing chronic illnesses aggravated by other problems such as social isolation or poverty, the resource patient is called upon based on her considerable experience living with the same disease. In practice, first, the resource patient assesses the needs of patients relative to the impact of the disease on their life projects and role in society. Then, she helps them develop self-care abilities, in addition to supporting their integration into a community support network. Therefore, as a result of resource patient input, the family physician can adjust treatment plans according to true problems faced by patients. This initiative is part of a wider approach to creating a caring community, which will be presented further.

Ghislaine Rouly's Testimony

As a patient myself, I have always known the health system and its paths well. When I first see a patient, it is certain that I tell him and repeat that I am not a health professional. That what he entrusts to me will remain confidential unless he wishes this information to be transmitted to his doctor Dr. Boivin.

My goal is to know or recognize the underlying problems that hinder its treatment. Why, despite the care provided, there are not so many improvements. Has the patient been asked about his or her life project, for example? Did we have time? Patients also do not take the time to talk to their doctor. They go to the most urgent and do not always share the real reasons for their meeting. Each of us sometimes needs to confide in each other. To be listened to, without judgment. Especially when living with a chronic disease. We are alone with our illness, and sometimes this loneliness weighs on us. So having someone to confide in, to talk to, becomes a real relief.

In this era where everything is managed at high speed, human beings are isolating themselves in this increasingly dense society. No one really talks to each other; no one listens to each other, and yet everyone needs to be listened to, heard, seen. Be visible. To be alive.

What touches me deeply and fascinates me is the speed with which the other, the patient, the citizen opens up to me. It's a valve that jumps, and the flow pours out ready to flood me. I find myself overwhelmed with information. Often relevant to their illness but not always. What I offer is very simple; a listening, real, attentive, humble, non-judgmental. I teach them to become patients, to know their rights, to discover unsuspected resources in them.

This project must continue in a sustainable way and become another way of treating people. To offer the possibility to any patient to have recourse to a patient partner just for him/her. A patient partner who listens to him, encourages him, educates him to become a better patient, partners in his own care and eventually becomes his mentor and ally by helping him to regain his place in the community.

Patient Participation in the Organization of Primary Care and Services

To improve the relevance of continuous quality improvement projects for primary care and services, the EQUIPPS-GMF project is currently being implemented in the Quebec City region (Haesebaert et al. 2018). As a pilot, it aims to co-create a partnership model between patients, relatives, managers and clinicians in two non-university family medicine groups (FMGs). Thus, a Continuous Improvement Committee, consisting of 12 patients/caregivers, a manager and a family physician meet from 90 minutes every six to nine weeks to identify priority topics, establish improvement measures and identify research themes.

Another initiative led by the MSSS and Quebec's national institute of excellence in health and social services known as INESSS (*Institut National d'Excellence en Santé et en Services Sociaux*) enables the creation of reflexive practice workshops for front-line teams based on quality practice indicators according to given pathologies (Vachon et al. 2013, 2015). After analysing these indicators, clinicians, in consultation with managers and patients, co-develop action plans to improve the quality of care and services. Also known as CoMPAS (*COllectif pour les Meilleurs Pratiques et l'Amélioration des Services en première ligne*), this programme integrates patients into its governance structures and workshops to foster best practices and primary service improvements (Vachon et al. 2017).

Patient Participation in Strategic Bodies (Primary Care)

In another U-FMG in Montreal, the *GMF-U de Verdun*, a new initiative was implemented in 2017, where patients participate in the group's management activities. Three patients from the U-FMG's clientele were recruited to sit on the group's Executive Committee, based on pre-established criteria (see Table 3.1) and results from telephone and in-person interviews. Stemming from their experiences with one or several illnesses, health services, personal and professional experiences, recruited patients share their experiential knowledge of the U-FMG's care and services to improve service quality with regard to patient care, as well as the organization of care, education and research in distinct disease areas.

To ensure that the project runs smoothly and successfully, two members of the DCPP (one patient coach and one quality improvement coach) assist managers, professionals and patients' advisors throughout the deployment process, attending committee meetings and providing continuous coaching to all participants. In addition to its managerial impact, this project aims to promote and support the dissemination of a patient partnership culture in all U-FMG activities. This initiative has been recognized as a pilot project by the MSSS, and the project's formative assessment has been planned accordingly (Trépanier et al. 2017).

Patient Participation in Public Health

The «Caring Community Project»

More recently, a local initiative in Montréal, created by a physician (A Boivin) and a patient (G Rouly), the «Caring community project» has piloted an intervention where primary care clinicians, patient partners and citizens work together to care for members of their community. Each partner's skills, knowledge and competencies are mobilized to bridge professional and community healthcare (Boivin and Rouly 2018). Although promising, most of these initiatives have been conducted solely within pragmatic research projects. Despite being implemented in real-world settings, few have been scaled up and implemented at the system level.

That said, this innovative model involves breaking down a series of barriers between the health system and the community; between health professionals and patients; and between sick and healthy citizens. In fact, a first "Caring Community" pilot has been set up in the south-central district of Montreal since June 2017.

As part of these Caring Communities:

- Partner clinicians integrate patients and citizens as full members of their care teams;
- Resource patients support other patients in developing self-care abilities and collaborating effectively with health professionals and community members;
- Partner citizens of different age groups, health status, income and cultural background engage in reciprocal relations of mutual assistance and exchange services backed by a social currency: time;
- Partner decision-makers mobilize collective action levers within their community with the aim of creating environments conducive to mutual social assistance and health.

Social Participation of Senior Citizens

Improving the social participation of seniors is considered as a decisive factor for maintaining this target population's health. (Holt-

Lunstad et al. 2010; Gilmour 2012). Since May 2017, a project was put in place with the aim of co-creating a shared vision of senior social participation as a health determinant in urban and multicultural settings. It helped establish a collaborative space between various actors and to collect, through focused discussion groups, the experiential knowledge of seniors regarding their social participation. Engaged seniors came from nursing homes or low-income housing projects and included those who regularly consult clinics or follow community centre activities. Of note, not all participants were Quebec natives; some were born abroad.

In terms of outcomes, analysis of discussion group data helped build a framework for analysing social participation and also served as basis for an action plan to reduce social isolation, which was co-developed by recruited seniors, health and social services network managers, city and regional public health teams and community partners (organizers and workers). Given the collaborative nature of this project, a genuine co-creation process involving senior citizens was achieved, and potential areas of intervention were identified thanks to elicited statements. Ultimately, the approach helped restore links which are fundamental to developing partnership spaces and generating collaboration for future initiatives (Lemieux et al. 2018).

Patient Participation in the Assessment of Technologies and Modalities of Interventions

Over the last decade, Quebec's national institute of excellence in health and social services (INESSS) has led some patient partnership initiatives and developed a structure for including patients and members of the public in its health technology assessment (HTA) and drug assessment processes (*Institut national d'excellence en santé et en services sociaux* 2018a). Founded in 2011, INESSS's mission is to promote clinical excellence and optimize the use of resources in healthcare and social services by evaluating new technologies, medication, as well as interventions. It provides recommendations for their implementation, optimal use and public application by integrating perspectives from healthcare professionals, managers, decision-makers and patients (*Institut national d'excellence en santé et en services sociaux* 2018b). Further, to operationalize patient participation in its assessments, based on the Montréal Model (Pomey et al. 2015b) which strives to implement experiential knowledge and partnership. However, until now, guidelines and recommendations issued by INESSS mainly benefited from patient consultation (not co-creation). In fact, the first project to benefit from actual co-creation between patients and professionals was an assessment with regard to decision-making in implantable cardioverter defibrillator (ICD) replacement.

The project was broken into four steps.

- Step (1) consisted in defining, for the first time, assessment questions related to the experience of patients living with an ICD and who may need a replacement. This led to a literature review on quality of life and shared decision-making.
- Step (2) was the creation of an expert patient group, complementing the professional expert group. All expert patients were ICD owners and, during two working session, provided feedback on the literature review to cover potential blind spots and help fit results within Quebec's context.
- For Step (3), in order to co-create recommendations, a modified Delphi method was used on members of both expert committees, and comments about proposed recommendations were synthesized, anonymized and incorporated.
- Finally, Step (4) allowed for a joint meeting with both committees to decide on issues and tools to be developed in support of proposed recommendations. As a result, out of 11 recommendations, seven related to patient experience (*Institut national d'excellence en santé et en services sociaux* 2018c).

An assessment of this first participative project revealed that: (1) at first, it was difficult for the Institute's scientists to understand the role of patients; (2) patients enjoyed their experience and were able to highlight encountered difficulties, despite the subject being technical; (3) it confirmed and validated observations made by health professionals regarding organizational modalities and the importance of changing their practices and the organization of services (Pomey et al. 2019; *Institut national d'excellence en santé et en services sociaux* 2018c).

Patient Participation in Healthcare Policy

Patient participation can include the development, implementation and evaluation of policies and programmes implemented by the MSSS. Involvement in this area can be undertaken either by patients, citizens or the public. Accordingly, representatives can work with policy-makers to find community-based solutions, help define policies, establish health priorities and resource allocations. At this level, engagement may either be individual, or through representatives of patient organizations or groups or even special interest groups. So far, in Quebec, a public policy for the partnership model does not exist. However, recently, the MSSS published a reference framework for partnership approaches between users, their relatives and health and social services stakeholders. This framework was developed in consultation with all stakeholders within the health network, including resource patients involved in various initiatives (Quebec Ministry of Health and Social Services 2018b).

Patient Participation in Research

Canadian Strategy for Patient-Oriented Research

In 2011, the Canadian Institutes for Health Research (CIHR), the main public research funding agency in Canada (equivalent to NIHR in the UK) launched its Strategy for Patient-Oriented Research. CIHR defines patient-oriented research as "a continuum of research that engages patients as partners, focusses on patient-identified priorities and improves patient outcomes" (Canadian Institutes for Health Research 2015). It further defined patient engagement as "meaningful and active collaboration in governance, priority-setting, conducting research and knowledge translation". Although a participatory research tradition with patients and communities already existed in the country (e.g. community-based participatory research with indigenous communities), CIHR's strategy for patient-oriented research offered new impetus, incentives, opportunities and infrastructure to support patient engagement in research. For example, Methodological Support Units were established in each province for patient-oriented research capacity building. The Quebec Support Unit strategy for patient and public partnership in research involved methodological advice, researcher–patient co-training to co-lead projects, patient recruitment and patient-research matchmaking support and evaluation of patient engagement in research (Boivin et al. 2018b, c). Quebec's strategy focuses explicitly on partnership approaches, supporting project co-leadership with patients at different levels of research governance (research projects, networks and infrastructure). For example, dyads of patient partners and researchers were established in each university network to support local research teams.

Transplant-Action

In preparation for a study assessing the impact of implementing a training programme for new kidney and liver transplant recipients, a research team collaborated, since the onset of the research protocol, with three transplant patients to facilitate the programme's implementation and patient recruitment.

The so-called "Transplant-Action" project met a need expressed by kidney and liver transplant patients for coaching in physical activity to help improve post-transplant heart function and quality of life (Rakel 2017). As such, Transplant-Action proposed to randomize newly transplanted kidney or liver patients so they could be assigned to either the exercise group—where they would train twice a week in cardiovascular training and resistance training supervised by a kinesiologist for six months at home or in a gym (Rakel 2017)—or to the control group—where they would receive basic advice on the benefits of physical activity.

Therefore, as full members of the research team, the three involved patients embraced various roles which evolved over time. The first patient, who was identified as co-principal investigator since the beginning of the project, participated in drafting the protocol and creating the training programme, which he tested himself to understand potential patient-related issues. Additionally, he participated in: writing documents introducing the programme as well as ethical information and consent forms for patients; producing video capsules to illustrate home exercises; data analyses and presentations at conferences.

The second patient, a retiree, worked on recruiting patients for the study. Twice a week, he visited the healthcare organization's transplant inpatient unit to meet with potential candidates. He also collaborated with care teams to identify patients and ensure that his visits were announced. During his visits, he explained the project and made offers to join.

As for the third patient, he took on a coaching role, as he followed patients in the exercise group, offered help and monitored progress according to exercise plans. Moreover, he handed follow-ups by calling patients once a week to enquire on potential issues and answer questions.

In all three cases, project participation significantly impacted the lives of patient researchers. For the first patient, this experience led to a career change: he was hired by the CEPPP—where he now trains researchers on how to work with patients as part of a Patient-Centred Research Strategy—and started a master's degree in Research. As for the second patient, Transplant-Action brought a new dimension to his retirement as he feels useful when in contact with patients and clinicians. And finally, the third patient researcher was motivated to engage in even more physical activity by participating in the Canadian Transplant Games (CTG).

The RUCCHES Project

Within a project designed to encourage meetings among patients/users, clinicians and researchers to improve primary care research, the RUCCHES project (*Rencontres patients-Usagers, Cliniciens et CHerchEurs*) helps create formal discussion spaces to better support the identification of research questions and the development of research projects within U-FMGs. As part of the project, a working group was created, which consisted of a researcher, a family physician, two residents, three primary care professionals and three patients, one of whom led the group. Themes were brought up by the researcher, followed by discussions to identify and prioritize research questions (Samson and Dogba 2016).

Patient Participation in Education

As mentioned previously, the Patient Collaboration and Partnership Directorate (DCPP) is located within the UofM Faculty of Medicine and aims to orchestrate a major cultural shift by facilitating the emergence, deployment and assessment of new partnership initiatives involving patients in medical education (*Direction collaboration et partenariat patient* 2018).

The DCPP's educational initiatives are intended to help medical and health sciences students develop skills for dealing with complex human healthcare issues through ethics, story-telling, collaboration and communication. In true patient partnership spirit, patients are systematically integrated throughout the process: from activity ideation, design and pedagogical engineering, to patient-faculty sessions co-facilitation and assessments, everything is co-led in partnership (Direction collaboration et partenariat patient 2018).

Three core principles support the DCPP's mission:

1. Develop students' abilities to manage complex human situations, address ethical issues and strengthen partnership with their patients;
2. Implement longitudinal and integrated learning in clinical ethics, collaboration and communication (reflective, narrative, simulation practices, etc.);
3. Work systematically with patient trainers for educational content design and use co-created content to train students.

In recent years, around the world, several medical education initiatives tried to integrate patients, with varying degrees of success. At the UofM, the undeniable growth of DCPP activities is a testament to internationally recognized success (see Fig. 3.2).

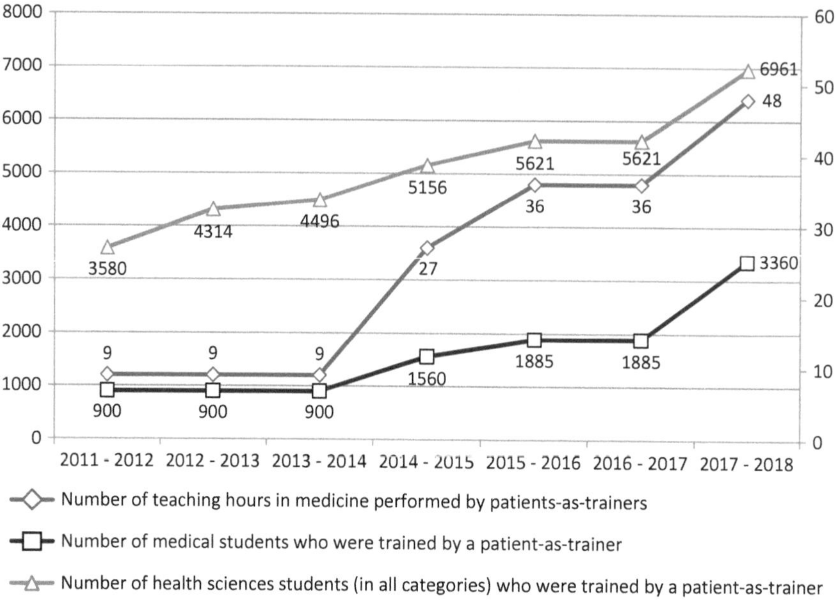

Fig. 3.2 Assessment of DCPP Activities between 2011 and 2017. (Source: Adapted from Dumez and Karazivan, 2018 and DCPP)

An important aspect distinguishes the DCPP approach from other initiatives: it is firmly anchored in the care partnership paradigm and not in the one of patient-centred approaches. Indeed, patients are no longer asked for mere testimonials; instead, they are asked to mobilize their experiential knowledge to serve students. Nowadays, not only must they know how to tell their stories, they must also do so pedagogically. Patients are no longer invited to meet students as part of pre-created coursework; they work alongside faculty from the start to co-create learning objectives and pedagogical methods to develop students' skills (see Fig. 3.3).

More than 200 patient partners (with trainer profiles) are already engaged in training medical students. All were carefully and rigorously recruited according to their partnership skills (*Direction collaboration et partenariat patient* 2015; Flora et al. 2016b) and take advantage of co-training sessions (for faculty and patients) provided by the DCPP in order to continuously develop their partnership and pedagogical skills.

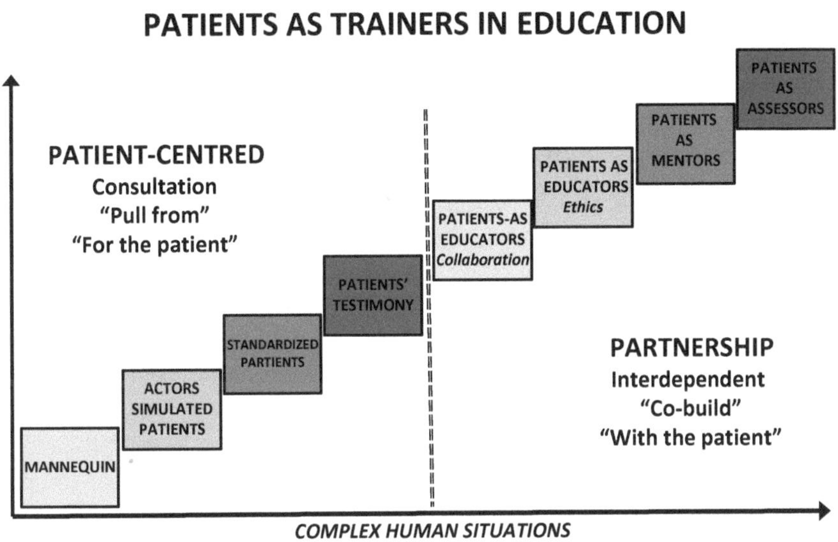

Fig. 3.3 Patients as trainers in education. (Source: DCPP)

Description of the DCPP's Pedagogical Activities for Medical Students

Throughout the medical school curriculum:

- Student mentorship by patient partners: eight patient trainers, 70 students per year.

Preclinical (1st and 2nd year students):

- Course CSS 1900 (Interprofessional Collaboration): 68 patient trainers, 1500 students in health sciences per year;
- Course CSS 2900 (Interprofessional Collaboration): 68 patients' trainers, 1500 students in health sciences per year;
- "Value Pluralism" course: two patients' trainers, 300 students per year.

Clinical clerkship (3rd and 4th year)

- Clinical Ethics Workshop 1: 12 patient trainers, 300 students per year;
- Clinical Ethics Workshop 2: 12 patient trainers, 300 students per year;
- Course CSS 3900 (Interprofessional Collaboration): 68 patient trainers, 1500 students in health sciences per year.

Residency (5th to 9th year)

- Storytelling Ethics Workshop 1: four patient trainers, 140 students per year;
- Storytelling Ethics Workshop 2: four patient trainers, 140 students per year.

New pedagogical initiatives in 2017–2018:

- "Professionalism in Medicine" workshop: 23 patient trainers, 300 students per year;
- "Conflicts of Interest" course: two patient trainers, 300 students per year;
- "Power and White Lab Coats" workshop: 23 patient trainers, 300 students per year;
- "Ethics in End-of-Life Care" course: 2 patient trainers, 300 students per year
- Storytelling Ethics Workshop 3: four patient trainers, 140 students per year

The following section will elaborate on four specific DCPP activity areas: (1) CSS courses, (2) clinical ethics workshops, (3) medical student assessments, and (4) support services.

Initial Training

Developing Collaboration Competencies: CSS Courses

To support major changes in healthcare practices and organizations, the next generation of healthcare professionals must be prepared to work in collaborative practice settings and contribute to the deployment of partnerships in clinical institutions. Accordingly, since 2011, the UofM integrated patients to act as co-facilitators in training courses, aiming for progressive development of interprofessional collaboration and care partnership skills (Fulmer et al. 2014; Vanier et al. 2014) for students in 13 distinct health-related professions and in psychosocial sciences. The interprofessional education (IPE) programme comprises three one-credit undergraduate mandatory courses embedded in the first three years of preclinical education.

In the first year, students meet and jointly explore the concept of "Partnership" through personal examples and testimonies brought by patient trainers. During the second year, students are required to become familiar with the interprofessional meeting sequence, clarify roles of different professions and apply the Partnership concept to a clinical case of an outpatient in paediatrics as the patient trainer advocates for patient and family interests and personal objectives regarding care. Finally, in the third year, students apply the Partnership concept to an interprofessional meeting simulation to develop an interdisciplinary intervention plan (IIP) for a hospitalized senior patient. In this case, the patient trainer advocates for the patient's role in building the IIP.

About 1400 students participated yearly in each of the three IPE courses while patient trainers were gradually integrated since the 2012–2013 academic year. Early exposure to the Partnership concept is expected to allow students to gradually develop their ability to build healthcare partnerships, apply concepts during clinical training and help them become agents of change once they join the workforce.

Student course evaluations revealed that over 85 per cent of them believed that patient experiences enriched class discussions and that professional-patient trainer collaboration or coordination is relevant (*Centre de pédagogie appliquée aux sciences de la santé* 2014). 94 per cent of students plan to implement the Care Partnership approach in their future practice. In addition to these courses, other interprofessional activities during internships, as well as mentoring by patients, are underway.

Clinical Ethics

The Clinical Ethics Bureau (*Bureau d'Éthique Clinique* [BEC]) of the UofM Faculty of Medicine is a group of physicians working daily alongside other ethics professionals (e.g. lawyers specialized in health law, ethicists, etc.) or professionals dealing with ethical issues in clinical settings (e.g. mediators, chaplains, spiritual life coaches, etc.) to develop and deploy an integrated and comprehensive initial and continuing training curriculum for faculty.

In 2014, the Bureau joined the DCPP for the co-creation, co-facilitation and co-evaluation of clinical ethics workshops geared towards medical students and residents, during which complex themes aimed at developing students' interpersonal skills and clinical reasoning were discussed (value pluralism, power dynamics in the care relationship, etc.). Workshops which are co-created and co-facilitated with patients aim to particularly develop the students' ability to recognize and solve ethical issues that are specific to clinical practices and care relationships, as well as develop their empathy, reflexivity and partnership skills.

Since 2014, many activities resulting from this partnership were developed and implemented, including the 4th edition (2018) of clinical ethics workshops for students in clinical clerkship (3rd and 4th year students). During these workshops, a resident/patient trainer/physician trio co-facilitate group discussions based on clinical scenarios written by students and co-trainers, describing complex clinical situations using narrative logic. Scenarios may include instances where students felt as if they were acting against their personal ethics, or were left alone in a medically complex situation, or had to initiate a difficult conversation with patients and their relatives.

Each year, through this activity alone, members of faculty read up to 300 clinical scenarios which help them realize how challenging student learning conditions could be on a daily basis. On the other hand, it also helps 300 students learn how to deal with complex situations and turn them into levers of personal and professional emancipation, not only for them but for patients and relatives they are bound to encounter during their careers.

Beyond this single activity, other discussion workshops in clinical settings were developed as well. For instance, smaller groups of four to six students discuss the real and perceived impact of physician authority on the care relationship—particularly through their social role and symbolically charged attributes such as the stethoscope, the white lab coat, etc.—as well as the way patients and students adjust their behaviours and opinions in consequence.

Evaluating Medical Students

A pan-Canadian effort has been taking place in recent years to reflect on the role that patients could play in medical student evaluations. The DCPP was invited to several national medical education forums to help the medical community better integrate patient perspectives into medical student training. Despite being a relatively new field, the DCPP is already playing a leading role in this movement by actively integrating patient trainers into faculty and departmental reflections on the assessment of students, programmes, faculty, as well as current and future health professionals.

In a meaningful way, the DCPP contributes to the recognition of the legitimacy and relevance of patient trainer skills to assess the abilities of medical students. The team is also conducting research to explore the limits of purely positivist approaches—which only consider what is measurable, palpable, visible, etc. in the assessment of what constitutes a "good/competent" physician—while thinking about the potential role of singular/experiential knowledge in assessing student competencies. To achieve this, and to better understand the added value of patients in the evaluation of health sciences students, the DCPP currently leads many activities at the Faculty of Medicine:

- Formal student evaluations by patient partners in several of the Faculty's pedagogic activities;
- Epistemological research on experiential knowledge developed by patients from and through living with diseases;

- Participation in a working group to reform admissions to medical residency;
- Project to involve patient partners and the DCPP in the central evaluation committee for residents in family medicine.

Continuing Professional Development

Support Services by the DCPP and the CEPPP

Support services provided by the DCPP follow the 2015 health system reorganization led by the Quebec ministry of health and social services.

Drawing from its deep expertise developed since 2010, the DCPP set up support services for organizations wanting to integrate, coordinate and institutionalize care and service partnerships within their structures. Of course, implementing a new relationship model requires expertise at various levels: raising awareness among organizational stakeholders and decision-makers; recruitment methodology for patient partners who contribute to improving care and services; support and coaching for pilot projects in which patient partners would be integrated; and day-to-day management of a patient partner data base.

Since 2016, the DCPP provided nearly 1000 hours of support for training courses (training practitioners on the Partnership concept, identifying and recruiting patients, developing IIPs in partnership with patients), as well as supporting new patient recruitment (individual meetings and follow-ups with patients showing latent partnership skills), and coaching (care teams welcoming patients, and patients starting new roles as partners).

The Partnership School

The Partnership School is one of the four pillars of the Centre of Excellence on Patient and Public Partnership (CEPPP). The School's mission is to facilitate the transfer of CEPPP expertise, skills and knowledge to all stakeholders in the health system. School activities are divided into three components: training, knowledge creation and pedagogical innovation.

The training component includes pedagogical support for various stakeholders in the health community who wish to engage in patient partnership initiatives. The School offers training via a variety of methods, including in-person training (e.g. workshops, lectures, simulations) as well as synchronous online training (e.g. webinars) and asynchronous training (e.g. online training, video capsules intended for the general public).

In addition to meeting the immediate needs of the healthcare community, new training content creation contributes to the emergence of a new disciplinary field; for instance: the development of a new credited university course on patient partnership foundations.

With regard to pedagogical innovation, a variety of educational initiatives contribute to the Patient Partnership society project which positions the School as a driver of social transformation within the CEPPP. Projects include, among others, engaging patient evaluators to develop new practices to assess future health professionals; conceptualizing a certification structure aimed at establishing standards of excellence in patient partnership and supporting the recognition of work performed by patients in the field; as well as popular education projects and disseminating underlying values of patient partnerships, for instance, in primary education or during various events, symposia or colloquia.

Training Peer Helpers in Recovery

In 2017, the first cohort of peer helpers in recovery graduated from the UofM. In this special programme, the concept of recovery is defined as strategies implemented by actual patients to live better with chronic disease.

This recovery experience is particularly conducive to exchanges between people experiencing or having experienced similar challenges. Referred to as Peer Helping Mentors, the role is becoming a positive recovery model in mental health for both care givers and receivers. Not only does it represent a source of hope and empowerment for patient partners but it also provides them with psychosocial support by facilitating the maintenance of a role in the community as a full and active citizen (University of Montreal 2018).

Inspired by principles of therapeutic education, the mentorship approach aims to help patients acquire or maintain disease management skills while maintaining and improving quality of life. It encompasses a set of organized activities which includes psychosocial support, disease and health awareness and information activities, care options, hospital and healthcare organization procedures, community group resources, behaviours related to health, illness and recovery.

In addition, to further train peer helpers/mentors in recovery, the Department of Psychiatry of the UdeM Faculty of Medicine developed a credited training programme, open to anyone wishing to convert experiential disease knowledge (personal or that of a relative) into accredited expertise for the benefit of others. Through this programme, students are exposed to basic medical information on the organization of care and services, as well as various recovery and self-management processes in chronic mental or physical illnesses. This knowledge is then applied to various training environments (public health and social services network, community groups and organizations, private companies, etc.).

The role of peer helping mentors is to contribute to the mobilization of personal skills and awaken resilience potential within peers suffering from health issues in the communities. Mentors help peers become and remain primary architects of their own recovery journey.

Success Factors of the Montréal Model

General Factors

In an article by Carman et al. (2013), three general factors are identified to explain the success of patient engagement (*Centre de pédagogie appliquée aux sciences de la santé* 2014). First in line are patient characteristics: values, knowledge, attitudes, beliefs and past experiences, education level, health condition, self-confidence and social status, which are factors that can affect a patient's degree of commitment. In the Montréal model, the idea is to first select patients that exhibit specific characteristics conducive to patient partnership. Then, selected patients can help other patients become involved in self-care before becoming patient advisors in other aspects or care and services.

Second, institutional culture may influence patient engagement in healthcare organizations. It mostly depends on the culture's openness towards patient opinions and that of their relatives, as well as its flexibility when implementing practices and policies. In Quebec, there is a long tradition of citizen participation, and the province is home to a culture that generally values innovation and change. The resilience of Quebec's health system is recognized as well. That said, although different practice areas have shown openness towards patient participation and that of their relatives, converting commitments into action is not always a simple task.

The third factor is related to social norms, which could impact the perceived value added by patient and citizen engagement at all levels. Compensation arrangements for professionals, health organizations and patients may have an impact on participation as well (Carman et al. 2013). However, in Quebec, volunteering and citizen engagement are socially valued activities. Therefore, even though it is not possible to financially compensate for patients participating in Quebec's health and social services system, it does not seem to hinder patient recruitment.

Specific Factors

The first noticeable factor is that the implementation of patient participation, in Quebec, is carried out jointly by patient/health professional duos in recognized structures. In fact, the Patient Partner Office (*Bureau du patient partenaire*), then the DCPP (*Direction collaboration et partenariat patient* 2018) within the UofM Faculty of Medicine, the Centre of Excellence on Partnership with Patients and the Public (CEPPP 2018) at the UofM Hospital Research Centre (*Centre de recherche du Centre hospitalier de l'Université de Montréal* [CRCHUM]) and now the patient partnership Community of Practice are co-directed by patients and health professionals. The Centre of Excellence (CEPPP 2018) is a place where the science of partnership and best practices are being developed. It houses two research chairs and brings together people working on partnership and having experiences in different fields to welcome students and researchers.

The second factor consists in working towards changing practice environments by implementing measures affecting initial and ongoing health professional and healthcare manager training. This helps bridge gaps between theory and reality on the ground.

Since the MSSS recognizes partnership as a fundamental value of the health and social services system, human resources trained in partnership are allocated to Quality, Evaluation, Performance and Ethics Directorates (*Direction de la qualité, de l'évaluation, de la performance et de l'éthique* [DQEPE]) in healthcare organizations. The patient partnership Community of Practice then allows for very fruitful exchanges among healthcare organizations so that they can benefit from each other's experiences.

Thanks to the CEPPP, the development of partnership approaches is fairly structured, and provides healthcare organizations with proven methodology to follow in specific care settings, which caters to the need of working simultaneously with professionals and patients to help them to become partners at various levels of the health system (Pomey et al. 2018d).

And lastly, a final important factor is to systematically implement assessment projects to properly measure patient engagement impacts and benefit from research funding to evaluate partnership impact on patients and relatives, clinicians, managers and different health system structures (Boivin 2018; Boivin et al. 2018c).

Conclusion

In Quebec, since the beginning, patient partnership was conceived as an approach to be conducted simultaneously in the training of healthcare actors, in research and in the health system. Having sprouted from academic circles, particularly from a faculty of medicine, the model's legitimacy was more easily recognized by various health system actors. Synergies have enabled the acceleration of cultural shifts in healthcare settings and in the way healthcare professionals perceive patients' roles and contributions to improve the quality and safety of care, which ultimately yields care and services that are better suited to patients' needs.

The integration of patients into all spheres that can have an impact on patient health also provides an opportunity to learn from experiences in some areas and how they can be transferred to others. Indeed, everything that has been learned for patient recruitment, training and coaching has first been tested in universities before being imported into health institutions and research. It is by working simultaneously on these different spheres that we will be able to change the culture more quickly and ensure that patient participation in a structured and evaluated way becomes a matter of course and allows the health system, the world of research and education to better meet the real needs of patients and their families (Pomey et al. 2018d).

Among the elements still to be worked on in the Montreal model, these focus more particularly on vulnerable populations and also on how to better structure the therapeutic coaching that patients can provide to each other to help them better live their daily lives with their disease.

By better meeting their needs and allowing them to take their place, the involvement of patients and their relatives, care relationships can hopefully become more humanized and contribute to improving the population's health and well-being (Boivin et al. 2018a).

Acknowledgements We would like to acknowledge the contributions of Jean-François Pelletier, France Laverdière and France Légaré for their suggestions to add examples in this chapter and also to patients who contribute to the Montréal Model.

References

Boivin, A. 2018. From craft to reflective art and science; comment on "metrics and evaluation tools for patient engagement in healthcare organization- and system-level decision-making: A systematic review". *International Journal of Health Policy and Management* 8 (2): 124–127.

Boivin, A., and G. Rouly. 2018. Communauté soignante: Prendre soin les uns des autres. *Journées annuelles de santé publique du Québec*, Montréal.

Boivin, A., P. Lehoux, R. Lacombe, J. Burgers, and R. Grol. 2014. Involving patients in setting priorities for healthcare improvement: A cluster randomized trial. *Implementation Science* 9: 24.

Boivin, A., V. Dumez, C. Fancott, and A. L'Esperance. 2018a. Growing a healthy ecosystem for patient and citizen partnerships. *Healthcare Quarterly* 21 (Sp): 73–82.

Boivin, A., A. L'Esperance, F.P. Gauvin, V. Dumez, A.C. Macaulay, P. Lehoux, and J. Abelson. 2018b. Patient and public engagement in research and health system decision making: A systematic review of evaluation tools. *Health Expectations* 21 (6): 1075–1084.

Boivin, A., T. Richards, L. Forsythe, A. Gregoire, A. L'Esperance, J. Abelson, and K.L. Carman. 2018c. Evaluating patient and public involvement in research. *BMJ* 363: k5147.

Cambon, L., and F. Alla. 2013. Transfert et partage de connaissances en santé publique: réflexions Sur les composantes d'un dispositif national en France. *Santé Publique* 25 (6): 757–762.

Canadian Institute for Health Information. 2018. How does health spending differ across provinces and territories? https://www.cihi.ca/en/how-does-health-spending-differ-across-provinces-and-territories-2017. Accessed 17 Nov 2018.

Canadian Institutes for Health Research. 2015. Canada's strategy for Patient-Oriented Research. Patient engagement framework at a glance. http://www.cihr-irsc.gc.ca/e/49232.html. Accessed 6 Nov 2018.

Carman, K.L., and T.A. Workman. 2017. Engaging patients and consumers in research evidence: Applying the conceptual model of patient and family engagement. *Patient Education and Counseling* 100 (1): 25–29.

Carman, K.L., P. Dardess, M. Maurer, S. Sofaer, K. Adams, C. Bechtel, and J. Sweeney. 2013. Patient and family engagement: A framework for understanding the elements and developing interventions and policies. *Health Affairs* 32 (2): 223–231.

Castonguay, C., and G. Nepveu. 1967. *Rapport de la Commission d'enquête sur la santé et le bien-être social.* Québec: Éditeur officiel du Québec.

Centre de pédagogie appliquée aux sciences de la santé. 2013. *Guide d'implantation du partenariat de soins et de services, vers une collaboration optimale entre intervenants et avec le patient.* Montréal, QC: CPASS, Université de Montréal.

———. 2014. *Programme partenaires de soins. Rapport d'étape (2011–2013) et perspectives.* Montréal, QC: CPASS, Université de Montréal.

Centre de recherche du CHUM. 2018a. Le Patient Accompagnateur, une Ressource Organisationnelle comme Levier pour une Expérience patient améliorée en oncologie (PAROLE-Onco). https://chaireengagementpatient.openum.ca/projets-de-recherche/parole-onco-2/. Accessed 6 Nov 2018.

———. 2018b. Communautés de pratique. https://chaireengagementpatient.openum.ca/communautes-de-pratique/. Accessed 6 Nov 2018.

CEPPP. 2018a. *Patients as trainers in educations*. Montreal: CEPPP.

———. 2018b. *Who we are*. https://ceppp.ca/en/about-us/. Accessed 6 Nov 2018.

Chouinard, M.-C., C. Hudon, M.-F. Dubois, P. Roberge, C. Loignon, É. Tchouaket, M. Fortin, É.-M. Couture, and M. Sasseville. 2013. Case management and self-management support for frequent users with chronic disease in primary care: A pragmatic randomized controlled trial. *BMC Health Services Research* 13 (1): 49.

Conseil pour la protection des malades. 2018. Service conseil. Notre approche. https://www.cpm.qc.ca/champs-dintervention/service-conseil. Accessed 6 Nov 2018.

Coulter, A. 2012. Patient engagement—What works? *The Journal of Ambulatory Care Management* 35 (2): 80–89.

Denis, J.-L., H. Davies, E. Ferlie, L. Fitzgerald, and A. McManus. 2011. *Assessing initiatives to transform health care systems—Lessons for the Canadian health care system*, 23. Ottawa: CHSRF.

Direction collaboration et partenariat patient. 2015. *Référentiel de compétences des patients*, 18. Montréal, QC: DCPP, Université de Montréal.

———. 2018. Mission. https://medecine.umontreal.ca/faculte/direction-collaboration-partenariat-patient/. Accessed 6 Nov 2018.

Dumez, V., and P. Karazivan. 2018. Évolution des activités de la DCPP entre 2011 et 2017. Direction collaboration et partenariat patient.

Fédération des centres d'assistance et d'accompagnement aux plaintes. 2018. L'historique de la Fédération des centres d'assistance et d'accompagnement aux plaintes. https://fcaap.ca/federation/historique/. Accessed 6 Nov 2018.

Flora, L., A. Berkesse, A. Payot, V. Dumez, and P. Karazivan. 2016a. Chapitre 3. L'application d'un modèle intégré de partenariat-patient dans la formation des professionnels de la santé: vers un nouveau paradigme humaniste et éthique de co-construction des savoirs en santé. *Journal international de bioéthique et d'éthique des sciences* 27 (1): 59–72.

Flora, L., P. Karazivan, V. Dumez, and M. Pomey. 2016b. La vision «patient partenaire» et ses implications: le modèle de Montréal. *La Revue du Praticien* 66 (4): 371.

Fulmer, T., M. Gaines, and F. Macy. 2014. *Partnering with patients, families, and communities to link Interprofessional practice and education*. Josiah Macy Jr Foundation: New-York.

Gilmour, H. 2012. Social participation and the health and well-being of Canadian seniors. *Health Reports* 23 (4): 23–32.

Godbout, J., M. Leduc, and J.-P. Collin. 1987. *La face cachée du système. Commission d'enquête sur les services de santé et les services sociaux*. Québec: Les publications du Québec.

Government of Quebec. 2002. Loi sur les services de santé et les services sociaux. *Québec Éditeur officiel du Québec* S-4.2.

——— 2015. LOI MODIFIANT L'ORGANISATION ET LA GOUVERNANCE DU RÉSEAU DE LA SANTÉ ET DES SERVICES SOCIAUX NOTAMMENT PAR L'ABOLITION DES AGENCES RÉGIONALES. *Québec Éditeur officiel du Québec* Chapitre O-7.2.

Haesebaert, J., I. Samson, H. Lee-Gosselin, S. Guay-Belanger, J.F. Proteau, G. Drouin, C. Guimont, L. Vigneault, A. Poirier, P.N. Sanon, G. Roch, M.E. Poitras, A. LeBlanc, and F. Legare. 2018. How to engage patients in research and quality improvement in community-based primary care settings: Protocol for a participatory action research pilot study. *Research Involvement and Engagement* 4: 30.

Holt-Lunstad, J., T.B. Smith, and J.B. Layton. 2010. Social relationships and mortality risk: A meta-analytic review. *PLoS Medicine* 7 (7): e1000316.

Institut de la Statistique du Québec. 2018. Banque de données des statistiques officielles sur le Québec. http://www.bdso.gouv.qc.ca/pls/ken/p_afch_tabl_clie?p_no_client_cie=FR&p_param_id_raprt=798.

Institut national d'excellence en santé et en services sociaux. 2018a. FORUM MÉTHODOLOGIQUE 2017. https://www.inesss.qc.ca/evenements/forum-methodologique-2017.html?sword_list%5B0%5D=forum&no_cache=1. Accessed 17 Nov 18.

———. 2018b. Mission. https://www.inesss.qc.ca/a-propos/a-propos-de-linstitut.html. Accessed 6 Nov 2018.

———. 2018c. *Les éléments facilitant la prise de décision dans le contexte du remplacement du générateur d'un défibrillateur cardiaque implantable*. Montréal, QC: Institut national d'excellence en santé et services sociaux (INESSS).

Instituts de recherche en santé du Canada. 2018. Stratégie de recherche axée sur le patient—Cadre d'engagement des patients. http://www.cihr-irsc.gc.ca/f/48413.html. Accessed 6 Nov 2018.

Karazivan, P., V. Dumez, L. Flora, M.-P. Pomey, C. Del Grande, D.P. Ghadiri, N. Fernandez, E. Jouet, O. Las Vergnas, and P. Lebel. 2015. The patient-as-partner approach in health care: A conceptual framework for a necessary transition. *Academic Medicine* 90 (4): 437–441.

Katz, A., N. Herpai, G. Smith, K. Aubrey-Bassler, M. Breton, A. Boivin, W. Hogg, B. Miedema, J. Pang, W. Wodchis, and S. Wong. 2017. Alignment of Canadian primary care with the patient medical home model: A QUALICO-PC study. *Annals of Family Medicine* 15 (3): 230–236.

Lebel, P., L. Flora, V. Dumez, A. Berkesse, A. Néron, and B. Débarges. 2014. Le partenariat en santé: une approche révolutionnaire pour mieux répondre aux besoins des personnes âgées et de leurs proches aidants par la co-construction. *Vie et Vieillissement* 12 (1): 15–20.

Legare, F., M. Labrecque, M. Cauchon, J. Castel, S. Turcotte, and J. Grimshaw. 2012. Training family physicians in shared decision-making to reduce the overuse of antibiotics in acute respiratory infections: A cluster randomized trial. *CMAJ* 184 (13): E726–E734.

Lemieux, V., P. Lebel, and M. Stanton Jean. 2018. *La participation sociale comme déterminant de la santé: Comment véritablement l'intégrer aux actions de santé publique? La participation sociale des ainés revisitée: des savoirs à l'action.* Québec: Université de Laval.

Pomey, M., and P. Lebel. 2016. Patient engagement: The Quebec path. *Healthc Papers* 16 (2): 78–83.

Pomey, M., V. Dumez, A. Boivin, H. Hihat, and P. Lebel. 2015a. Le partenariat de soins et de services: une voix/voie pour donner un sens à la loi 10? (2015). *Le point en administration de la santé* 11 (1): 38–42.

Pomey, M., L. Flora, P. Karazivan, V. Dumez, P. Lebel, M. Vanier, B. Debarges, N. Clavel, and E. Jouet. 2015b. The Montreal model: The challenges of a partnership relationship between patients and healthcare professionals. *Santé Publique* 27 (1 Suppl): S41–S50.

Pomey, M., D.P. Ghadiri, P. Karazivan, N. Fernandez, and N. Clavel. 2015c. Patients as partners: A qualitative study of patients' engagement in their health care. *PLoS One* 10 (4): e0122499.

Pomey, M., K. Vigneault, J. Arsenault, J. Higgins, V. Lahaie, O. Fortin, M. De Guise, and A. Michel Dnino. 2015d. Une intervention à l'impact décisif pour le nouveau patient. *La revue du praticien* 65: 1215–1218.

Pomey, M., E. Morin, C. Neault, V. Biron, L. Houle, L. Lavigueur, G. Bouvette, N. St-Pierre, and M. Beaumont. 2016. Patient advisors: How to implement a process for involvement at all levels of governance in a healthcare organization. *Patient Experience Journal* 3 (3): 99–112.

Pomey, M.-P., J.I. Efanov, J. Arseneault, A.-M. Mercier, V. Lahaie, O. Fortin, M. Haineault, and A.M. Danino. 2018a. The partnership co-design lab: Co-constructing a patient advisor programme to increase adherence to rehabilitation after upper extremity replantation. *The Journal of Health Design* 3 (1): 94–101.

Pomey, M., N. Clavel, L. Normandin, C. Del Grande, and D. Ghadiri. 2018b. *Development and pre-testing of the CADICEE questionnaire to assess the degree of care partnership between users and healthcare professionals.* Montreal: University of Montreal.

Pomey, M., G. Dumais Levesque, A. Fournier and E. Drouin. 2018c. *Patient advisor roles for positive experiences among young patients—The PAROLE-pediatric transition program.* 8th international conference on patient- and family-centered care, Baltimore, MD.

Pomey, M., P. Lebel, N. Clavel, E. Morin, M. Morin, C. Neault, B. Tetrault, and A. Ewalds. 2018d. Development of patient-inclusive teams: Towards a structured methodology. *Healthcare Quarterly* 21 (SP): 38–44.

Pomey, M.P., P. Brouillard, I. Ganache, L. Lambert, L. Boothroyd, C. Collette, S. Bédard, A. Grégoire, S. Pelaez, O. Demers-Payette, M. Goetghebeur, M. de Guise, and D. Roy. 2019. Engaging patients in the co-construction of recommendations in health technology assessment: An example with replacement of an implantable cardiac defibrillator. *Health Expectations.* (Forthcoming).

Quebec Ministry of Health and Social Services. 2009. *Regards sur le système de santé et de services sociaux du.* Québec, QC: MSSS, Gouvernement du Québec.

———. 2015. Système de santé et de services sociaux en bref. Financement des services. http://www.msss.gouv.qc.ca/reseau/systeme-de-sante-et-de-services-sociaux-en-bref/financement-des-services/. Accessed 6 Nov 2018.

———. 2017. *Plan stratégique du ministère de la Santé et des Services sociaux 2015–2020*, 33. Québec: MSSS, Gouvernement du Québec.

———. 2018. Système de santé et de services sociaux en bref. http://www.msss.gouv.qc.ca/reseau/systeme-de-sante-et-de-services-sociaux-en-bref/le-ministere-et-ses-partenaires/. Accessed 17 Nov 2018.

———. 2018a. *Cadre de référence relatif aux comités des usagers et aux comités de résidents.* Québec: MSSS, Gouvernement du Québec.

———. 2018b. *Cadre de référence de l'approche de partenariat entre les usagers, leurs proches et les acteurs en santé et en services sociaux*, 46. Québec: MSSS, Gouvernement du Québec.

Rakel, A. 2017. *Projet Transplant-Action: Impact de l'implication d'un programme d'entraînement créé en collaboration avec des patients partenaies sur le fonction cardiaque et le contrôle des facteurs de risques cardio vasculaires en post greffe rénale et hépatique.* Montréal, QC: Centre Hospitalier de l'Université de Montréal.

Regroupement provincial des comités des usagers. 2018. Le RPCU. Notre mission. http://www.rpcu.qc.ca/fr/mission.aspx. Accessed 6 Nov 2018.

Rochon, J. 1988. *Rapport de la commission d'enquête sur les services de santé et les services sociaux*, 221. Québec: Les publications du Québec.

Samson, I., and J. Dogba. 2016. Les Rencontres patients-Usagers, Cliniciens et CHercheurS pour améliorer la recherche en première ligne. RUCCHES, Université Laval. https://docplayer.fr/86835430-Les-rencontres-patients-usagers-cliniciens-et-chercheurs-pour-ameliorer-la-recherche-en-premiere-lignerucches.html.

Trépanier, E., M. Pomey, and P. Lebel. 2017. *La participation des patients à la gouvernance du groupes de médecins de famille au*. Québec: Université de Montréal.

University of Montreal. 2018. Université de Montréal. Microprogramme de 1er cycle en santé mentale: mentorat pour pairs aidants. https://admission.umontreal.ca/programmes/microprogramme-de-1er-cycle-en-sante-mentale-mentorat-pour-pairs-aidants/. Accessed 6 Nov 2018.

Vachon, B., B. Desorcy, M. Camirand, J. Rodrigue, L. Quesnel, C. Guimond, M. Labelle, J. Fournier, and J. Grimshaw. 2013. Engaging primary care practitioners in quality improvement: Making explicit the program theory of an interprofessional education intervention. *BMC Health Services Research* 13: 106.

Vachon, B., B. Désorcy, I. Gaboury, M. Camirand, J. Rodrigue, L. Quesnel, C. Guimond, M. Labelle, A.-T. Huynh, and J. Grimshaw. 2015. Combining administrative data feedback, reflection and action planning to engage primary care professionals in quality improvement: Qualitative assessment of short term program outcomes. *BMC Health Services Research* 15: 391–391.

Vachon, B., A.T. Huynh, M. Breton, L. Quesnel, M. Camirand, J. Leblanc, and S. Tardif. 2017. Patients' expectations and solutions for improving primary diabetes care. *International Journal of Health Care Quality Assurance* 30 (6): 554–567.

Vanier, M., V. Dumez, E. Drouin, I. Brault, S. MacDonal, and A. Boucher. 2014. *Université de Montréal case study. Partners in Interprofessional Education: Integrating patients-as-trainers. Engaging patients, families and communities to link Interprofessional practice and education.* Arlington: Virginia Macy Jr Foundation.

4

Implementing Patient and Carer Participation in Self-Care and Co-Care in Sweden: Policy, Practice and the Future of Person-Centred Care

John Øvretveit and Eskil Degsell

Introduction

Sweden has universal health coverage achieved through a decentralized national health service which counts 21 regions responsible for financing, purchasing and providing all individual health services. Sweden spends 11 per cent of its GDP on healthcare and ranks third for health spending compared to other EU countries. Public expenditure accounts for 84 per cent of health spending and voluntary health insurance represents a small but increasing part of health funding (OECD 2017).

Sweden's population of 10 million is spread across a territory of 450,295 kilometres^2, with a relatively low density of population of 22.6 per kilometre^2. Life expectancy at birth was 82.2 years old in 2015, 80.4 years for men and 84.1 for women, and is among the highest in the EU (OECD 2017). In Sweden, behavioural risk factors including smoking, alcohol, dietary risks and physical inactivity are below most of the EU countries, and 26 per cent of the overall burden of disease in 2015 can be

J. Øvretveit (✉) • E. Degsell
Karolinska Institute, Stockholm, Sweden
e-mail: Eskil.degsell@ki.se

M.-P. Pomey et al. (eds.), *Patient Engagement*, Organizational Behaviour in Healthcare,
https://doi.org/10.1007/978-3-030-14101-1_4

attributed to such risk factors. For example, only 12 per cent of people smoke daily and 13 per cent of the population suffers from obesity (OECD 2017). However, Sweden faces relatively high rates of cardiovascular diseases and cancer, which account for nearly two-thirds of deaths. In 2014, cardiovascular diseases accounted for 37 per cent of all deaths among women and 36 per cent of all deaths among men, and cancer accounted for 23 per cent of all deaths among women and 27 per cent of all deaths among men (OECD 2017). Heart disease is the most common cause of death followed by Alzheimer's disease and other forms of dementia, and musculoskeletal problems and depression are among the leading causes of poor health which have important life-limiting consequences (OECD 2017).

In terms of health system performance, Sweden has a relatively low rate of preventable mortality (98 preventable deaths/100,000 population in 2014). Although there are long waiting times and care coordination issues, access to healthcare is generally good. Finally, Sweden has a relatively high number of doctors and nurses which is above the EU average (4.2 doctors per 1000 population and 11.1 nurses per 1000 population). However, the efficient use of workforce remains challenging in Sweden. The 2014 Commonwealth Fund International Health Policy Survey highlights challenges for chronic management in primary care settings, since only 53 per cent of patients report that they are often or always informed about the care they have received from healthcare professionals (OECD 2017).

Sweden is experiencing a widening gap between the supply of and the demand for healthcare. There are more older people living longer, many with chronic diseases, but fewer qualified and unqualified workers to care for them. There is a growing gap between the cost of care and the ability to pay for care, and this gap is increasing with new treatments and technologies which, in the past, have added to the costs of care. One response is for healthcare to enable patients to perform self-care more effectively, which includes preventing avoidable illness. How can this best be done in ways which benefit all, rather than burdening patients and their families with work they are not able to undertake?

This chapter provides an answer to this question which includes our "co-care" programme of research. It also draws on our experiences as a researcher with a chronic illness and a patient representative who is also a close-carer for his partner with a brain tumour.

The two changes we discuss are the

- changes needed for public services to enable patients and healthcare workers to work more fully in a co-caring partnership, which also includes the patient's close-carers (family and friends) in that partnership;
- changes to enable more people to perform more effective self-care, to prevent or reduce health deterioration when they contract a disease or experience trauma, as well as to avoid having to use healthcare services that arise from an illness.

We concentrate on what healthcare services and health systems can do to enable self-care rather than the broader population changes needed also to promote wellness and a "culture of health" (RWJF 2018). We highlight successful examples and consider how organizational behaviour, implementation and improvement sciences, and digital technologies can be used to make this transition to a new "co-care" and "person-centered" health service.

The chapter puts forward two propositions. The first is that to reduce the widening gaps noted above, we need to engage and support citizens, patients and health workers to carry out more effective self-care and co-care. The second is that organizational, implementation and improvement sciences can assist the movement towards more person-centred services.

Our starting perspective is that:

- most healthcare is provided by ourselves and to ourselves, as well as to our family or friends as "close-carers" for them;
- this self-care can be more effective with the right support from health and other services, and appropriate government health and healthcare policies and financing;
- co-care, which also involves shared decision-making about treatment, is effective for choosing and implementing the right treatments;
- people vary in the amount and type of support they need, which may change at different stages of their illness, and they also vary in the support they need to enable wellness activities and prevent disease;
- research can help the changes needed to achieve more self-care and co-care which is appropriate and effective;

- not all changes to support self-care and co-care are cost-saving for healthcare, but those that are should be prioritized first so as to show what can be achieved and to speed implementation.

There is some evidence to support these contentions which we present in this chapter, as well as our personal experience. We conceptualize patient, citizen and carer engagement and participation as being possible at different levels: (a) in formulating policy for health and healthcare, (b) in decisions and planning the overall structure of a healthcare system, including the siting of services; (c) in designing the organization of care at a service level, (d) in planning and taking part in their own individual care and (e) in providing information about outcomes of care and experiences of care.

The chapter first presents the history of and current policy in Sweden regarding patient participation. It describes the different types of participation and some of the research and experience into these, including how digital health technology is both helping and hindering different types of patient participation. It then presents the two authors' experiences of participation in brain tumour care and orthopaedic surgery care. To consider how to advance participation, the chapter then shows the contribution of research to faster and more widespread change for effective participation, as well as sharing the authors' research, experience and perceptions. The focus is on changes in healthcare practice, organization and attitudes that have enabled patients to play a greater role in their care and in self-managing their health, and on effective ways to enable these changes.

What Is Co-Care and Self-Care and Why Is It a Challenge to Current Healthcare Services?

In this chapter we use the terms "co-care" and "self-care" rather than "patient engagement" (PE) or "patient participation" (PP). We do so because these are more specific aspects of PE and PP, and we focus on these as we see them as the most important to the future. The latter two terms (PE and PP) are more general and refer to the many different ways in which patients are involved in different activities, and the terms are also defined in different ways (INVOLVE 2012).

The meanings of the terms that we use in this chapter are given in Appendix 4.1. Our focus is on how patients are involved in their own care and in the organization and implementation design to support co-care and self-care. We define "co-care" simply and in a way that could be measured as "sharing decisions and activities about care and self-care". Co-care combines shared decision making as well as activities to enable a person to engage in self-care.

Central to the concept is "expert patient knowledge": knowledge that a patient has about their symptoms and about "what works for me", the strategies that they perform which help them to manage their symptoms and their health. More patients are sharing and learning from other patients about such strategies (Patients like me 2018; Recovery college 2018). This individual and collective patient knowledge is different to clinical professionals' knowledge about disease and treatment effectiveness, much of which relates to "the average patient" (Kent and Hayward 2007).

Patient knowledge is also about the activities and life goals which are now important to them after their diagnosis and experiencing the effects of their illness. We define patient-driven care and treatment as choosing treatments, care and self-care strategies that enable a patient to perform the activities and achieve the life goals which are important to them at different times.

Patient capacity for sharing care and self-care can be developed into competences for these activities, especially in people classified as "disadvantaged" (Lima et al. 2016). However, an important criticism of co-care is that this approach may meet the wishes of educated and wealthier patients, but may not benefit patients who are limited in the extent of shared decision making and self-care that they can undertake by capacity or circumstance, by education or socio-economic factors. It is unknown whether or how more self-care by the privileged might release resources to invest in more support for those more challenged to perform self-care.

Developing self-care presents challenges to healthcare because it requires changes in attitudes, and an ability to judge when and how a person is able and willing to perform more self-care and which extra and new services are required, which can often include medically-related social services. Some self-care can damage a person's health, for example when patients self-medicate or exercise inappropriately. Self-care and co-care present new demands for health services including often requiring clinicians to learn new ways to enable patients to "do it for themselves" rather than "deciding and doing" for patients. It requires healthcare organizations and IT systems to change so as to support clinicians and patients to carry out effective self-care and co-care, and to do so economically. We later describe some of these changes and some examples of co-care.

Context for Co-Care and Self-Care in the Nordic Countries

There is a history to bear in mind that provides a context for the co-care in Sweden. Part of this is a culture of physical activity and independence which is generally compatible with health promotion activities. Compared to some other high-income countries there is a long history of and substantial investment in health promotion and wellness programmes. In addition, there is a financial incentive for local county government taxpayer-funded services, which provide most healthcare, to encourage and support health promotion and wellness programmes: effective preventative illness and health promotion activities reduce avoidable illness and utilization of healthcare among a population that tends to remain in the geographic areas served by their county.

This culture and the health promotion activities are supportive of those aspects of co-care and self-care which help to prevent illness, and are also factors contributing to the reduction of health deterioration when illness does strike: there is a generally high engagement in healthy lifestyles and a desire to maintain such a lifestyle when experiencing illness, although there are differences between and within different social groups, especially in the larger cities.

A further part of the context is the "Ombudsman" arrangement, which is a government officer and an administrative system which acts to protect the interests of individual citizens who complain about an organization. This originated in Sweden 300 years ago: it both builds on and contributes to a democratic culture that has an even longer history in the Nordic countries. This is part of the background that led to the Nordic countries being the first to establish patients' rights in law in the 1990s (Fallberg and Øvretveit 2003). Since then, various quality-improvement and safety initiatives and policies have been the main vehicles shaping healthcare towards a more co-care approach. This includes making data available to patients to assist them in choosing a healthcare provider.

However, over the last 30 years there has not been a widespread and effective implementation of person-centred and co-care approaches, and the examples we cite later are isolated ones that are yet to be spread widely. A study and report in 2012 concluded that "Sweden's health care system often fails to anticipate and respond to patients as individuals with particular needs, values and preferences. Failure to meet patient expectations can have demonstrable costs to patients, the health system and the public purse" (Docteur and Coulter 2012). An evaluation in 2017 of the enhanced 2015 Swedish patients' rights law concluded that it was an "Act without impact", that "many patients do not feel that the health care services are seeking their participation", "and think that they have been given a somewhat lower level of support by the health care service in adapting the self-care they provide to themselves to their individual needs". The following is one of the later recommendations by the local government association:

> *Patients should be given better tools to enable them to participate more and become more involved in their care. This mostly involves providing access to information and guiding patients correctly, when they are looking for information, but also enabling patients themselves to share their information with the health care service to a greater extent.* (Vardanalysis 2017)

Building on our own experience with applied improvement research and on the experience of others in Sweden with service improvement, we are carrying out a programme of co-care research and development in partnership with Stockholm county healthcare and patient organizations. Two of the research project team members are "patient researchers" and we describe their role as part of this chapter's discussion of the co-care approach. The earlier-noted external assessment of patient-centredness of Swedish healthcare in 2012 commented that "Patients and patient representatives are an untapped resource in Sweden's health care in the progress towards a more patient-centered health care" (Docteur and Coulter 2012).

Supporting Patients and Carers

The Karolinska Patient-Driven Co-Care Programme

The second author of this chapter is a carer for a patient with a brain tumour and a patient representative on a number of hospital and national bodies. As such, he and other patients have been successful in establishing the idea of patient involvement in planning changes in healthcare in Sweden, and locally in clinic re-organization for the patient-flow processes in the new Karolinska hospital. Cancer patients have been among those most involved in advancing co-care and self-care and in contributing to service redesign from the patient perspective.

As part of a research project with the USA Mayo Clinic, the second author has also developed a model for co-care and the learning health system (Fig. 4.1). This describes the most important needs from the patient's perspective, as well as the corresponding activities that healthcare workers need to undertake to perform co-care and enable self-care.

Some of the important principles underlying this model and the use of patient knowledge in individual care include:

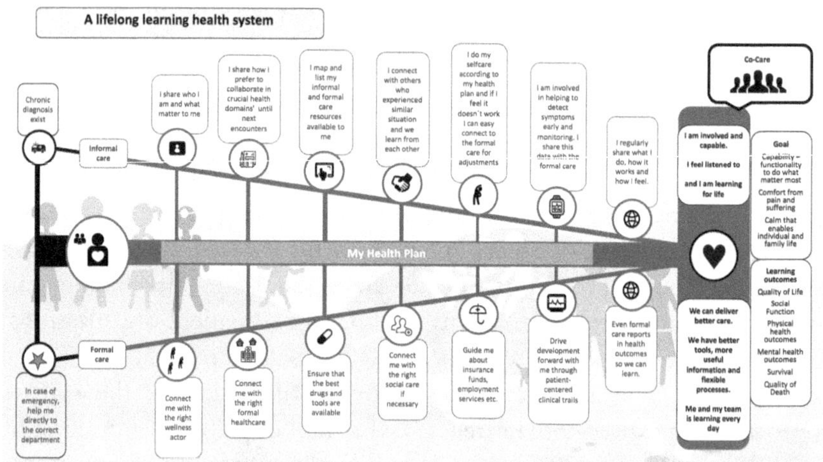

Fig. 4.1 The model for co-care and the learning health system[1]

1. Recognition of different personal capacities and wishes for self-care, and how this may change at different times in the course of treatment and illness;
2. Values clarification and goal setting: What was done/not done to enable you and/or your partner being treated to clarify what they most hoped to be able to do in the future that the treatment should make possible?
3. Shared decision making;
4. Collecting and acting on patient health monitoring data;
5. Incentives for and against co-care for clinical providers and the service-providing organization, and the healthcare system as a whole;
6. Service delivery organization design to support co-care (including digital data and technologies).

The "co-care" programme has developed and is studying the use of a number of tools to help implement co-care in the different stages of the model for co-care and the learning health system (Fig. 4.1). Some are being developed in private—public partnerships, and some privately and independent of the public health system. Some involve patient—clinician—researcher partnerships (PCRPs).

One is a symptom-monitoring tool used by patients to enhance the everyday management of cystic fibrosis (CF). This tool was developed by the chair of the Cystic Fibrosis Association, who funded the company that owns and distributes the tool (Genia 2018). The CF Association organizes networking, collaboration and shared learning among CF patients. The Association works with all CF Centres of the six university hospitals in Sweden to help develop the use of the CF national clinical registry and the Genia tool.

Another self-tracking tool is the "ParkWell" smart phone application, developed by a patient-engineer in collaboration with the company Cambio, which tracks patients' medication administration and related short-term motor symptoms (Parkwell 2018).

A third tool is the patient evaluation of co-care survey (PECS). This is a tool for patients to assess how much the service they have received has assisted them to perform the activities they now wish to engage in and which are made more difficult by their health condition (Degsell and Øvretveit 2018; Degsell 2018).

A further patient-driven innovation is one that also uses an internet platform for sharing information and providing education: this is a website and applications associated with Swedish "Recovery Colleges". This follows the examples established in the National Health Service in England (Recovery College 2018). These colleges aim at increasing people's self-confidence in the self-management of their mental health and well-being. This is believed to help people experiencing mental ill-health to take control of and overcome or manage the challenges posed by their mental health difficulties.

Enabling Self-Care and Co-Care for Hip Replacement

The second patient example is from the first author of the chapter who recently received a hip replacement. The following describes the experience of examples of co-care, and examples of opportunities missed for co-care, as well as the national clinical register programmes in Sweden that contribute to co-care.

Generally, my experience of being engaged by healthcare workers in decisions and self-care was positive. This experience was different to my negative experience in accessing care and the time-consuming and frustrating process before I arrived for the operation at the surgery centre. It took time to book and gain an appointment with my primary care doctor, who then referred me for an X-ray of my hip. I waited weeks and was later told the referral had been lost, and I had to start again to make an appointment with my primary care doctor to get another referral, and then to get the X-ray.

I then had to go back to my primary care doctor to be referred to an orthopaedic surgeon, who I then met after further delays in making an appointment as I could not go on the date sent to me. This surgeon did not respond well to my asking what type of operation and implant he was thinking of using, and I chose to go back to my primary care doctor to ask for a referral to a small centre that showed low infection and complication rates in the data base I had been able to access.

I finally received a referral to the doctor assigned to me at this centre, who could not access the X-ray so I had to get another X-ray and revisit later before the operation could be scheduled. Overall, the time and costs wasted because of poor coordination were considerable, and those that I saw and spoke to on the telephone were not encouraging of questions from me and appeared surprised to have a patient asking such questions.

These challenges in navigating the system were in marked contrast to the experience of the actual operation and after-care, which was an excellent experience. Staff did all they could to motivate me to move and then walk as soon as I could, and also gave very clear and comprehensive answers to all my many questions. I also note that my preference was for no information about the operation—I thought I would feel more pain if I heard what they were going to do: my request was "just do what you think best and make sure I wake up after and do not get an infection".

Six months after the operation I received a letter which invited me to score any pain or complications on a patient-reported outcome measure (PROM) diagram, and to send this back (Øvretveit et al. 2017). The diagram was simple and easy for most patients to understand and complete, but there was no option to complete it online or to view the experience of other patients like me. Importantly, it did not ask for or provide a place to comment on my bad experience in stopping the opioid pain medications over a one-week period: I was not told about the side effects which I experienced and during recovery was not able to use a website to see other patients' experience. The latter is an important part of the developments which needs to take place to improve self-care; this is discussed in a later section of this chapter.

The PROM collected one set of data that was entered into the national hip replacement quality registry, which is one of over 106 national quality registers in Sweden. This register did not allow patient interaction, which is a notable feature of some other register systems described below.

Other Examples of Co-Care and Self-Care Support

The Karolinska co-care research programme includes two sub-projects for patients experiencing rheumatoid arthritis and Parkinson's disease. Recent developments have built on the Swedish rheumatology quality registry system to provide an information system that supports co-care and self-care. In this system, a patient reports her symptoms, health and quality of life before she visits a clinician. She does this either at a clinic using a computer tablet or at home using the internet and a patient portal. The patient answers questions shown on a series of simple screens and scores her symptoms, health and quality of life (Øvretveit et al. 2013). The clinician also inputs clinical examinations and laboratory data—this is now done by abstracting the data from the electronic medical record (EMR) on the physician's order.

The system takes these data and combines these with other data to give to the patient and care provider a graphical display of the patient's health status, as well as a time graph of trends in the patient's health and treatment. The patient and clinician can see these data on a visual display, either together at the consultation or separately, and this helps them to work together to optimize the medications and lifestyle to achieve the best health outcomes. Because the patient-reported outcomes measures were developed with patients regarding the outcomes they valued, this presentation of the data also helps the physician and patient to concentrate on understanding the effects of the treatment on these patient-valued outcomes.

These structured data from each visit are exported to the national clinical registry, which builds data sets that can be analysed to contribute to improving patient population health and for research. Evaluations have found that patients greatly value this system for the knowledge it gives them about their changing condition and symptoms over time (Hvitfeldt et al. 2009). This is an example of a new generation of "smart clinical registries" which enable patients to track and self-manage their condition.

Challenges and Ways Forward for Developing Co- and Self-Care

Our experience and our overview of the research on the subject led us to identify key challenges hindering the development of co- and self-care, as well as possible solutions. The context of our discussion is Nordic health and social care services, mostly publicly financed and provided, and an educated and computer-literate population, with a generally healthy lifestyle. The issues and solutions would be different for other countries.

Organization for Standard Services

Healthcare and information services are currently organized to provide one type of standard service for all citizens and patients. Any tailoring to meet individual needs is carried out by individual physicians and other clinicians within a fixed appointment "time slot" and from a limited "menu" of choices available to them. To date, public services have not been able to design and organize their workforce and resources to provide more individual services, based on patients' goals, as described in the co-care discussion above, due to constraints on budgets, old technology, inflexibilities regarding workforce roles and limited capacity to use and implement quality-improvement methods.

Differences in Capability for Self- and Co-Care and Disempowering Visit Environments and Encounters

Traditionally, care has been provided in a way which discourages patients from being active in their care (Alexander et al. 2012). However, there may be an optimal balance between the two extremes of excluding a patient from decision making in their own care and placing full responsibility on a patient for care decisions and self-care. Some patients may not be able to, or may not want to, take responsibility for self-care, or for making decisions about treatment. For acute trauma, it is appropriate that providers take responsibility for the patient's care. But for long-term illnesses there are ethical and economic reasons for encouraging patients to take a greater role in their self-care. The pervasiveness of a reciprocal "care co-dependence" and responsibility-avoidance on the part of patients may have been underestimated.

Assessment

People vary in their ability to engage in self-care and co-care and in their preference for taking control of their own care. Their ability and preference style often vary at different stages in illness episodes. Care providers have a difficult task in judging patients' capabilities and motivating and "stretching" patients to take more responsibility, when many patients' psychological tendency is to avoid responsibility. There are few easy and quick-to-use tools that can be used to elicit and assess patients' and close-carers' preference and capability for self-care and co-care. The education and training of care workers to be able to assess patients' capability and preference for co-care and self-care is limited.

Attitudes and Values

Two sets of attitudes mitigate against increasing co-care and self-care. The first is an overprotective or paternalistic attitude on the part of care providers, often one they are not aware of and similar to an implicit stereotype bias towards different social groups (Norman and Eva 2010). The second is a public concern that, to contain or reduce government expenditure, current care responsibility will be moved from government to individuals, and often to already over-burdened female carers. There is some evidence that this has occurred during the last years of Swedish neo-liberal governments and in the UK.

Given the care and affordability gaps noted in the introduction, there is evidence that any future government in Sweden—social democrat, neo-liberal or libertarian—will need to find politically-acceptable ways to constrain public spending and allocate finance in better ways to achieve the most health. There are ways to develop co- and self-care that result in more or less help being available to those most in need: changing attitudes will require a debate about the role of the individual and the state, and a "contract with the public" that upholds social values.

Developing Co- and Self-Care Approaches to Meet our Health Challenges

Our experience and research have led us to suggest changes and areas for attention that we consider below for developing the co- and self-care approaches that are wanted by citizens and patients: these are changes in financing, organization, digital technology and the use of the modern applied change sciences, especially to develop evidence-based tools and support. The general approach we propose is to reduce the hindrances and barriers to co- and self-care, to carry out and spread evaluated pilots and best practices, and to focus on care and system redesign and attitude change that make possible more support for self-care and co-care approaches.

Financing and Budgets

There are financial incentives for Swedish counties, which provide most healthcare, to encourage people to stay healthy and to reduce their use of services by carrying out more self-care. The incentive is that this could reduce costs and hence the amount of tax funding that would otherwise be required. However, this incentive may be limited in its influence, for two reasons.

First, there is certainly strong evidence that self-care exercise, nutrition and sleep are effective. In addition, there is evidence that co-care approaches can support these self-care activities and are also effective for reducing use of healthcare by people experiencing long-term conditions or a recent hospital visit (Ziebland et al. 2013; Da Silva 2012). However, whether these outcomes could be achieved in most local services is less certain. Evidence about implementation in routine services gives less certainty about which strategies are effective for increasing self-care and co-care for different groups and in different settings, and the costs of these strategies. Counties cannot be certain about how effective and cost-effective their implementation strategies may be for changing healthcare practices and patient lifestyles.

The second factor which reduces the power of the financial incentive to promote self-care and co-care is accounting practices for departmental and service budgeting. A county, overall, could save money with self-care and co-care, but some departments and services would need to spend more to implement these approaches and would not experience savings. For example, to transition people home after hospital care, a hospital would need to spend money and time to develop and then operate a proven self-care and co-care model. This model is likely to result in patients making less use of primary care and other community services and savings in these services. A budget-adjusting arrangement would be needed to spread the costs and savings fairly between different budgets funding the different facilities and services (Øvretveit 2012).

Spreading the costs and savings fairly is further complicated by budgeting for services for "social support" at home for frail older people that provided by local government municipality organizations that are different to the county local government responsible for healthcare. The number and type of municipality services affects people's ability to perform health-related self-care and co-care. These budgets are separate from county healthcare budgets and there are not normally cost- and saving-sharing mechanisms in operation, and indeed, laws that make it difficult to do so. Thus, the practicalities of organizational budgets and absence of cost- and saving-sharing mechanisms reduce the power of the overall financial incentive to keep people healthy and enable co-care.

In addition, other current financing methods for healthcare services are hindering the development of co- and self-care. The payment system is for items for service payment for providing a patient visit or an item of treatment or diagnostics, and is one which provides few rewards for preventative services. The type of activities by healthcare that support co- and self-care that we have described are mostly not funded: activities such as helping patients define goals, tailoring the support provided, coordinating care, developing and providing e-health services, and many other activities to prevent deterioration or illness. Experiments have been carried out with value-based financing, and several services such as orthopaedic hip replacement are financed in this way with patient-reported outcome measures (PROMs) influencing the reimbursement. However, PROMs are not strong incentives for co-care: what would be needed are outcome indicators more strongly influenced by the degree to which services enable the patient to share in decision making and perform more effective self-care.

Time, Workload and Organization

Some private services can give more individualized care because they allow clinicians to spend more time per patient and invest in technologies and tools that allow support to be tailored and patient-centred, but the cost is higher. Examples are some occupational health services and private concierge primary healthcare services in the USA. The lessons for public healthcare for developing co- and self-care from these and other models are that organization and system changes can be made which allow more economical approaches to conducting the activities noted in the last section to be effective and to increase efficiency.

One change is to provide tools or methods for making explicit a patient's hopes and goals, in order that staff can be clearer about what the patient wants to achieve from their treatment. These tools and methods need to be quick and easy to use, but also to give clear guidance for care and treatment. One method is for patients to work through a series of questions on their own, or with help, to define what their health condition is restricting them from achieving. A number of tools exist for this purpose which can be adapted for different health conditions and patient groups.

As regards the efficiency changes, too much of the time of expensive qualified care professionals is taken up with tasks that lower-cost staff could undertake or which could be automated. To date, healthcare services have found it difficult to carry out workforce redesign and care organization changes that redistribute work and train staff for the new roles and teamwork required. Examples are teams which support self-care and co-care for patients with long-term conditions such as heart failure, diabetes and asthma. Such teams are made up of clinicians and others who are from the same communities as their patients or who know the language and culture, and are structured to combine and facilitate working between the nurses, community workers, peer educators and pharmacists in the team and any physicians necessary.

To complement efficient workforce redesign, carefully designed digital health technologies are needed.

Digital Health Technology

Decision-support technologies within the electronic health record and on mobile devices can help care professionals at all qualification levels to provide more effective treatments and services than they would be able to carry out if they relied only on what they had learned from their training. These technologies enable staff to "work at the top of their licence" and can also reduce the burden of data collection and allow more accurate and comprehensive patient data to be collected.

A great benefit of digital data and technologies is that they enable information to be sent and interventions to be provided that are tailored to the needs and wishes of an individual. A simple example is how historical data about our choices or searches are collected and algorithms are used to combine these data with other data to target us with advertisements for products that the system assumes we would be interested in. In healthcare, there are opportunities to tailor information to individual patients based on data about the patient, thus increasing the chances that the information is relevant and will increase patient activation (Hibbard and Mahoney 2010). The benefit of digital data and technologies is that individual tailoring can be performed economically on a large scale, allowing mass-customization of strategies for engaging and activating patients.

Modern Applied Change Sciences

The last key element in developing self- and co- care is better application of knowledge from four of the applied change sciences: the sciences of business case economics, implementation, behaviour changes and improvement. We summarize below the contributions each can make to designing, implementing and evaluating cost-effective self- and co-care interventions:

Business case economics: Budget impact analysis and return on investment estimation are two accounting methods that make it possible to make pragmatic estimates of the costs and savings of a particular intervention or change designed to develop self-care and co-care. This information is necessary for management and others to decide whether and how to invest in a change to support self- and co-care. Budget impact analysis can be applied to assess the costs and savings to different departmental or other budgets and to help devise a "fair cost-savings spreading contract" (Sullivan et al. 2014). This can also be used as a basis for estimating a return on investment in different situations and for different stakeholders, at one-year, three-year and ten-year timescales (AHRQ 2017, 2018; Øvretveit 2009).

Implementation science: This knowledge describes, understands, explains and evaluates how clinicians and healthcare organizations "take up" into routine practice a proven "improvement change", such as a new and more effective treatment. The chapter noted a number of interventions to healthcare and direct to patients that enable them to carry out more and better self- and co-care. Implementation science helps to plan and revise evidence-based strategies to enable staff and patients to perform self- and co-care, but to date it has been little used: one example is taxonomies of strategies that have been in use (73 different implementation strategies and 93 different behaviour change methods (Powell et al. 2015; Michie et al. 2013)).

Behaviour change science: A number of disciplines contribute to the growing behaviour and organizational change sciences. These provide insights about how to change social, financial and physical environments so as to enable clinicians and patients to change their routines. These sciences reveal the emotional and unconscious factors underlying success and failure in behaviour change, and provide additional insights and tools for enabling self- and co-care.

Improvement science: This comprises a set of theories and tools typically used by workplace project teams to diagnose, test and carry out changes that improve healthcare processes and outcomes (Langley et al. 1996; Batalden and Stoltz 1993). Part of this science that is already contributing to developing co-care is the application of approaches for improving patient flow through a care service, and for building in time and systems to support co-care at different stages (Nelson et al. 2016; Sabadosa and Batalden 2014).

We can therefore summarize here the conditions allowing the development of self- and co-care:

(1) A recognition of different personal capacities and wishes for self-care, and how this may change at different times in the course of treatment and illness;

(2) Values clarification and goal setting: What was done/not done to enable you and/or your relative being treated to clarify what they most hoped to be able to do in the future that the treatment should make possible?
(3) Shared decision making;
(4) Collecting and acting on patient health monitoring data;
(5) Incentives for and against co-care for clinical providers and the service-providing organization, and the healthcare system as a whole;
(6) Service delivery organization design to support co-care (including digital data and technologies).

Conclusion

This chapter provides examples and research to support our two propositions. The first is that, to reduce the widening gaps between needs and supply and between cost and affordability, we need to engage and support citizens, patients and health workers to carry out more effective self-care and co-care. The current physician- and provider-centric model of visit-based health services is not able to meet needs, even when the threshold for needs is set high and when services are made more difficult for ordinary working people to access. The second proposition is that certain changes and greater use of modern change sciences can help to move healthcare towards the more person-centred services represented by self-care and co-care approaches.

We therefore both agree and disagree with the contention implied by this book's title that "patient knowledge is a cornerstone for the transformation of care and health organizations". We agree that patient knowledge is central to self-care and co-care and that patients can demand support from healthcare for this. However, we believe that more than patient knowledge is needed both for patient self-care and to drive changes in care and health organizations. Behavioural science shows clearly that knowledge is necessary, but not sufficient for change, and that features of the environment decide whether a change will take place or not.

We drew on our experience and research to describe the changes to organizational, finance and digital health technologies that will be necessary. We also suggested how modern applied change science disciplines can contribute to building a more patient-centred health system. We proposed that experimentation with pilot schemes informed by these sciences and involving partnership research is one way forward. Such schemes need to investigate how self-care and co-care are best developed, especially for the most disadvantaged members of our community who could be harmed by a simplistic strategy to cut costs by reducing services and not providing the support and environments that those most in need require to enable self-care and co-care.

Appendix 4.1: Definitions

Table 4.1 Definitions used in this chapter

Self-care: People taking responsibility for being the principal provider of their own healthcare and illness prevention, and actively carrying out activities needed for this
Co-care: Sharing decisions and activities about care and self-care. Co-care supports self-care through help from others such as clinicians and family, and includes shared decision making, to maximize health and wellness before, during and after disease
Goal-concordant Treatment Plan: The outcome of the shared decision-making process is a goal-concordant treatment plan. This is a treatment plan that reflects the patient's needs, values and preferences regarding the trade-offs between benefits and risks of treatment options; spans the full range of care needs, including financial counselling and support, psychosocial support and palliative care; is captured digitally, in a dynamic way, so that patients and providers can track their progress, and provide data and feedback related to their care goals; and is readily accessible to, understood by and digestible for the patient (NAPF 2018)
Patient activation: an "individual's knowledge, skill, and confidence for managing his/her own health and health care".
Patient and family engaged care (PFEC): "care planned, delivered, managed, and continuously improved in active partnership with patients and their families (or care partners as defined by the patient) to ensure integration of their health and health care goals, preferences, and values. It includes explicit and partnered determination of goals and care options, and it requires ongoing assessment of the care match with patient goals" (Frampton et al. 2016)

(continued)

Table 4.1 (continued)

Person-centred Care: Meeting an individual's needs and wants, as far as is possible, with available resources and technology, and enabling a patient to engage in self-care, as wanted and appropriate, including informal carers (Øvretveit 2017)
Patient-driven care and treatment: Choosing treatments, care and self-care strategies that enable a patient to perform the activities and achieve the life goals which are important to them at different times
PER: a Swedish internet patient portal which allows patients to enter in their patient-reported outcome and other data, and for this to be exported to a clinical register data base ("Patient Service")
Patient empowerment: Acquisition of motivations and abilities that patients might use to improve participation in decision making, and thus improve their power in their relationship with professionals (Fumagalli et al. 2015)
Patient engagement: The experience and behaviour of being involved or occupied in a decision or activity
Patient participation: "involvement of the patient in decision making or expressing opinions about different treatment methods, which includes sharing information, feelings and signs and accepting health team instructions" (Vahdat et al. 2014) "Patient participation can relate to aspects of health care as diverse as decision making, self-medication, self-monitoring, patient education, goal setting, or taking part in physical care" (Longtin et al. 2010)

Appendix 4.2: Patient Evaluation of Co-Care Survey (PECS) (Degsell and Øvretveit 2018)

1. **Does your illness make everyday activities more difficult**?
   (0 not at all, 1 a little, 2 yes but no major difficulties, 3 yes quite difficult, 4 yes very difficult, 5 yes because of my illness it is impossible to perform many activities important to me).
2. Has any care provider asked you **which activities your disease makes difficult** for you to carry out?
   (2 yes, 1 no, 0 don't know)
3. If yes to 2) **have they asked you what you want the treatment or care to help you to do**, or what you want the goals of treatment or care to be?
   (2 yes, 1 no, 0 don't know)

4. If yes to 3) or 2) **how much do you think they considered your views about which activities your disease makes difficult**, when they were advising you about your treatment and care?
   (0 not at all, 1 they know but do not seem to have considered this, 2 they have taken this into consideration a little, 3 they are very good at discussing which treatment and care choices are best for helping with different activities that are important to me)
5. **Have they asked you what you are doing yourself to make living with your illness less difficult**?
   (2 yes, 1 no, 0 don't know)
6. If yes to 2 or 3, **have they discussed with you what you could do yourself so as to be able to carry out activities important to you which your illness is making more difficult**?
   (0 not at all, 1 they suggested some things but did not discuss how I could arrange my life differently to be able to do these things, 2 they suggested some things and we discussed how I could arrange my life differently to be able to do these things)
7. **Have you discussed with other patients what they do themselves** to be able to carry out activities important to them which their illness is making more difficult?
   (2 yes, 1 no, 0 don't know)
8. Have healthcare or other services **made it possible to meet with other patients** to share and discuss what they do themselves to carry out activities important to them which their illness is making more difficult?
   (2 yes, 1 no, 0 don't know, 3 not healthcare but other services)

Note

1. Reproduced with permission from Eskil Degsell

References

AHRQ. 2017. Tool 1D: Business Case Form, from https://www.ahrq.gov/professionals/systems/hospital/fallpxtoolkit/fallpxtk-tool1d.html. Accessed 18 Feb 2018.

———. 2018. Return on Investment Estimation, (in Toolkit for Using the AHRQ Quality Indicators). https://www.ahrq.gov/sites/default/files/wysiwyg/professionals/systems/hospital/qitoolkit/pdi/f1_pdi_returnoninvestment.pdf. Accessed 18 Feb 2018.

Alexander, J.A., L.R. Hearld, J.N. Mittler, and J. Harvey. 2012. Patient–physician role relationships and patient activation among individuals with chronic illness. *Health Services Research* 47: 1201–1223. https://doi.org/10.1111/j.1475-6773.2011.01354.x.

Batalden, P.B., and P.K. Stoltz. 1993. A framework for the continual improvement of health care. *Joint Commission Journal on Quality and Patient Safety* 19: 424–452.

Da Silva, D. 2012. *Helping people share decision a review of evidence considering whether shared decision making is worthwhile*. London: The Health Foundation.

Degsell, E. 2018. *A model for co-care and the learning health system, available from Eskil Degsell, Patient representative for liaison co-care and patient centred care and researcher*. LIME/MMC, Tomtebodavägen 18A. Karolinska Institutet, Stockholm 17177, Sweden.

Degsell, E., and Øvretveit. 2018. *Patient evaluation of co-care survey (PECS)*. Available from MMC, Karolinska Institutet, Stockholm.

Docteur, E., and A. Coulter. 2012. *Patient-centeredness in Sweden's health system—An external assessment and six steps for progress*. Stockholm: Swedish Agency for Health and Care Services (Vårdanalys).

Fallberg, L., and J. Øvretveit. 2003. Introduction to patient ombudsmen schemes in Europe. Chap. 1 in *Protecting Patient's Rights?*, ed. S. Mackenney and L. Fallberg. Oxford: Radcliffe Medical Press.

Frampton, S.B., S. Guastello, L. Hoy, M. Naylor, S. Sheridan, and M. Johnston-Fleece. 2016. *Harnessing evidence and experience to change culture: A guiding framework for patient and family engaged care*. Discussion Paper, National Academy of Medicine, Washington, DC. https://nam.edu/wp-content/uploads/2017/01/Harnessing-Evidence-and-Experience-to-Change-Culture-A-Guiding-Framework-for-Patient-and-Family-Engaged-Care. pdf.

Fumagalli, L.P., G. Radaelli, E. Lettieri, P. Bertele', and C. Masella. 2015. Patient empowerment and its neighbours: Clarifying the boundaries and their mutual relationships. *Health Policy* 119: 384–394.

Genia. 2018. Bromma, Sweden. http://www.genia.se/homepage/. Accessed 16 May 2018.

Hibbard, J.H., and E. Mahoney. 2010. Toward a theory of patient and consumer activation. *Patient Education and Counseling* 78 (3): 377–381. https://doi.org/10.1016/j.pec.2009.12.015. Epub 2010 Feb 25.

Hvitfeldt, H., C.A. Carli, E.C. Nelson, et al. 2009. Feed-forward systems for patient participation and provider support: Adoption results from the original US context to Sweden and beyond. *Quality Management in Health Care* 18: 247–256.

INVOLVE. 2012. *INVOLVE: Briefing notes for researchers: Public involvement in NHS, public health and social care research*. National Institute for Health Research, Hamphire UK, February. www.involve.nihr.ac.uk. Accessed 1 June 2018.

Kent, D.M., and R.A. Hayward. 2007. Limitations of applying summary results of clinical trials to Langley G, Nolan K, Nolan T, Norman C, Provost L. The Improvement Guide: A Practical Approach to Enhancing Organizational Performance. San Francisco: Jossey-Bass, 1996.

Langley, G.J., K.M. Nolan, T.W. Nolan, et al. 1996. *The improvement guide: A practical approach to enhancing organizational performance*. San Francisco: Jossey-Bass.

Lima, A., et al. 2016. Effectiveness of an intervention to improve diabetes self-management on clinical outcomes in patients with low educational level. *Gaceta Sanitaria* 2017 31 (1): 40–47. https://doi.org/10.1016/j.gaceta.2016.05.017.

Longtin, Y., H. Sax, L. Leape, S. Sheridan, L. Donaldson, and D. Pittet. 2010. Patient participation: Current knowledge and applicability to patient safety. *Mayo Clinic Proceedings* 85 (1): 53–62. https://doi.org/10.4065/mcp.2009.0248.

Michie, S., M. Richardson, M. Johnston, C. Abraham, J. Francis, W. Hardeman, M.P. Eccles, J. Cane, and C.E. Wood. 2013. The behavior change technique taxonomy (v1) of 93 hierarchically clustered techniques: Building an international consensus for the reporting of behavior change interventions. *Annals of Behavioral Medicine* 46 (1): 81–95. https://doi.org/10.1007/s12160-013-9486-6.

Nelson, E.C., M. Dixon-Woods, P.B. Batalden, K. Homa, A.D. Van Citters, T.S. Morgan, E. Eftimovska, E.S. Fisher, J. Ovretveit, W. Harrison, C. Lind, and S. Lindblad. 2016. Patient focused registries can improve health, care, and science. *BMJ* 354: i3319. https://doi.org/10.1136/bmj.i3319. (Published 1 July 2016).

Norman, N., and K. Eva. 2010. Diagnostic error in clinical reasoning. *Medical Education* 44: 94–100. https://doi.org/10.1111/j.1365-2923.2009.03507.x.

OECD/European Observatory on Health Systems and Policies. 2017. Sweden: Country Health Profile 2017, State of Health in the EU, OECD Publishing, Paris/European Observatory on Health Systems and Policies, Brussels. https://doi.org/10.1787/9789264283572-en.

Øvretveit, J. 2009. *Does improving quality save money? A review of evidence of which improvement to quality reduce costs for health service providers*. London: The Health Foundation. www.health.org.uk; http://www.health.org.uk/publication/does-improving-quality-save-money.

———. 2012. *Do changes to patient-provider relationships improve quality and save money? A review of evidence*. London: The Health Foundation. http://www.health.org.uk/publications/do-changes-to-patient-provider-relationships-improve-quality-and-save-money/.

———. 2017. Digital technologies supporting person-Centered integrated care. *International Journal of Integrated Care* 17 (4): 6. https://doi.org/10.5334/ijic.3051.

Øvretveit, J., C. Keller, H. Hvitfeldt Forsberg, A. Essén, S. Lindblad, and M. Brommels. 2013. Continuous innovation: The development and use of the Swedish rheumatology register to improve the quality of arthritis care. *International Journal for Quality in Health Care* 25 (2): 118–124. https://doi.org/10.1093/intqhc/mzt002.

Øvretveit, J., L. Zubkoff, E. Nelson, S. Frampton, J. Lehmann Knudsen, and E. Zimlichman. 2017. Using patient-reported outcome measurement to improve patient care. *International Journal for Quality in Health Care* 29 (6): 874–879.

Parkwell. 2018. https://www.openratio.com/category/enterprise-mobility/page/2/. Accessed 16 May 2018.

Patients like me. 2018. A chance to change the future of personalized health. https://www.patientslikeme.com/. Accessed 11 May 2018.

Powell, B., T. Waltz, M. Chinman, L. Damschroder, J. Smith, M. Matthieu, E. Proctor, and J. Kirchner. 2015. A refined compilation of implementation strategies: Results from the expert recommendations for implementing change (ERIC) project. *Implementation Science* 10: 21. https://doi.org/10.1186/s13012-015-0209-1.

Recovery college. 2018. The power of peer support at the Severn & Wye Recovery College. https://www.health.org.uk/content/power-peer-support-severn-wye-recovery-college. Accessed 16 May 2018.

RWJF. 2018. Building a Culture of Health, from Robert Wood Johnson Foundation. https://www.rwjf.org/en/how-we-work/building-a-culture-of-health.html. Accessed 1 June 2018.

Sabadosa, K.A., and P.B. Batalden. 2014. The interdependent roles of patients, families and professionals in cystic fibrosis: A system for the coproduction of healthcare and its improvement. *BMJ Quality and Safety* 23: i90–i94.

Sullivan, S., J. Mauskopf, F. Augustovski, J. Caro, K. Lee, M. Minchin, E. Orlewska, P. Penna, J. Barrios, and W. Shau. 2014. 2012 budget impact analysis—Principles of good practice: Report of the ISPOR 2012 budget impact analysis good practice II task force. *Value in Health* 17: 5–14.

Vahdat, S., L. Hamzehgardeshi, S. Hessam, and Z. Hamzehgardeshi. 2014. Patient involvement in health care decision making: A review. *Iranian Red Crescent Medical Journal* 16 (1): e12454. https://doi.org/10.5812/ircmj.12454. Published online 2014 Jan 5.

Vardanalysis. 2017. *From the patient's perspective.* Stockholm. https://www.vardanalys.se/rapporter/varden-ur-patienternas-perspektiv-65-ar-och-aldre/. Accessed 1 June 2018.

Ziebland, S., A. Coulter, J. Calabrese, and L. Locock, eds. 2013. *Understanding and using health experiences: Improving patient care.* Oxford: Oxford university press.

5

Patient and Family Engagement in the United States: A Social Movement from Patient to Advocate to Partner

Maureen Maurer, Pam Dardess, and Tara Bristol Rouse

Introduction

The United States healthcare system is multifaceted, complex, and costly. Given the lack of a unified system, providing a simple overview of how health care is delivered and financed is challenging. As context for patient and family engagement in the United States, we briefly describe core characteristics of the system in terms of overall spending, insurance, the workforce, and the population.

M. Maurer (✉)
American Institutes for Research, Chapel Hill, NC, USA
e-mail: MMaurer@air.org

P. Dardess
Institute for Patient- and Family-Centered Care (IPFCC), Durham, NC, USA
e-mail: pdardess@ipfcc.org

T. B. Rouse
American Hospital Association, Raleigh, NC, USA

M.-P. Pomey et al. (eds.), *Patient Engagement*, Organizational Behaviour in Healthcare,
https://doi.org/10.1007/978-3-030-14101-1_5

In 2017, US healthcare spending increased 3.9 per cent to reach $3.5 trillion, or $10,739 per person, and the overall share of gross domestic product related to healthcare spending was 17.9 per cent. While federal, state, and local governments are significant payers, nearly half of U.S. healthcare spending comes from private sources, including individual households and private employers (CMS 2018).

Lacking a single nationwide system of health insurance, individuals obtain insurance via private and public health insurance programmes. Major sources of coverage include (1) private employer-sponsored insurance, in which some employers voluntarily provide insurance coverage to employees and their dependents; (2) individual insurance, in which people can purchase health insurance directly from an insurer or through the health insurance marketplace created by the Affordable Care Act in 2010; and (3) public programmes, such as Medicare and Medicaid, which provide coverage to people ages 65 and older, individuals with a severe disability, or those who have very low incomes (CMS 2018). In 2017, among adults ages 18–64, 69 per cent had private health insurance, 1 per cent had public coverage, and 1 per cent were uninsured (AHRQ 2018b). Within and across insurance programmes, there can be significant differences with respect to benefits covered, payments to medical providers, and costs to beneficiaries.

The US healthcare industry employs millions of workers who provide billions of services each year. Workers include 951,000 active medical doctors, 2.9 million registered nurses, 2.4 million health technologists, and 2.6 million nursing and other aides (AHRQ 2018b). An array of clinicians, hospitals, and other healthcare facilities operate in various configurations of groups, networks, and independent practices to provide services. These entities can be public—federal, state or local—and private—both not-for-profit and for profit (IOM 2003).

Life expectancy was 78.6 years in 2016, 76.1 years for men and 81.1 for women (Kochanek et al. 2017). The population of 326.6 million people is spread over 50 states and a federal district spanning an area of 9.8 million square kilometres. Although population density varies by state, 82 per cent of the total population live in urban areas (CIA 2018). State-level data show that healthcare quality and disparities vary widely depending on state and region. Variation in access to care and care delivery contributes to disparities in health and health care related to race, ethnicity, sex, and socioeconomic status (AHRQ 2018b).

Recent decades have seen a significant ageing of the population and major changes in diet, exercise, stress, environment, and social connections (Manahan 2011). The leading causes of death, years of potential life lost, and years with disability illustrate the overall disease burden of complex and chronic health problems caused by multiple lifestyle and environmental factors. In 2015 and 2016, the leading causes of death for the overall population were heart disease, cancer, unintentional injuries, chronic lower respiratory diseases, cerebrovascular disease, Alzheimer's disease, and diabetes. In 2016, the leading diseases and injuries contributing to years of potential life lost were unintentional injury, cancer, and heart disease. In 2015, mental health and substance use disorders, musculoskeletal disorders, and endocrine disorders, including diabetes and kidney disease accounted for most years lost to disability (AHRQ 2018b).

In this chapter, we describe the history of patient and family engagement in the United States, highlight three case studies illustrating current practice, and identify lessons learned. Today's focus on patient and family engagement is the result of nearly seven decades of evolving changes in the culture and practice of health care that have created opportunities for patients, family members, caregivers, and community members to partner in decisions about health care and its delivery. Exemplified by the slogan "nothing about me without me," partnership is now happening at the point of care, within healthcare organizational structures and governance, and in health research.

Tara's Story: Transition from Patient to Advocate to Partner

Lying on the exam table, I watched the triage nurse fill the last in an assemblage of blood collection tubes on her tray. Clueless as to what was to come, I asked her how long I should expect to be there.

Crisp and emotionless, if not curt and annoyed, she responded that it would be "awhile."

Yearning for some clarity, I tried again and, with all earnestness, asked how long "awhile" might be.

Her answer was nothing less than shocking—I would be there until my baby was born. Handing me a gown and instructing me to put it on, the nurse quickly left the room—the thick, heavy wooden door pulled shut behind her.

As it turned out, my baby would be born less than 12 hours later. At 27 weeks gestation and weighing just 1 lb. 13 oz., my early bird, Jack, would take up residence in the Newborn Intensive Care Unit (NICU) for 83 days; my own 11-day stay paling by comparison. And so began my family's intimate relationship with the healthcare system.

I can't say that I was a shrinking violet when I began the journey, but I felt ill prepared and insecure in this new environment that had its own language, culture, customs, and etiquette. The first days in the hospital felt like baptism by fire. A revolving door of people, equipment and terms filled my days while I struggled to manage my physical and emotional health, precarious as it was. But my salvation would come on day 13, by way of a nurse who, without even knowing she was doing it, invited me into what I had believed to be the unassailable fold of the healthcare team. She assured me that I was not a visitor, but an essential person whose role it was to care for my baby, be a partner in decision-making, and educate care providers about my family and our goals.

In the coming weeks and months, this empowerment translated into what are now considered staples of patient and family engagement at the bedside:

- Participation in daily rounds
- Open communication with and timely updates from the care team
- Access to the medical chart
- Training in the use of medical equipment
- Presence during procedures
- Participation in discharge planning, education and goal-setting

Towards the end of our NICU stay, I found myself mentoring other parents as they began their own journeys, struggling to stay afloat amidst all the loss they were experiencing. The need was clear, but the consistency of support was not.

As we eventually settled into life at home and the new routines that come with raising a high-risk infant, the NICU was never far from my mind and—as the saying goes—I soon found myself in the right place at the right time. A call came from the NICU Medical Director letting me know that she was recruiting parents to become founding members of a family advisory board and offering me a seat at the table.

Over the next six years it would be my great pleasure and honor to serve as the first parent co-chair, and later as a staff member in the hospital's first paid parent support position. The group's work was the most beautiful example of co-design—and what started out as a committee soon led to integrating patients and family members on hospital quality committees and teams. Consistency and reliability of patient and family support, communication, and engagement in quality and safety became a priority—formalized and strengthened by the devotion of resources and unwavering support from leadership.

These days I am fortunate to continue this work in partnership with nationally recognized leaders in healthcare quality improvement. The landscape has changed, and I am humbled to have had the opportunity to be part of the efforts that led to those first hard-earned wins. I am also grateful—grateful that patient and family engagement has become woven into the fabric of our healthcare system in ways that we always hoped for, but never thought possible.

History of Patient and Family Engagement

Recognizing that individual behaviours are shaped and influenced by systems and structures, partnership efforts in the United States have often focused on promoting patient and family engagement within the context of healthcare system redesign. As an early example of the relationship between these reforms and engagement, during the establishment of federally funded community health centres, the Economic Opportunity Act of 1964 and subsequent legislation specified that patients must make up at least 51 per cent of a centre's community advisory board, which provided patients with a governing voice in finance and operations (Sharma et al. 2018). Most recently, the passage of the Affordable Care Act in 2010 not only created the health insurance marketplace but also instituted payment reforms that recognized patient and family engagement as an essential function of healthcare delivery and a promising pathway to improve care quality, value, and patient outcomes.

To describe the history of the patient and family engagement in the United States, we have conceptualized four areas of influences, highlighting key actors and organizations in each, which have collectively informed the current state of engagement:

- Patients as care recipients: Changing the traditional patient-provider dynamic
- Patients as consumers: A marketplace orientation to health care
- Patients as an active community: ePatient movement advocating for collective change
- Patients as partners: Patient-centred care and patient safety movements

Although presented separately, these areas overlap and are interconnected. For example, the patient safety movement has advocated for greater partnership with patients while also calling for information-sharing that influences changes in the patient-provider dynamic. As healthcare consumers, patients have advocated for greater transparency related to healthcare costs, quality, and safety. And, as voices within the healthcare system, ePatients have fought for access to information about their own health and health care, and a changed view of what it means to partner with patients and families.

Patients as Care Recipients: Changing the Traditional Patient-Provider Dynamic

For most of American history, physicians made medical decisions on behalf of their patients, in what they perceived to be the patient's best interest. This paternalistic approach led most physicians to control the disclosure of information that they believed appropriate, and making decisions about which disclosures would and would not harm the patient. In this traditional "doctor knows best" approach, the physician was expected to direct care and decide treatment, while the patient's job was to follow through and comply with treatment orders (Sisk et al. 2016; Will 2011a).

In the 1950s, the bioethics movement and informed consent doctrine sought to equalize the power dynamic in the physician–patient relationship, particularly in terms of the imbalance of knowledge in clinical practice and medical research. Prompted by the Nazi trials after World War II, Henry Beecher's 1966 publication in the *New England Journal of Medicine* outlined 22 examples of questionable post-war experiments in human research in the United States, none of which involved consent. High-profile legal cases also contributed to public questioning of the trust in physicians to protect the well-being of their patients. In 1979, the Belmont Report served as the foundation for future government regulation and oversight of research with human subjects and its principles: respect for persons, beneficence, and justice (Will 2011b).

Concurrently, an evolution towards greater patient autonomy arose, particularly in the field of mental health care. Between 1950 and 1970, deinstitutionalization, new psychotropic drug treatments, and legal conceptions of patients' autonomy resulted in a completely restructured mental health care system (Tomes 2006). Judi Chamberlin's 1978 book, *On Our Own*, which spurred the creation of consumer groups in the late 1970s and 1980s, argued that the key to improving the mental health system was giving patients control over their own treatments (Chamberlin 1978). Families of people with serious mental health illness also became involved, forming the first branch of what would become the National Alliance on Mental Illness (NAMI) in 1979 and advocating for more research funds for mental illness (Tomes 2006).

In addition, there was an associated push to increase transparency and patient and family involvement in making decisions about health and health care. In 1973, the American Hospital Association published the Patient Bill of Rights, stating that "The patient has the right to and is encouraged to obtain from physicians and their direct caregivers relevant, current, and understandable information concerning diagnosis, treatment, and prognosis" (Will 2011b; Sisk et al. 2016). In 1982, a U.S. Presidential Commission on medical decision-making ethics recommended increased patient involvement in decision making as the "appropriate ideal for patient–professional relationships that a sound doctrine of informed consent should support." A survey conducted by the Commission revealed that 56 per cent of physicians and 64 per cent of the public felt that increasing the involvement of patients would improve quality of care, with physicians citing patient compliance and cooperativeness as the main facilitators (President's Commission 1982). Another impetus for this involvement was the assumption that consumers were integral members of the care team (Von Korff et al. 1997) and that consumers, particularly those with chronic illness—and their providers—needed information, motivation, tools, skills, and system-level support to shift towards greater patient engagement in their care (Bodenheimer et al. 2002).

By the late 1980s, the foundation for shared decision making—the process whereby health professionals and patients work together to make healthcare choices—was laid. As part of the shared decision-making movement, two Dartmouth-Hitchcock Medical Center physicians—

John Wennberg and Albert Mulley Jr.—started the Informed Medical Decisions Foundation (IMDF) in 1989. IMDF's goal was to produce and disseminate decision aids designed to provide patients with the available medical evidence on screening and treatment options and associated outcomes specific to their circumstances, help elicit and clarify patients' values and preferences, and support patients in making choices together with their physicians. In 1990, the foundation published its first decision aid—a video helping patients understand the pros and cons of prostate cancer treatments (Billings 2004).

The American Medical Association's (AMA) current Code of Medical Ethics reflects the transformation in expectations for patient-provider dynamics, stating "the health and well-being of patients depends on a collaborative effort between patient and physician in a mutually respectful alliance (AMA 2018)." With a new set of expectations, much of the current engagement-related work focuses on training and supporting patients, families, and partners in these new roles.

Here is Tara's testimony recounting how the traditional patient-provider dynamic changed over time.

Patients as Consumers: A Marketplace Orientation to Health Care

Since 1960, healthcare spending in the United States has grown steadily, with various approaches used to control costs. In the 1960s and early 1970s, advances in medicine and expanded access to care resulting from the creation of Medicare and Medicaid led to increased use of healthcare services. Employers controlled costs by offering healthcare plans at lower annual costs with more tightly managed access to care, while governments passed legislation that curbed spending on Medicare and Medicaid. Yet, in the late 1990s and early 2000s, consumers demanded less restrictive managed care, which was followed by increases in spending (Catlin and Cowan 2015). Cost-controlling strategies then moved to approaches that shift financial responsibility to consumers and providers. Within the employer-sponsored health insurance market, consumer-driven plans such as health savings accounts and high-deductible plans, where consumers bear more of the costs associated with health care, have become more commonplace. These plans encourage patients to take on more responsibility in choosing plans with the best value for their situation.

At the same time, payment reforms and other efforts encouraged providers to change behaviours. Value-based care, for example, shifts the focus from traditional fee-for-service medicine, where higher volume means more reward, to rewarding the quality and value of services. Healthcare organizations also began to pursue the Triple Aim, a framework designed by the Institute for Healthcare Improvement in 2008 to refer to simultaneously "improving the individual experience of care; improving the health of populations; and reducing the per capita costs of care for populations." In addition, to meet consumer needs in the competitive marketplace, new types of providers have moved into the care delivery space, providing retail-like care delivery services—for instance, retail clinics, pharmacist-administered immunizations, and a growing array of diagnostic tests available over the counter or online. As a result, traditional healthcare organizations also look for strategies to differentiate their organizations.

With the shifts in power in the patient–physician relationship and increasing attention to healthcare costs, people began to emphasize the power of patients to affect the healthcare market. Language evolved to reflect this shift—from "patients" as passive recipients of care to "consumers" as purchasers of goods and services. Although both providers and patients have found the term "consumer" objectionable (Deber et al. 2005; Levine 2015), the terms "patient" and "consumer" are often used interchangeably today in the U.S.

With a marketplace orientation, expectations related to patients' responsibilities changed. Patients were being asked to engage in myriad behaviours—many of them new—to manage their care. The Center for Advancing Health, under the direction of Jessie Gruman who drew on her own experience of treatment for five cancer diagnoses, summarized 42 behaviours that patients must take "to find good health care and make the most of it" (Gruman et al. 2010). These behaviours fall into 10 categories:

1. Find good health care
2. Communicate with your doctors
3. Organize your health care
4. Pay for your health care
5. Make good treatment decisions
6. Participate in your treatment
7. Promote your health
8. Get preventive care
9. Plan for your end-of-life care
10. Seek knowledge about your health

In looking for ways to understand patients' ability to engage in their health and understand how to support them in new roles, the concept of patient activation emerged. Judith Hibbard and colleagues conceptualized and developed the Patient Activation Measure (PAM) to assess and categorize patients' self-efficacy and capacity to manage their own health and health care (Hibbard et al. 2004). As research using the PAM exploded, findings from multiple studies have confirmed that activated, engaged patients, who have the skills and confidence to manage their health and healthcare experience better outcomes. PAM scores are predictive of most healthy behaviours, such as getting immunizations, regular exercise, medication management, and health information seeking. In addition, patient activation skills can be acquired and are fluid depending on the situation (Greene and Hibbard 2012; Greene et al. 2015).

Yet, the vision of activated, informed consumers making value-based, rational healthcare decisions has faced a major challenge: the U.S. healthcare system is not designed to prepare or support patients in a consumer role. As early as 1996, a Picker Institute and American Hospital Association report summarized the public's concerns and dissatisfaction about health care: "The system is a nightmare to navigate; caregivers don't provide enough information; patients are not involved in decisions about their healthcare and hospital caregivers are not emotionally supportive" (AHA and Picker Institute 1997). Patients have lacked access to accurate, easy-to-understand, and personalized information to make value-based decisions, such as comparative information to evaluate providers and healthcare plans based on quality and costs of healthcare services, specifically related to out-of-pocket expenses.

An early attempt to provide patients with standard, comparative, evidence-based information was the Consumer Assessment of Healthcare Providers and Systems (CAHPS®) programme. Launched in 1995 with financing from the federal Agency for Healthcare Research and Quality (AHRQ), this national, multi-institutional collaborative project was intended to provide consumers with information about health plan enrollees' own perspective on the quality of their plans (AHRQ 2018a). The CAHPS surveys ask patients to report on their experiences with care and covered such topics as communication with healthcare professionals, access to care and information, customer service, and coordination of care. The surveys now assess experience for a variety of settings, including commercial and public health insurance programmes, inpatient stays at hospital facilities, and primary or specialty care received in ambulatory settings. The results of CAHPS surveys are used to monitor and drive improvements in care and are made available publicly to help inform patients' decisions about where to get care (AHRQ 2016).

Currently, consumers have access to comparative information for nearly all health plans in report cards published by the National Committee for Quality Assurance, *Consumer Reports*, and other national sponsors. Similarly, some quality information is available for hospitals across the country through the national Hospital Compare website maintained by the Centers for Medicare & Medicaid Services. However, little information is available at the medical practice level and even less so, for individual physicians; physician-level comparative quality information is only available through some health plans and a few dozen collaborative organizations covering metropolitan areas or states. Another issue is that, while comparative quality information is available to consumers, less attention has been paid to increasing awareness, relevance, or appropriate timing of public quality reports (Maurer et al. 2017). Thus, despite an emergence of public quality reports in the past 20 years, studies show that only a small minority of Americans have seen information on healthcare quality and only a fraction of those have actually used the information to inform healthcare choices (KFF 2008; Yegian et al. 2013; Fox and Duggan 2013). Furthermore, public quality reports have been more likely to be associated with changes in provider behaviours (Ketelaar et al. 2011) than consumer behaviours (Totten et al. 2012).

In terms of cost transparency, there is a general lack of consumer-friendly information and a complex billing process; often, patients do not know the costs of services until the bill arrives after the care experience. With costs varying based on type of insurance coverage, patients not only have to understand and navigate their own financial responsibilities in terms of insurance premiums, deductibles, copays, and provider networks, they also need skills to use and interpret this information when making decisions. Not surprisingly, consumers struggle with cost and medical terminology (Quincy 2011); have difficulty calculating their costs when presented with health plan cost structure information (Kutner et al. 2006); find it difficult to move into an active purchasing role to weigh complex information (Greene and Peters 2009); and have limited ability to objectively weigh risk trade-offs associated with different deductibles and copays against premium costs (Tennyson 2011).

While insurers are developing cost calculators and other price transparency tools to help patients make informed, value-based decisions, there remains a significant gap between the information available and the information needed. As a result, independent groups, including crowd-sourced information as well as private vendors, have stepped in to meet consumers' needs for personalized price information. For instance, Jeanne Pinder, a former *New York Times* reporter, founded and runs ClearHealthCosts.com, a company that systematically gathers and reports actual prices paid for healthcare procedures with the goal of giving patients more information to make informed decisions (Pinder 2010).

Simply making information available may be insufficient to address issues associated with overuse of care that contribute to rising healthcare costs. Deeply ingrained beliefs that more care is better or that higher quality care costs more may hinder evidence-informed choices (Carman et al. 2010). Also, concerned that providers prioritize financial returns over patients' health, consumers mistrust the profit motives of insurers when decisions are made to limit care (Richmond et al. 2017). Engaging patients and providers in discussions and decisions about what constitutes necessary care may be a promising approach to mitigating these conflicts. For example, Choosing Wisely, an initiative of the ABIM Foundation, have asked organizations representing medical specialists to identify commonly used tests or procedures "whose necessity should be questioned and discussed." The initiative then promotes partnership and conversations between clinicians and patients to help patients choose care that is evidence-based, not duplicative, free from harm, and truly necessary (ABIM Foundation 2018).

Patients as an Active Community: ePatient Movement Advocating for Collective Change

With the advent of the Internet, social networking, and mobile wireless technology, user-generated health-related content and groups proliferated. Patients and families were able to more rapidly learn, on their own or in collaboration with their providers, how to optimize health and functional status; manage both acute and chronic illnesses; and share what they learn with other patients and families via general or health-specific social networking websites, or in face-to-face peer-support groups.

Writing about the empowered medical consumer since 1975 and about online health resources for consumers since 1987, Tom Ferguson coined the term "ePatient." He envisioned health care as an equal partnership between ePatients—those who were equipped, enabled, empowered, and engaged in their healthcare decisions—and health professionals and systems that support them (SPM 2017a). After Ferguson's death, others built on his work and formed the Society for Participatory Medicine in 2009, a not-for-profit membership organization working to transform the culture of health care (SPM 2017b). Since then, the term ePatient has expanded to include patients' use of information technologies in managing their health: Stanford Medicine X's ePatient Program now uses the term "ePatient scholar" to describe those who have become leaders in the movement, serving as "an educator and role model for other patients and healthcare stakeholders" (MedicineX 2018).

Examples of such scholars include David deBronkart and Regina Holliday. David deBronkart, widely known as e-Patient Dave, is a cancer patient and blogger who, in 2009, became an activist for participatory medicine and personal health data rights (deBronkart 2018). Regina Holliday, an artist and advocate, speaks about the benefits of health information technology and timely data access for patients. She began an advocacy movement called the Walking Gallery, which is made up of business jackets with individually designed art work portrayed on the back of the jacket. Each jacket uses representational imagery to create a patient-centric narrative, illustrating their own or their loved ones' experiences with the healthcare system. With more than 400 individuals in this gallery, the owners wear jackets to medical conferences where patient voices are underrepresented to change the healthcare conversation (Holliday 2018).

As patients have advocated for change, the healthcare system has made steps to improve patient access to their data. In 2009, the Health Information Technology for Economic and Clinical Health Act made funds available for healthcare organizations to adopt electronic health records and spurred the development of secure online patient portals as a way to exchange information between patients and providers. While patient portals gave patients convenient, protected access to their healthcare providers' services or health records, the medical record is still largely owned and managed by healthcare providers, and certain aspects, such as the notes clinicians write after a visit, remain hidden from the patient's view. Designed to help clinicians and healthcare systems share medical visit notes with patients, Open Notes allows patients to contribute to and correct personal health data in the medical record. In 2010, Beth Israel Deaconess Medical Center, Geisinger Health System, and Harborview Medical Center launched an exploratory study to examine the effects of sharing notes on both patients and doctors. Funded by the Robert Wood Johnson Foundation, the study included 105 primary care doctors and more than 20,000 of their patients (OpenNotes 2018). Patients reported an increased sense of control, greater understanding of their medical issues, improved recall of their plans for care, better preparation for future visits, and better medication adherence. Physicians commented that Open Notes strengthened relationships with some of their patients and that participation did not adversely affect their workloads (Delbanco et al. 2012).

The ePatient movement has also affected clinical research, with patient-driven studies using open science approaches. For example, PatientsLikeMe is a patient network and real-time research platform that connects patients with others who have the same disease or condition; they track and share their own experiences with the goal to improve outcomes. As another powerful example, Eric Valor, diagnosed with amyotrophic lateral sclerosis (ALS) in 2004 and working from his bed, designs patient-driven drug trials and manages a non-profit bringing new treatments from the lab to clinical trials (Valor 2018).

Patients as Partners and Patient Safety

The patient- and family-centred care and patient safety movements propelled the belief that patients and families had an important role to play in ensuring the quality and safety—not only at the point of care but also at the organizational level, partnering in the design, implementation, and evaluation of healthcare practices, procedures, and policies. Advocates in these areas advanced the practice of working "with" patients and families, rather than just providing care "to" or "for" them.

The idea of patient-centred care was introduced in the medical literature in the mid-1950s (Balint 1955), and the concept of family-centred care is intertwined with the evolution of care and support for children and youth with special needs. In the 1960s, with families advocating to be part of medical decisions about their children, civil rights legislation outlined rights and responsibilities of families, initially in education, and subsequently in health care, and acknowledged the important role families play in their children's health (Wells 2011). The 1970s and 1980s saw continued support for the important role of families in ensuring positive outcomes for children, particularly regarding education and health care, along with the development of family support models that focused on building capacity through access to resources, information, and peer support.

Families also began to have a seat at the table for national-level discussions. In the 1970s and 1980s, leaders within the federal Maternal and Child Health Bureau (MCHB) fostered and nurtured concepts of family and professional partnerships that began a revolution in health care for children and families (Wells 2011). In 1987, then U.S. Surgeon, General

C. Everett Koop, launched a National Agenda for Children with Special Healthcare Needs that established family-centred, community-based, coordinated care as the standard of care. For the first time, significant numbers of parents were invited to participate with healthcare professionals, researchers, and public policy makers at a national meeting sponsored by MCHB (Johnson 2000).

Fueled by the desire to drive progress in family-centred care, two consumer-driven institutions were created in 1992 that continue to provide leadership in the field: Family Voices and the Institute for Family-Centered Care (now known as the Institute for Patient- and Family-Centered Care, or IPFCC). Formed as a "grassroots network of families and friends of children and youth with special health care needs and disabilities," Family Voices helped advocate for the creation of Medicaid waivers—financial mechanisms that allow children with special healthcare needs to live at home with their families while receiving the care needed. Another key component of the organization was peer-to-peer support, providing valuable lifelines between families of children with special needs. The organization continues to work broadly to promote authentic patient and family partnerships with the healthcare system at the national, state, and local level, advocating for family engagement in both clinical and community settings (Family Voices 2018). Recognizing the need for meaningful partnerships in health care, IPFCC was formed by a group of parents and health professionals involved in the family-centred care movement. Designed to serve as a leader in the field—independent of changing political and funding priorities, IPFCC's work initially focused on five areas: strengthening family/professional collaboration, changing care in hospitals, improving healthcare facility design, transforming medical education, and advising on health policy (Johnson 2000). The Institute also advanced a definition of patient- and family-centred care as "an approach to the planning, delivery, and evaluation of health care that is grounded in mutually beneficial partnerships among health care providers, patients, and families." The four core concepts of patient- and family-centred care—dignity and respect; information sharing; participation; and collaboration—serve as a foundation for IPFCC's work and the field more broadly. IPFCC has continued to work across care settings and the care continuum to ensure that patients and families are "essential allies for quality and safety," not just in direct care interactions, but also in the design and delivery of health care.

Over the years, other patient- and consumer-led organizations, such as PFCCpartners, have emerged to help healthcare organizations work in partnership with patients and families in ways that respect and incorporate patients' and families' preferences, needs, and values. Organizations such as the non-profit Planetree, founded in 1978 by Angelica Theiriot after a series of traumatic personal healthcare experiences, provide models that focus on humanizing health care through the delivery of patient-centred care in nurturing environments (Planetree 2018).

While there has been a long-standing spotlight on patient safety issues, the 1990s saw the growth of patient safety advocates and advocacy organizations, arising in many cases from personal experiences with the healthcare system. Patient safety groups, such as the Pulse Center for Patient Safety Education and Advocacy (PULSE), formed to advocate for transparency and accountability, particularly for medical errors. In some instances, preventable medical errors created an unenviable pathway into the world of patient safety advocacy for grieving parents, spouses, and family members. In 2000, in response to her son Lewis's death, Helen Haskell formed Mothers Against Medical Error, a patient safety advocacy organization (Mothers Against Medical Errors 2018). In 2001, the death of Sorrel King's 18-month old daughter Josie from a preventable medical error led to the creation of the Josie King Foundation to "unite healthcare providers and consumers to create a culture of patient safety" (Josie King Foundation 2016). These groups argued for legislation—such as Lewis Blackman Patient Safety Act in South Carolina, which required, for the first time, that healthcare providers be clearly identified and that patients be provided with an emergency response system in hospitals—and advocated for transparency around medical errors and the inclusion of patients and their family members as active and involved members of healthcare teams.

In October 2003, a workshop funded by the federal Agency for Healthcare Research and Quality (AHRQ) brought together consumers who saw themselves as constructive partners and change agents with other stakeholders interested in partnering. Led by Roxanne Goeltz and Susan Sheridan, both of whom had experienced healthcare system failure, outcomes of the workshop included a mission, goals, and a new nonprofit organization, Consumers Advancing Patient Safety to carry this work forward (Hatlie 2014).

Adding to the clarion call of patient advocacy groups were several high-profile incidents in which preventable medical errors led to the death of patients and created the impetus for organizational changes. One such widely publicized case occurred at the Dana-Farber Cancer Institute, where breakdowns in standards of care contributed to the death of a *Boston Globe* reporter who was receiving treatment for breast cancer. As part of their organizational response to this sentinel event, Dana Farber outlined a six-point plan that included "letting patients into the process of leading the organization." Progress was made towards this goal through increasing transparency, improving communication, and working with patients and families as members of Patient and Family Advisory Councils (PFACs) and hospital committees, where they have decision-making roles (Conway and Weingart 2015). Other organizations have made efforts to improve communication with patients and families around medical errors, emphasizing transparency and relationship-building. For example, the University of Michigan Health System pioneered a programme of disclosure of medical error and apology to patients and families. Although fears of litigation still prevent many hospitals from full disclosure, full disclosure policies have led to decreases in malpractice claims and average settlement amounts (Wachter et al. 2015; Moffatt-Bruce et al. 2016).

As momentum grew around patient safety, federal agencies and national organizations began to expand their emphasis on patient and family engagement as a pathway towards improved healthcare quality and safety. In 1999, the Institute of Medicine (now known as the National Academy of Sciences) published a landmark report on patient safety. *To Err is Human: Building a Safer Health System* laid out the serious impact of medical errors in hospitals, noting that preventable safety events contributed to as many as 98,000 deaths per year (IOM 1999). The IOM's strategy for addressing patient safety included specific roles for key stakeholders, including the federal government, healthcare providers, and patients. A subsequent report issued in 2001, *Crossing the Quality Chasm*, identified patient-centredness as one of the six domains that define quality care—the others being safety, timeliness, effectiveness, efficiency, and equity. They defined patient-centred care as "care that is respectful of and responsive to individual patient preferences, needs, and values and [ensures] that patient values guide all clinical decisions" (IOM 2001).

As a result, partnerships with patients and families to improve quality and safety also grew. The National Patient Safety Foundation integrated PULSE representatives and other patient advocates into its Board and established a PFAC. Other national organizations such as the Joint Commission on Accreditation of Healthcare Organizations and the National Quality Forum also expanded the role of patient advocates as advisors in patient safety efforts (Hatlie 2014). AHRQ funded the *Guide to Patient and Family Engagement in Hospital Quality and Safety* that focused on four strategies to promote engagement (AHRQ 2017). Most recently, the federal Centers for Medicare & Medicaid Services (CMS) has had a significant role in encouraging patient and family engagement within and across care settings as a way to improve quality and safety.

The Current State of Patient and Family Engagement: Case Study Examples

These three case studies illustrate the current state of patient and family engagement: the first describes efforts to unite related engagement efforts; the second highlights how federal initiatives promote engagement as a quality improvement strategy; the third is an example of a cultural paradigm shift in care delivery.

Case 1. Bringing Together All-Related Efforts: A Framework and Roadmap

Over the years, various areas of work in patient and family engagement developed separately while working towards a similar vision—that of a transformed healthcare system in which patients and families partner with healthcare providers and systems to achieve high-quality, cost-effective care that responds to and addresses patients' needs. Separate areas of influence led to a disjointed system in which even the term "patient and family engagement" and the vision of the patient and family engagement differed among key stakeholders. As a result, concerns arose that various efforts to promote and improve patient and family engagement would begin to compete with, rather than complement each other.

There was a need for a unified definition and conceptualization of patient and family engagement—one that would drive meaningful change towards a vision of shared leadership, with patients as active partners in their care and in the organizations and structures that provide care. In response to this need, the Carman et al. Patient and Family Engagement Framework articulated several key elements of patient and family engagement (Carman et al. 2013):

- **Engagement at multiple levels in health care**: Patients and families partner not only in direct care (i.e., point of care interactions) but also in organizational design and governance, and policy making
- **Continuum of engagement**: Efforts labelled as "engagement" can range from merely consulting patients and families in one-sided interactions to interactions in which there is shared power and decision-making authority—with the goal being to move along the continuum to shared leadership.
- **Factors that influence whether and to what extent patients are able to engage**: Grouped into three categories—those related to patients, organizations, and society—each set of factors acts on its own and in conjunction with the others to affect patients' actions and engagement.

Building on the concepts in this framework, the Gordon and Betty Moore Foundation funded the creation of the *Roadmap for Patient and Family Engagement in Healthcare Practice and Research* to translate the shared vision and understanding into concrete action (Maurer et al. 2015). To develop the Roadmap, a team from the American Institutes for Research, led by Kristin Carman and Pam Dardess, convened a multi-stakeholder meeting of more than 70 individuals who had been involved in the key areas influencing patient and family engagement practice and research and asked them to create a shared vision of patient and family engagement along with key strategies for advancing progress towards this vision.

The resulting road map has eight strategies for change, which include (Carman et al. 2014):

- **Patient and family preparation**: Educate, prepare, and empower patients and family members to engage effectively in their health and health care.
- **Clinician and leadership preparation**: Educate, prepare, and empower clinicians and healthcare leaders to partner effectively with patients and families.
- **Care and system redesign**: Redesign system processes, policies, and structures to provide opportunities for and support of partnerships between patients, families, and the healthcare team.
- **Organizational partnership**: Redesign healthcare organizations to make patients and families part of the governance structure.
- **Measurement and research**: Create measures and conduct research to improve care, facilitate changes in processes, and assess the relationships between outcomes, experiences, and engagement.
- **Transparency and accountability**: Make data and information transparent to promote organizational accountability for quality and safety and to enable patients and families to be active in their health and health care.
- **Legislation and regulation**: Encourage patient and family engagement through regulation and legislation.
- **Partnership in public policy**: Identify and provide opportunities to integrate patient and family perspectives into public policy.

These strategies represent central, but distinct efforts that, when combined together, can drive progress towards true patient and family engagement.

The Roadmap has been used to organize action across levels of engagement. For example, the North Carolina Institute of Medicine Task Force on Patient and Family Engagement, which included patient and family representatives, used the Roadmap as a way of organizing work to increase patient and family engagement across healthcare organizations in North

Carolina and recommend actions to further catalyse engagement (NCIOM 2015).

Case 2. Promoting Person and Family Engagement: Centers for Medicare and Medicaid Services (CMS) Quality Improvement Initiatives

In the past decade, quality improvement and patient safety initiatives through the federal CMS—that include technical support and changes in payment policies—have promoted patient and family engagement strategies within and across care settings.

In 2012, CMS established the Partnership for Patients (PfP) programme, a large national quality improvement learning collaborative, to improve safety in acute care hospitals and to improve coordination of care at discharge to prevent readmissions. As a public—private partnership, the programme sought national change by setting clear aims, aligning and engaging multiple stakeholders, and establishing networks of hospitals to support these aims. Over 4000 hospitals work to accomplish the PfP goals. Simultaneously, CMS pursued aligned changes in payment policy, a nationwide programme of technical assistance aimed at improving hospital safety and care coordination through the nation's Quality Improvement Organizations (QIOs), and a programme of work through the CMS Innovation Center known as the "Community-based Care Transitions Program" to improve care transitions from inpatient hospitals to other care settings for high-risk Medicare beneficiaries. Then, in 2015, CMS launched the Transforming Clinical Practice Initiative (TCPI) to support more than 140,000 clinician practices in developing comprehensive quality improvement strategies.

For these initiatives, CMS has identified person and family engagement as a mechanism for achieving quality and safety goals. CMS's *Person and Family Engagement Strategy*, published in 2016, outlines the Agency's vision for engagement along with specific goals and actions for incorporating the principles of engagement into action. CMS defines person and family engagement as follows: "Patients and families are partners in defining, designing, participating in and assessing the care practices and systems that serve them to assure they are respectful of and responsive to individual patient preferences, needs and values. This collaborative engagement allows patient values to guide all clinical decisions and drives genuine transformation in attitudes, behavior and practice." Of note, the strategy uses the term "person" to recognize that individuals may not always be patients. The specific goals and actions include partnering with patients and families across the care continuum and within communities; promoting tools and strategies that enable patients and their families to engage in care self-management; creating environments where patients and families can partner with healthcare providers to make evidence-based decisions aligned with patient and family values and preferences; and spreading best practices in person and family engagement as identified in CMS models and initiatives (CMS 2016).

To demonstrate progress by participating hospitals, PfP identified five person and family engagement metrics and adapted six of the strategies from the *Roadmap for Patient and Family Engagement in Healthcare Practice and Research* to help hospitals achieve those metrics. The metrics are intended to assess whether hospitals have, at a minimum, structures and practices that enable active patient and family partnership at three levels of the hospital setting (AIR 2017):

- Point of care, including preparing patients for scheduled hospital admissions and conducting nurse bedside shift report or bedside rounding
- Policy and protocol, including designating an accountable leader for patient and family engagement, and working with patient and family advisors in PFACs
- Governance, including having patient representatives on the Board of Directors

Similarly, TCPI identified six metrics to address strategies that can be adopted by primary care practices to engage patients and families as partners at the levels of the primary care setting (PCPCC 2018):

- Point of care, including supporting shared decision making and using an electronic tool where patients can access their medical record and communicate with their providers

- Policy and procedure, including assessing patient activation, using a health literacy survey, and supporting patients and families with medication management
- Governance, including patient and family participation on PFACs, as members of practice improvement teams, and as board representatives

Metrics for both initiatives reflect practices designed to include patients as partners in the care team, increase structural opportunities for partnership, and include the perspectives of patients and families into governance and organizational decision making.

Within PfP and TCPI, CMS provides specific technical assistance and support for the implementation of person and family engagement. For example, within TCPI, CMS has funded a Support and Alignment Network to facilitate greater patient engagement in practice change at the sites participating in the programme (Sharma et al. 2018).

CMS initiatives have also focused on the intersection between person and family engagement and achieving health equity. Persistent racial, ethnic, and socioeconomic disparities demonstrate that health care is not equitable across all populations. Per the National Healthcare Quality and Disparities Report chartbook on patient safety, patients without Medicaid or who have no insurance, of lower socioeconomic backgrounds, and minority groups received worse care than whites and experienced poor outcomes in a variety of safety areas (AHRQ 2018b). Although significant progress has been made in narrowing the gap in health outcomes, eliminating disparities in health and health care has yet to be achieved (National Academies of Sciences 2017). To address health equity in Medicare, the CMS Office of Minority Health unveiled a plan in 2015 that has six priority areas and aims to reduce health disparities (CMS 2015). The CMS PfP Roadmap also offers six patient and family engagement strategies to help achieve health equity, noting that equitable application of person and family engagement means that every person in the hospital—including patients and families from all backgrounds—gets the benefit of engagement in improving equity in quality and safety (AIR 2017).

Case 3. Redesigning Health Care: Customer-Owners in Southcentral Foundation

"Nuka" is an Alaska Native word that means "strong, giant structures, and living things." It is also the name given to the nonprofit Southcentral Foundation's (SCF) healthcare system, which provides medical, dental, behavioural, traditional, and healthcare support services to more than 65,000 Native people in the state of Alaska. The Nuka System of Care is a relationship-based approach where patients are "customer-owners" who have a meaningful role in decision-making, both regarding their own health care, but also the organization as a whole. This idea of "customer-owners" reflects a mindset in which the healthcare system exists to meet the needs of the Alaska Native people, who share leadership for the design and delivery of health care.

SCF was established in 1982 to deliver health and other services to Alaska Native people in the areas of Anchorage, the Matanuska-Susitna Valley, and villages within the rural Anchorage Service Unit. Over the years, SCF has taken over a range of services from the federal Indian Health Service, starting with dentistry, optometry, and community health, and moving on to primary, paediatric, and obstetric care. In 1997, Congress passed legislation that enabled Alaska Native people to obtain ownership and management of all Alaska Native healthcare services. As a result, SCF assumed co-ownership—with the Alaska Native Tribal Health Consortium—of the Alaska Native Medical Center, which delivers secondary and tertiary services to the Alaska Native population across the entire state. Currently, SCF employs more than 2000 people across more than 80 programmes.

SCF's broad mission is to partner with the Alaska Native population to achieve physical, mental, emotional, and spiritual wellness. Underlying the services provided by SCF is a strong belief that Native culture and health are intertwined. Multidisciplinary teams provide health services that incorporate both traditional medicine and cultural practices, in a vision of integrated health that addresses the full continuum of care while respecting and empowering Native Alaskans. Primary care clinics provide most health services complemented by home-based programmes for elders and adults with physical disabilities. SCF also offers programmes to address whole health and specific issues in the Alaska Native community, including programmes focusing on domestic violence and abuse, a women's talking circle, a Native Men's Wellness Program focusing on physical and mental health and community connectivity, and a healing garden with access to traditional healing plants.

In the Nuka Model of Care, the term "customer-owners" reflects a paradigm shift in how patients and families are viewed and treated. The Nuka System of Care is described as being managed by Alaska Natives, for Alaska Natives. Rather than acting as recipients of services within the confines of a paternalistic, provider-focused model, patients are owners of their own health and have a role in how services are designed and delivered. Customer-owners serve as part of SCF's management and governance structure and include over half of the SCF workforce. Orientation and onboarding for all new hires emphasizes the importance of relationships, including information about the customer-owner philosophy of care and the culture of the Alaska Native people. SCF obtains regular input and feedback from customer-owners via mechanisms such as surveys and focus groups, with a strong focus on incorporating feedback into care delivery. The Nuka System of Care also emphasizes the development of strong partnerships with the populations being served. SCF conducts outreach to engage the local and regional community, particularly to address gaps in services.

Along with system-level ownership, the expectation is that customer-owners have a significant level of personal responsibility for their own personal health outcomes. While the community served by SCF has high rates of poverty, chronic disease, and mental health issues, the Nuka System of Care adopts a strengths-based approach, looking to empower individuals and families. This means that customer-owners are active partners in their own health and healthcare decision making. There is also recognition that individual health outcomes feed into the system as a whole.

In addition to serving as an exemplar of engagement, SCF's operating principles explicitly note goals related to increased access, improved care coordination through system design, reducing unnecessary or duplicative care, and ensuring financial sustainability. In these areas, SCF has demonstrated positive outcomes that have garnered international attention. For example, SCF has seen a 50 per cent reduction in urgent care visits and emergency room utilization, along with a 53 per cent drop in hospital admissions. In many cases, SCF is able to offer same-day access for primary care appointments. In addition, survey results demonstrate that the system works for both customer-owners and staff, with satisfaction rates for both populations above 90 per cent.

At the heart of the Nuka System of Care is a transformative approach to healthcare delivery that relies on building strong and lasting relationships between patients, families, and their healthcare team. There is respect for and incorporation of Native culture and values, and a deliberate fostering of relationships with the community. Leadership for patient partnership comes from the highest levels of the organization, with the idea of "customer-owners" as central to SCF's philosophy of care. In the Nuka System, the individuals receiving services have control, helping drive changes to address the needs of the Alaska Native population. This approach translates into increased accountability for both providers and customer-owners, promising outcomes, and increased satisfaction for customer-owners and staff alike. With a commitment to continuous evaluation, learning, and improvement, SCF is poised to serve as a model for patient and family engagement for years to come.

Lessons Learned in Patient and Family Engagement

Progress has been made in shifting the paradigm from patients solely as recipients of care to patients as partners in care. As the United States continues to move forward with patient and family engagement efforts, prior work suggests the importance of three lessons learned, including the need for

- System-level incentives and support to promote engagement
- Intentional efforts to engage patients and families from diverse backgrounds
- Building an evidence base to improve and increase engagement

Importantly, advancing the practice and science of patient and family engagement requires active partnership with patients and families in all of these areas to achieve desired goals and outcomes.

System-Level Incentives and Support Promote Patient and Family Engagement

Patient and family engagement has been and will continue to be shaped by the structure of the U.S. healthcare system and the forces affecting that structure. Thus, advancing the practice of patient and family engagement requires working within this complex system, while also advocating for changes to the system that encourage and sustain engagement efforts.

Change is more likely to happen when there is alignment of incentives, measurement, technical support, and oversight. For example, the CMS quality initiatives described in this chapter include clear safety goals accompanied by changes in payment models, metrics related to patient and family engagement practices, technical assistance and learning support, and oversight by a federal agency. As a result, these initiatives have motivated a broader set of healthcare organizations to focus on patient and family engagement, and specifically to start partnering with patients and families at the organizational, design and governance level.

Likewise, the Patient-Centered Outcomes Research Institute (PCORI) is an example of aligning incentives, measurement, and oversight to promote patient and family engagement in research. Created under the Affordable Care Act of 2010, PCORI was established to fund research that can help patients and those who care for them make better informed decisions, guided by those who will use that information. To date, PCORI has funded more than 400 patient-centred comparative effectiveness research projects. PCORI models partnership with patients and other stakeholders in all aspects of their work—from identifying research priorities to evaluating the merit of research proposals to disseminating results. By requiring engagement of patients and other stakeholders in the project to receive funding, researchers started partnering with patients and other stakeholders in the design, conduct, and dissemination of research. PCORI's efforts to empower patients as research partners can also be seen influencing culture changes in other areas of healthcare delivery and practice (Sharma et al. 2018).

Intentional Efforts to Engage Patients and Families from Diverse Backgrounds Are Needed to Support Health Equity

The CMS quality initiatives and the SCF case study highlight the intersection between patient and family engagement and health equity. Done well, partnership with patients and families is part of the path towards achieving health equity and eliminating health disparities; however, to do so requires thinking about partnership in new ways.

Examining engagement efforts more holistically may help illuminate issues that affect whether and how individuals engage at the point of care. Because most actions related to health and health care occur outside of the healthcare system, looking at social determinants of health may improve partnership and address equity. According to the World Health Organization, social determinants of health are "the conditions in which people are born, grow, work, live, and age, and the wider set of forces and systems shaping the conditions of daily life" such as "economic policies and systems, development agendas, social norms, social policies and political systems." More efforts are starting to focus on these social determinants and creating supportive environments in which patients and families can better access and engage in their care.

At the organizational level, engagement efforts require concerted outreach to patients and families from diverse cultural, ethnic, or socioeconomic backgrounds. Even with the best of intentions, some populations are not currently engaged at all or at the same level as others. Potential barriers, such as implicit biases, mistrust, and cultural or language differences may preclude successful engagement of patients and families from diverse cultural, ethnic, or socioeconomic backgrounds—a necessary component for achieving equity (AIR 2017). Actively seeking to address barriers in engagement for diverse populations is critical in promoting equity in health care and health. For example, to increase diversity among PFAC members, some hospitals have started to cover travel and parking costs, provide childcare, use teleconferencing, or have flexible meeting times.

Finally, examining and acknowledging how institutional racism has operated within the healthcare system—for patients and providers—is an integral part of building trust in partnerships with patients and families and a starting point in achieving health equity (Yonas et al. 2006). For example, as the movements for parity in healthcare decision making were starting in the 1950s, people of colour in the United States were marching for civil rights and equal opportunities in work, education, and public spaces. Further, prior to the 1960s, the U.S. healthcare system was segregated. In the south, hospitals excluded blacks entirely or relegated them to receiving care in basements. In the north, hospitals dominated by white physicians did not allow black physicians to obtain practice privileges. Black patients were also sent to historically black institutions that had fewer resources and equipment. In 1964, Medicare forced desegregation by threatening to withhold federal funding from any hospital that practised racial discrimination as required by Title VI of the Civil Rights Act (Sternberg 2015). Acknowledging and apologizing for the larger history—and the role of individual institutions in it—is an important step in creating equal partnerships.

Building the Evidence Base May Improve and Increase Uptake of Engagement

While evidence supports the positive impact of patient and family engagement at multiple levels in health care, the field, as a whole, suffers from the criticism that it is not evidence-based. Systematic reviews find that the quality of the evidence is not as strong as it could be (Park et al. 2018; Sawesi et al. 2016; Oldfield et al. 2018), or that the research does not demonstrate associations between engagement and patient outcomes of interest (Clayman et al. 2016). Before investing resources into patient and family engagement efforts, many healthcare organizations want to see the evidence that engaging patients and families leads to better health and health care while reducing costs.

Adding to the complexity of measurement, patient and family engagement is a broad concept that encompasses a variety of behaviours, activities, and interventions at the individual, system, and policy levels. For practical and methodological reasons, when studying engagement, research often focuses on a specific or narrow intervention, such as evaluating the impact of a decision aid as part of shared decision making. However, this narrow focus makes it difficult to demonstrate how the body of evidence for patient and family engagement as a whole affects patient and system outcomes. Research studies have also used a variety of definitions, conceptualizations, and measures to assess patient and family engagement approaches. Developing and using a standard approach to define, conceptualize, and measure engagement will help to build the evidence base.

Finally, in building this evidence base for engagement, it is important to consider not only *whether* healthcare organizations implement patient and family engagement activities but *how* those activities are implemented. Engagement activities can be operationalized in different ways, and not always in ways that reflect meaningful partnership with patients and families. For example, family-centred rounds may give patients and families opportunities to collaborate in care and planning, but they do not guarantee that participation occurred (Cypress 2012). Likewise, when examining the impact of nurse bedside shift report, it would be important to know whether nurses actively engaged the patient and family while giving shift change report at the bedside, or whether they primarily interacted with each other. To address these issues, measurement efforts should be guided by frameworks that enable a more complete assessment of engagement, such as the Carman et al. Framework, which encourages attention to the level and extent of engagement.

Ultimately, having stronger, more reliable and valid evidence that demonstrates the connection between practices and outcomes will not only improve the practice of engagement but also help to implement and disseminate effective engagement practices.

Conclusion

The shift from patients as passive recipients of care to patients as advocates to patients as partners in the United States reflects multiple areas of influence that included changing the traditional patient-provider dynamic, recognizing the power of patients as consumers of health care, a community of ePatients advocating for collective change; and partnerships in the patient-and family-centred care and patient safety movements. Advancing the practice and science of engagement requires system-level incentives and support, intentional efforts to engage patients and families from diverse backgrounds, and stronger evidence to improve and increase uptake of effective engagement practices. Patient and family engagement inspires a vision of care that is centred on patients and families. The core elements of this vision are a system that acknowledges and respects the life a person has outside of the healthcare system, invites participation and is conducive to active partnership at all levels of decision making, and makes it easy to access and pay for care. Progress towards achieving this vision is possible with meaningful, sustained, multi-level engagement and partnership with patients and families.

Acknowledgements We would like to acknowledge the contributions of Thomas Workman and Tandrea Hilliard at the American Institutes for Research for reviewing an early draft of this chapter.

References

ABIM Foundation. 2018. Choosing wisely: Our mission. http://www.choosingwisely.org/our-mission/. Accessed 21 Sept 2018.

AHA and Picker Institute. 1997. *Eye on the patients: A report of the American Hospital Association and the Picker Institute*. Washington, DC: Author.

AHRQ. 2016. *CAHPS: Assessing health care quality from the patient's perspective*. Rockville, MD: Agency for Healthcare Research & Quality.

———. 2017. *Guide to patient and family engagement in hospital quality and safety | agency for healthcare research & quality*. Agency for Healthcare Research and Quality. https://www.ahrq.gov/professionals/systems/hospital/engagingfamilies/index.html. Accessed 25 Sept 2018.

———. 2018a. *Agency for healthcare research & quality: The CAHPS program*. https://www.ahrq.gov/cahps/about-cahps/cahps-program/index.html. Accessed 14 Sept 2018.

———. 2018b. *National healthcare quality & disparities report chartbooks*. Rockville, MD: Agency for Healthcare Research and Quality.

AIR. 2017. *PfP strategic vision roadmap for person and family engagement (PFE)*. Achieving the PFE metrics to improve patient safety and health equity. Centers for Medicare & Medicaid Services.

AMA. 2018. *Patient rights | American medical association code of medical ethics*. https://www.ama-assn.org/delivering-care/patient-rights. Accessed 21 Sept 2018.

Balint, M. 1955. The doctor, his patient, and the illness. *Lancet* 268 (6866): 683–688.

Billings, J. 2004. Promoting the dissemination of decision aids: An odyssey in a dysfunctional health care financing system. *Health Affairs (Millwood)* 23 (Suppl): Variation:Var128–32. https://doi.org/10.1377/hlthaff.var.128.

Bodenheimer, T., E.H. Wagner, and K. Grumbach. 2002. Improving primary care for patients with chronic illness. *JAMA* 288 (14): 1775–1779.

Carman, K.L., M. Maurer, J.M. Yegian, P. Dardess, J. McGee, M. Evers, and K.O. Marlo. 2010. Evidence that consumers are skeptical about evidence-based health care. *Health Affairs (Millwood)* 29 (7): 1400–1406. https://doi.org/10.1377/hlthaff.2009.0296.

Carman, K.L., P. Dardess, M. Maurer, S. Sofaer, K. Adams, C. Bechtel, and J. Sweeney. 2013. Patient and family engagement: a framework for understanding the elements and developing interventions and policies. *Health Affairs (Millwood)* 32 (2): 223–231. https://doi.org/10.1377/hlthaff.2012.1133.

Carman, K.L., P. Dardess, M. Maurer, T. Workman, D. Ganachari, and E. Pathak-Sen. 2014. *A roadmap for patient and family engagement in healthcare research and practice*. Palo Alto, CA: Gordon and Betty Moore Foundation.

Catlin, A.C., and C.A. Cowan. 2015. *History of health spending in the United States, 1960–2013*. Retrieved from https://www.cms.gov/Research-Statistics-Data-and-Systems/Statistics-Trends-and-Reports/NationalHealthExpendData/Downloads/HistoricalNHEPaper.pdf

Chamberlin, J. 1978. *On our own: Patient-controlled alternatives to the mental health system*. New York: Hawthorn Books.

CIA. 2018. *World Factbook: United States*. https://www.cia.gov/library/publications/the-world-factbook/docs/summary/US_general_one_pager.pdf. Accessed 13 Dec 2018.

Clayman, M.L., C.L. Bylund, B. Chewning, and G. Makoul. 2016. The impact of patient participation in health decisions within medical encounters: A systematic review. *Medical Decision Making* 36 (4): 427–452. https://doi.org/10.1177/0272989x15613530.

CMS. 2015. *CMS equity plan for medicare*. Centers for Medicare & Medicaid Services Office of Minority Health. https://www.cms.gov/About-CMS/Agency-Information/OMH/equity-initiatives/equity-plan.html. Last Modified 15 Aug 2018 3:12 PM; Accessed 22 Sept 2018.

———. 2016. *Centers for medicare & medicaid services person and family engagement strategy*. Centers for Medicare & Medicaid Services. https://www.cms.gov/Medicare/Quality-Initiatives-Patient-Assessment-Instruments/QualityInitiativesGenInfo/Downloads/Person-and-Family-Engagement-Strategic-Plan-12-12-16.pdf. Accessed 22 Sept 2018.

———. 2018. *Centers for medicare and medicaid services national health expenditures 2016 highlights*. https://www.cms.gov/Research-Statistics-Data-and-Systems/Statistics-Trends-and-Reports/NationalHealthExpendData/Downloads/highlights.pdf. Accessed 21 Sept 2018.

Conway, J.B., and S. Weingart. 2015. *Organizational change in the face of highly public errors I. The Dana-Farber cancer institute experience*. AHRQ Patient Safety Network. https://psnet.ahrq.gov/perspectives/perspective/3/organizational-change-in-the-face-of-highly-public-errorsi-the-dana-farber-cancer-institute-experience.

Cypress, B.S. 2012. Family presence on rounds: A systematic review of literature. *Dimensions of Critical Care Nursing* 31 (1): 53–64. https://doi.org/10.1097/DCC.0b013e31824246dd.

Deber, R.B., N. Kraetschmer, S. Urowitz, and N. Sharpe. 2005. Patient, consumer, client, or customer: What do people want to be called? *Health Expectations* 8 (4): 345–351. https://doi.org/10.1111/j.1369-7625.2005.00352.x.

deBronkart, Dave. 2018. *About e-patient dave*. @epatientdave. https://www.epatientdave.com/about-dave/. Accessed 21 Sept 2018.

Delbanco, T., J. Walker, S.K. Bell, J.D. Darer, J.G. Elmore, N. Farag, H.J. Feldman, R. Mejilla, L. Ngo, J.D. Ralston, S.E. Ross, N. Trivedi, E. Vodicka, and S.G. Leveille. 2012. Inviting patients to read their doctors' notes: A quasi-experimental study and a look ahead. *Annals of Internal Medicine* 157 (7): 461–470. https://doi.org/10.7326/0003-4819-157-7-201210020-00002.

Family Voices. 2018. *Family voices*. http://familyvoices.org/. Accessed 21 Sept 2018.

Fox, S., and M. Duggan. 2013. Peer-to-peer health care. http://www.pewinternet.org/2013/01/15/peer-to-peer-health-care/. Accessed 14 Sept 2018.

Greene, J., and J.H. Hibbard. 2012. Why does patient activation matter? An examination of the relationships between patient activation and health-related outcomes. *Journal of General Internal Medicine* 27 (5): 520–526. https://doi.org/10.1007/s11606-011-1931-2.

Greene, J., and E. Peters. 2009. Medicaid consumers and informed decision-making. *Health Care Financing Review* 30 (3): 25–40.

Greene, J., J. Hibbard, R. Sacks, V. Overton, and C.D. Parrotta. 2015. When patient activation levels change, health outcomes and costs change, too. *Health Affairs* 34 (3): 431–437.

Gruman, J., M.H. Rovner, M.E. French, D. Jeffress, S. Sofaer, D. Shaller, and D.J. Prager. 2010. From patient education to patient engagement: Implications for the field of patient education. *Patient Education and Counseling* 78 (3): 350–356. https://doi.org/10.1016/j.pec.2010.02.002.

Hatlie, M. 2014. *Consumers and the patient safety movement: Past and future, here and there.* Lioneart Publishing, Inc. https://www.psqh.com/octdec04/consumers.html. Accessed 14 Sept 2018.

Hibbard, J.H., J. Stockard, E.R. Mahoney, and M. Tusler. 2004. Development of the Patient Activation Measure (PAM): Conceptualizing and measuring activation in patients and consumers. *Health Services Research* 39 (4 Pt 1): 1005–1026. https://doi.org/10.1111/j.1475-6773.2004.00269.x.

Holliday, Regina. 2018. *Regina Holliday's medical advocacy blog.* http://reginaholliday.blogspot.com/. Accessed 21 Sept 2018.

IOM. 1999. *To err is human: Building a safer health system.* Ed. L.T. Kohn, J.M. Corrigan, and M. Donaldson. Washington, DC: National Academy of Sciences.

———. 2001. *Crossing the quality chasm: A new health system for the 21st century.* Washington, DC: National Academy Press.

———. 2003. *The future of the public's health in the 21st century.* Washington, DC: The National Academies Press.

Johnson, B.H. 2000. Family-centered care: Four decades of progress. *Families, Systems, & Health* 18 (2): 137–156.

Josie King Foundation. 2016. *About Josie King Foundation.* http://josieking.org/home/. Accessed 14 Sept 2018.

Ketelaar, N.A., M.J. Faber, S. Flottorp, L.H. Rygh, K.H. Deane, and M.P. Eccles. 2011. Public release of performance data in changing the behaviour of healthcare consumers, professionals or organisations. *Cochrane Database of Systematic Reviews* 11: Cd004538. https://doi.org/10.1002/14651858.CD004538.pub2.

KFF. 2008. *Kaiser Family Foundation 2008 update on consumers' views of patient safety and quality information.* https://www.kff.org/health-reform/poll-finding/2008-update-on-consumers-views-of-patient-2/. Accessed 14 Sept 2018.

Kochanek, Kenneth D., Sherry Murphy, Jiaquan X. Xu, and Elizabeth Arias Arias. 2017. *Centers for disease control and prevention, mortality in the United States, 2016.* https://www.cdc.gov/nchs/products/databriefs/db293.htm. Accessed 13 Dec 2018.

Kutner, M., E. Greenburg, Y. Jin, and C. Paulsen. 2006. *The health literacy of America's adults: Results from the 2003 National Assessment of Adult Literacy*. Washington, DC: National Center for Education Statistics.

Levine, S. 2015. Patients as consumers: We are all patients and consumers. *NEJM Catalyst*. https://catalyst.nejm.org/we-are-all-patients-we-are-all-consumers/. Last Modified 28 Dec 2015; Accessed 14 Sept 2018.

Manahan, B. 2011. The whole systems medicine of tomorrow: A half-century perspective. *Explore (NY)* 7 (4): 212–214.

Maurer, M.E., P. Dardess, D.L. Frosch, and K.L. Carman. 2015. Creating change in health care: Developing a shared understanding and roadmap for action. *North Carolina Medical Journal* 76 (3): 161–164. https://doi.org/10.18043/ncm.76.3.161.

Maurer, M., K.L. Carman, M. Yang, K. Firminger, and J. Hibbard. 2017. Increasing the use of comparative quality information in maternity care: Results from a randomized controlled trial. *Medical Care Research and Review*: 1077558717712290. doi: https://doi.org/10.1177/1077558717712290.

MedicineX. 2018. Medicine X 2018 ePatient scholarship program. https://medicinex.stanford.edu/2018-epatient-program/. Accessed 21 Sept 2018.

Moffatt-Bruce, S.D., F.D. Ferdinand, and J.I. Fann. 2016. Patient safety: Disclosure of medical errors and risk mitigation. *The Annals of Thoracic Surgery* 102 (2): 358–362. https://doi.org/10.1016/j.athoracsur.2016.06.033.

Mothers Against Medical Errors. 2018. Mothers against medical errors: Supporting victims of medical harm. http://www.mamemomsonline.org/. Accessed 14 Sept 2018.

National Academies of Sciences. 2017. *Communities in action: Pathways to health equity*. Ed. A. Baciu, Y. Negussie, A. Geller, and J.N. Weinstein. Washington, DC: National Academies Press.

NCIOM. 2015. *Patient and family engagement: A partnership for culture change. A report of the NCIOM task force on patient and family engagement*. Morrisville, NC: North Carolina Institute of Medicine.

Oldfield, B.J., M.A. Harrison, I. Genao, A.T. Greene, M.E. Pappas, J.G. Glover, and M.S. Rosenthal. 2018. Patient, family, and community advisory councils in health care and research: A systematic review. *Journal of General Internal Medicine*. https://doi.org/10.1007/s11606-018-4565-9.

OpenNotes. 2018. *Our history: Fifty years in the making*. https://www.opennotes.org/history/. Accessed 21 Sept 2018.

Park, M., T.T. Giap, M. Lee, H. Jeong, M. Jeong, and Y. Go. 2018. Patient- and family-centered care interventions for improving the quality of health care: A review of systematic reviews. *International Journal of Nursing Studies* 87: 69–83. https://doi.org/10.1016/j.ijnurstu.2018.07.006.

PCPCC. 2018. *Patient-centered primary care collaborative: Improving care through partnership with patients, families & communities.* https://www.pcpcc.org/tcpi. Accessed 14 Sept 2018.

Pinder, Jeanne. 2010. About—Clear health costs. https://clearhealthcosts.com/about/. Accessed 21 Sept 2018.

Planetree, Inc. 2018. *History of planetree.* https://planetree.org/reputation/. Accessed 14 Sept 2018.

President'sCommission. 1982. *The president's commission for the study of ethical problems in medicine and biomedical and behavioral research: A report on the ethical and legal implications of informed consent in the patient-practitioner relationship.* Washington, DC.

Quincy, L. 2011. Making health insurance cost-sharing clear to consumers: Challenges in implementing health reform's insurance disclosure requirements. *Commonwealth Fund Issue Brief* 2: 1–17.

Richmond, J., W. Powell, M. Maurer, R. Mangrum, M.R. Gold, E. Pathak-Sen, M. Yang, and K.L. Carman. 2017. Public mistrust of the U.S. health care system's profit motives: Mixed-methods results from a randomized controlled trial. *Journal of General Internal Medicine* 32 (12): 1396–1402. https://doi.org/10.1007/s11606-017-4172-1.

Sawesi, S., M. Rashrash, K. Phalakornkule, J.S. Carpenter, and J.F. Jones. 2016. The impact of information technology on patient engagement and health behavior change: A systematic review of the literature. *JMIR Medical Informatics* 4 (1): e1. https://doi.org/10.2196/medinform.4514.

Sharma, A.E., M. Knox, L.E. Peterson, R. Willard-Grace, K. Grumbach, and M.B. Potter. 2018. How is family medicine engaging patients at the practice-level?: A national sample of family physicians. *Journal of American Board of Family Medicine* 31 (5): 733–742. https://doi.org/10.3122/jabfm.2018.05.170418.

Sisk, B., R. Frankel, E. Kodish, and J. Harry Isaacson. 2016. The truth about truth-telling in American medicine: A brief history. *The Permanente Journal* 20 (3): 74–77. https://doi.org/10.7812/tpp/15-219.

SPM. 2017a. *About us | society for participatory medicine.* https://participatorymedicine.org/epatients/about-e-patientsnet. Last Modified 11 Oct 2008; Accessed 21 Sept 2018.

———. 2017b. *Society for participatory medicine founders circle.* https://participatorymedicine.org/about/board-of-directors/founders-circle/. Last Modified 2 June 2010; Accessed 21 Sept 2018.

Sternberg, S. 2015. *Desegregation: The hidden legacy of Medicare*. US News & World Report. https://www.usnews.com/news/articles/2015/07/30/desegregation-the-hidden-legacy-of-medicare. Accessed 14 Sept 2018.

Tennyson, Sharon L. 2011. *Consumers' insurance literacy*. In Networks Financial Institute Policy Brief No. 2011-PB-06: SSRN.

Tomes, N. 2006. The patient as a policy factor: A historical case study of the consumer/survivor movement in mental health. *Health Affairs (Millwood)* 25 (3): 720–729. https://doi.org/10.1377/hlthaff.25.3.720.

Totten, A.M., J. Wagner, A. Tiwari, C. O'Haire, J. Griffin, and M. Walker. 2012. Closing the quality gap: Revisiting the state of the science (vol. 5: public reporting as a quality improvement strategy). *Evidence Report/Technology Assessment (Full Report)* 208 (5): 1–645.

Valor, E. 2018. *About me—EricValor.org*. @surfiving. http://www.ericvalor.org/about-me/. Accessed 14 Sept 2018.

Von Korff, M., J. Gruman, J. Schaefer, S.J. Curry, and E.H. Wagner. 1997. Collaborative management of chronic illness. *Annals of Internal Medicine* 127 (12): 1097–1102.

Wachter, R., G.S. Kaplan, T. Gandhi, and L. Leape. 2015. You can't understand something you hide: Transparency as a path to improve patient safety. *Health Affairs Blog*. https://www.healthaffairs.org/do/10.1377/hblog20150622.048711/full/.

Wells, N. 2011. Historical perspective on family-centered care. *Academic Pediatrics* 11 (2): 100–102. https://doi.org/10.1016/j.acap.2011.01.007.

Will, J.F. 2011a. A brief historical and theoretical perspective on patient autonomy and medical decision making: Part I: The beneficence model. *Chest* 139 (3): 669–673. https://doi.org/10.1378/chest.10-2532.

———. 2011b. A brief historical and theoretical perspective on patient autonomy and medical decision making: Part II: The autonomy model. *Chest* 139 (6): 1491–1497. https://doi.org/10.1378/chest.11-0516.

Yegian, J.M., P. Dardess, M. Shannon, and K.L. Carman. 2013. Engaged patients will need comparative physician-level quality data and information about their out-of-pocket costs. *Health Affairs (Millwood)* 32 (2): 328–337. https://doi.org/10.1377/hlthaff.2012.1077.

Yonas, M.A., N. Jones, E. Eng, A.I. Vines, R. Aronson, D.M. Griffith, B. White, and M. DuBose. 2006. The art and science of integrating Undoing Racism with CBPR: Challenges of pursuing NIH funding to investigate cancer care and racial equity. *Journal of Urban Health* 83 (6): 1004–1012. https://doi.org/10.1007/s11524-006-9114-x.

6

Connections: The Power of Learning Together to Improve Healthcare in the United Kingdom

Rachel Matthews, Stuart Green, Rowan Myron, Catherine French, Susan Barber, Dionne Matthew, Sandra Jayacodi, Jenny Trite, Adrian Brown, Justin Baker, Howard Bluston, Ron Grant, Jean Straus, Richard M Ballerand, Maurice Hoffman, Fran Husson, Laura Fischer, and Cherelle Augustine

"It's your job, but this is my life"
Cherelle Augustine, Improvement Leader Fellow and Service User

R. Matthews (✉) • S. Green • R. Myron • S. Barber • D. Matthew • S. Jayacodi • J. Straus • M. Hoffman • F. Husson • L. Fischer • C. Augustine
Collaboration for Leadership in Applied Health Research and Care, National Institute for Health Research, London, UK
e-mail: r.matthews@imperial.ac.uk; stuart.green@imperial.ac.uk; r.myron@imperial.ac.uk; s.barber@imperial.ac.uk; d.matthew@imperial.ac.uk; laura@laurafischer-trauma.co.uk; c.augustine@imperial.ac.uk

C. French
Royal Brompton and Harefield NHS FT and King's Health Partners AHSC Partnership Programme, London, UK
e-mail: catherine.french@gstt.nhs.uk

M.-P. Pomey et al. (eds.), *Patient Engagement*, Organizational Behaviour in Healthcare,
https://doi.org/10.1007/978-3-030-14101-1_6

Introduction

Patients are essential to the transformation of care and health organizations. There are well-established service user movements in the UK which advocate for a stronger patient and public voice and draw attention to inequalities in health and discrimination in services. Policy publications refer to the desire for and perceived value of patient and public involvement (PPI). Meaningful PPI requires a systematic approach underpinned by emergent and experiential learning to generate evidence of what works well. Practice should demonstrate inclusivity and mutual respect.

This chapter is organized into three parts. Part one summarizes the background to the National Health Service (NHS) in the UK, drawing attention to the emergence and strengthening of the patient voice in contemporary healthcare. Part two reports our PPI practice within the context of an applied health research programme over ten years, drawing attention to three lessons gained through emergent and experiential learning. Part three shares personal reflections from service users and patients who are involved in improving care. The conclusion summarizes important messages from all three parts.

The History and Grassroots of Patients Voice in the United Kingdom

The National Health Service and the Voice of Patients

The NHS in the UK celebrated its 70th birthday in 2018. Introduced by the Labour government in 1948 as the country was recovering from war,

---

J. Trite • A. Brown • J. Baker
Central and North West London NHS Foundation Trust, London, UK
e-mail: jenny.trite@nhs.net; ade.brown@nhs.net

H. Bluston
London North West Healthcare NHS Trust, London, UK

R. Grant • R. M. Ballerand
Chelsea and Westminster Hospital NHS Foundation Trust, London, UK
e-mail: rwgrant@talktalk.net

it was visionary in its goal to provide universal healthcare free at the point of need and funded through general taxation. Today few people can recall health and social care before the NHS when people were required to pay or if they were unable to seek help from charitable and voluntary organizations and rely on the support of family, friends, and neighbours. The creation of the NHS was not universally supported and was perceived by some to be a threat to professional autonomy (Klein 2010). Predictions were made early on that there would be insufficient resources to provide all care and treatment. Over time, the role of patients and service users has changed from being passive recipients of care to increasingly active participants.

The Nuffield Trust (Nuffield Trust n.d.) provides a helpful historical timeline documenting significant reports, reforms, and legislation that influenced the NHS from 1948 to the present day. Unease about the management of patient care led for example, in 1957, to the Percy Commission which called for the abolition of institutionalized care for people with disability, mental illness, and learning difficulties (Percy Commission 1957).

Structural reform continued in the 1960s. The district general hospital model was introduced in early attempts to integrate care, professional, and managerial activity. Patients continued to be viewed as passive recipients of care delivered by experts. The medical model and paternalism were dominant and increasingly contested (Illich 1975; McKeown 1976; Skrabanek 1994; Coulter 2001; Schramme 2015).

The 1970s are remembered for economic, social, and political unrest in which reforming legislation was passed including the Equal Pay Act (1970), the Sex Discrimination Act (1975), and the Race Relations Act (1976). During this period, service user movements emerged, notably in mental health, and disability as minority groups exercised their rights in response to discrimination (Beresford and Branfield 2012). In 1972, the influential Cochrane report (Cochrane 1972) was published recommending the adoption of more randomized controlled trials to generate evidence about the effectiveness of clinical treatment.

The 1980s and 1990s introduced managerialism and an internal market under Conservative governments. The Black Report (Black 1980) presented evidence about growing inequalities in health. In 1983, the Mental Health Act was passed allowing people deemed to be a danger to themselves or others to be detained with or without their consent, leading to concerns about patients' rights. Priority areas for health improvement were identified as cancer, coronary heart disease, mental health, HIV/AIDS, and inequalities in health outcomes. Those affected by HIV and AIDS organized and campaigned for research and better treatment, ushering in an activism not commonly seen in the UK at the time (Manganiello and Anderson 2011).

Consumerist ideology became more influential in the 1990s and the Patient's Charter introduced in 1991 (Department of Health 1991) set out patient rights and expectations in service areas including GP services, hospital services, and ambulance services. Patients were invited to provide feedback and NHS organizations could be nominated for a Charter Mark if exceptional care was provided. In 1997, a new Labour government was elected and by 1998 health policy was decentralized through devolution in Scotland, Wales, and Northern Ireland (Greer 2008).

In 2001, Professor Ian Kennedy published *Learning from Bristol* (Kennedy 2001), documenting failures in children's heart surgery at the Bristol Royal Infirmary and the attendant disregard for parents who raised concerns. The report served as a blueprint for wider NHS reform and provided the impetus for renewed policy and legislation agendas such as the 2001 Health and Social Care Act and the publication of the NHS Plan. The NHS Plan set out an ambitious plan of reform developing further choice and competition (Department of Health 2000). It intended to strengthen the accountability of the NHS to consult with patients and the public. Foundation trusts were created with membership boards to which the public could be elected. Patients were increasingly viewed as informed consumers who are able and willing to make choices within the system. However, this was not borne out in practice, with the Acheson Report (Acheson 1998) recognizing continued concern about inequalities in relation to socioeconomic position, ethnicity, and gender.

The NHS Constitution for England (Department of Health 2009) sets out the rights for patients, public, and staff in the NHS. Regulatory and inspection mechanisms such as the Care Quality Commission (CQC) were set up to monitor services and provide an independent voice for people. The coalition government elected in 2010 reinforced their commitment to engaging the public through the Five Year Forward View

(NHS England 2014), and the 2012 Health and Social Care Act resulted in significant service restructuring. It reinforced the duty to consult and involve patients and the public in the commissioning, delivery, and evaluation of services. In 2019, NHS England published the NHS Long Term Plan (NHS England 2019), setting out the strategic direction of the health service for the next ten years. The NHS Long Term Plan (NHS England 2019) is perceived by some commentators (Beresford 2019; Denegri 2019) as a missed opportunity to build on the maturing patient and public involvement movement. Despite policy commitment, failures in care suggest that patient and carer voices can still struggle to be heard.

Patient and Public Involvement (PPI) in the NHS and Publicly Funded Research in the United Kingdom

The UK and other countries including Australia, Canada, Demark, Norway, and Sweden (Boivin et al. 2010; Wiig et al. 2013; Farmer et al. 2018) have maturing movements and commitment to the involvement of patients, carers, and service users in the design, delivery, evaluation, research, and improvement of healthcare (INVOLVE n.d.). The involvement of patients, the public, and citizens is not a new concept in the UK (Hogg 2007; Coulter 2011; Barnes and Cotterell 2012). There is a history of user movements which have influenced aspects of health in both service provision and research, for example, in mental health and disability (Beresford and Branfield 2012; Hallsor 2017; Terrence Higgins Trust n.d.). This difficult and pioneering work is recognized. However, it can be easily obscured by the proliferation of policies, toolkits, political ideology, and frequent and fragmented health service structural reform.

Hogg (2007) provides a useful account of the seismic changes in England introduced by the abolition of Community Health Councils (CHCs). CHCs were introduced as state sponsored scrutiny arrangements in 1974 and abolished in 2003. The councils were initially replaced by Patient and Public Involvement (PPI) Forums, followed by Local Involvement Networks (LINks) in 2006 and subsequently by Healthwatch England in 2012. Healthwatch England is described as 'the independent national champion for people who use health and social care services'

(Healthwatch n.d.), with a Healthwatch in each of the 152 local authority areas in England. They are funded by central government and administered through the local authority. Healthwatch is therefore affected by the economic and fiscal policies of the elected government.

There are different statutory arrangements for the involvement of patients and the public in Wales, Scotland, and Northern Ireland. Wales introduced a Board of Community Health Councils in 2004 (Community Health Council n.d.). Their role is to enhance and improve the quality of local health services. In 2015, the regulations were updated to give the board responsibility for setting standards for the local councils and to monitor their performance. In Scotland, the Scottish Health Council (Scottish Health Council n.d.), established in 2005, promotes improvements in the quality and extent of public involvement in the NHS in Scotland. NHS Boards in Scotland have a statutory duty to involve patients and the public in the planning and delivery of NHS services. In Northern Ireland, the 2009 Health and Social Care Reform Act placed a statutory duty on health and social care organizations to involve and consult patients, families, carers, and communities in the planning, delivery, and evaluation of services (Department of Health Northern Ireland n.d.). In Northern Ireland, PPI refers to personal and public involvement, with the Public Health Agency responsible for implementation of policies.

In health and social care research, there is an established support organization in England, INVOLVE, funded by the Department of Health and Social Care and hosted by the NIHR. INVOLVE emerged from the Consumers in NHS Support Unit established in 1999 which developed from the 1996 Standing Advisory Group on Consumer Involvement in the NHS Research and Development Programme (Evans 2014). The creation of the NIHR in England in 2006 and the appointment of the first NIHR National Director for Patients and the Public in Research in 2012 intensified interest and activity. The first national review of PPI across the NIHR in England was conducted and published as *Going the extra mile: Improving the nation's health and wellbeing through public involvement in research* (National Institute for Health Research 2015; Staniszewska et al. 2018). This report recommended exploring the nature of co-production in research. It summarized recommendations to guide strategic direction of PPI in research over the following ten years under four areas:

(1) Reach—to widen involvement across the diverse population.
(2) Relevance—minimize waste by ensuring research is grounded in the problems faced by people living with health and social care needs.
(3) Refinement—to continuously learn and improve practice.
(4) Relationships—to keep the focus on involvement relationships which transcend the politics, policy, and structural maelstrom to seek new insight and knowledge.

Academic debate explores the difficult relationship between theory, policy, and practice and the differing perception of and variation in impact (Martin 2009; Tritter and McCallum 2006; Gibson et al. 2017; Madden and Speed 2017; Hickey 2018).

Involvement in Healthcare Improvement

High-profile care failures in England suggest that there are persistent barriers to learning *with* patients about what needs to be improved (Francis 2013; Kennedy 2001). This may in part be due to the complex and challenging healthcare landscape in which the patient and carer perspective can quickly become obscured. Further progress is required to evolve from a system characterized by paternalism and institutional power towards collaboration and networks (Malby and Anderson-Wallace 2017). Efforts are being made to foster a change in culture that recognizes the potential for patients and healthcare professionals to work more closely (Berwick 2016; Batalden 2018; Seale 2016; Pereira and Creary 2018).

NIHR CLAHRC Northwest London works from the INVOLVE definition which describes involvement as any activity that is done 'with' or 'by' patients and not 'to' 'for', or 'about' them. Other terms are used, sometimes interchangeably, for example 'engagement' and 'participation'. The INVOLVE definition is helpful to facilitate research and improvement teams and with individuals to clarify what they want to achieve. Involvement can take place at different levels. Carman and colleagues (Carman et al. 2013) offer a useful framework to conceptualize involvement at individual, service, and policy level. This framework uses a continuum to indicate how power can be shared between professionals and patients from consultation to partnership. In recent years, more attention has been paid to the idea of co-production suggesting a move towards an acknowledgement of and reduction in power differentials. Batalden and colleagues (Batalden 2018; Batalden et al. 2016) emphasize the uniqueness of the healthcare setting when exploring the concept of co-production and the necessary understanding and trust that are required to achieve shared planning and execution of services. Filipe et al. (2017) explores co-production as an experimental space. Whilst involvement in healthcare is not new, disquiet is being expressed about persistent barriers and constraints (Ocloo and Matthews 2016; Wicks et al. 2018; Gilbert 2018; deBronkart 2018; Batalden 2018). In part two, we share learning about how some of these challenges can be approached despite the complexity of the policy, evidence, and structural landscape.

Patient and Public Involvement Practice Within the Context of an Applied Health Research Programme

Applied Health Research: An Unusual Space to Foster Involvement

In 2009, the NIHR introduced a competitive infrastructure funding call inviting partners from the NHS and academia to secure funding to speed up the translation of research evidence into everyday practice to benefit patients (Cooksey 2006). The aims of the CLAHRC programme in England funded from 2013 are set out in the following textbox.

The NIHR CLAHRC Northwest London programme presented an unusual space for the involvement of patients, carers, and service users in quality improvement and the translation of research evidence into practice. The NIHR CLAHRC programme does not commission or provide health services and is heavily reliant on effective partnership working between the NHS, Higher Education Institutions (HEI) and Third Sector, and community organizations.

Aims of the Collaboration for Leadership in Applied Health Research and Care (CLAHRC) Programme

- **Develop and conduct applied health research** relevant across the NHS and translate research findings into improved outcomes for patients
- Create a **distributed model** for the conduct and application of applied health research that links those who conduct applied health research with all those who use it in practice **across the health community**
- Create and embed approaches to research and its dissemination that are specifically designed to take account of the way that healthcare is delivered **across the local Academic Health Science Network**
- Increase the country's **capacity** to conduct high-quality **applied health research** focused on the needs of patients, particularly research targeted at **chronic disease and public health interventions**
- **Improve patient outcomes** locally and across the wider NHS
- **Contribute to the country's growth** by working with the life sciences industry

Source: National Institute for Health Research (2016)

NIHR CLAHRC Northwest London was the first programme of its kind in the capital and one of nine funded across England in 2009. It secured further funding from 2014 when the number of CLAHRC programmes increased to 13.

NIHR CLAHRC Northwest London made an explicit commitment to involve patients, carers, and service users in its activity from the beginning, building this into all levels including governance, shared learning, and local improvement research funding calls. From the outset, our programme combined practice with research. A partnership was established with social science researchers at the London School of Hygiene and Tropical Medicine. This unusual combination enhanced our ability to practise and study involvement in a variety of settings across acute hospital, primary and community care. We describe emergent learning that evolved our practice and provided data for ethnographic research (Renedo and Marston 2015a, b). It is worth noting that as a research programme funded for two consecutive five-year periods between 2008 and 2018, our position, by comparison with other healthcare organizations in our local health system, has been stable. During this period, there were two general elections, four acute (hospital) NHS trusts in northwest London merged into two organizations, and the health reforms of 2010 changed the commissioning and public health landscape. Our research programme remained a constant with a limited turnover in team membership. This is an important factor which supports the development of work and relationships over time. Next, we draw attention to three important lessons about the foundation of meaningful PPI practice from 'doing'.

Emergent and Experiential Learning

Learning by doing, gaining experiential knowledge, and being alert to emergent understanding is a significant and distinguishing feature of PPI in our programme approach. Emergent learning is described by Darling and Parry (Darling and Parry n.d.):

> *Learning from experience is mostly done retrospectively. Engaging in emergent learning means taking an intentional, evolutionary approach to learning 'through' experience—by conducting iterative experiments using a group's real work as the experimental field. Taking this approach often produces new and powerful learning simultaneously to making headway on key business issues.*

We report three significant lessons from this approach at NIHR CLAHRC Northwest London. These lessons may be unsurprising but we propose that they reflect the overlooked work of involvement that needs to be better attended to in practice and more fully explored in research:

1. Establishing connections and relationships—the need to make connections and build relationships over time from which shared improvement and transformation interests can be identified.
2. Democratizing learning spaces—include learners without professional or employment status and loosen the traditional rituals and practices that influence and characterize learning in healthcare.
3. Testing frameworks in practice—rather than creating something new, test and adapt existing evidence-based frameworks to understand acceptability and utility in the real world.

Lesson One: Establishing Connections and Relationships

From the outset, we communicated the purpose of NIHR CLAHRC Northwest London to the wider community and identified potential opportunities for people to be involved. Working in partnership with InHealth Associates, a consultancy dedicated to the promotion of patient and public engagement and involvement, and later with the Centre for Patient Leadership, we offered a free learning programme called 'The Effective Patient and Community Representative' to support people who wanted to be influential in improving healthcare services. We approached local NHS, third sector, and community voluntary organizations to recruit participants. The programme ran five times between 2009 and 2012 enrolling a total of 76 patients, service users, and community representatives. It differed from traditional, episodic deficit-model induction and introductory courses and focused instead on working with the experiences and skills participants brought with them and what they wanted to achieve. Each programme had four consecutive monthly sessions. This approach established peer relationships over time and enabled facilitators and participants to work together to identify further opportunities for collaboration.

Three important outcomes emerged from this experience. First, programme participants alerted us to a community-based idea focused on people living with diabetes—Diabetes Improvement through Mentoring and Peer Led Education (DIMPLE)—that we subsequently funded (Chita et al. 2012). Second, some participants were invited to critique their learning experience and in doing so challenged our inclusion criteria for our Improvement Leader Fellowship launched in 2010. Third, summative participant evaluation suggested we consider co-designing a new opportunity where patients, carers, and service users could learn more collaboratively *with* clinicians, researchers, and managers. They expressed a desire for a *shared* learning space. This influenced the development of the Exchange Network which is described in lesson two.

Lesson Two: Democratizing Learning Spaces

The way people come together, and how they learn, can model and reinforce collaborative behaviour (Clarke et al. 2018). Education and training in healthcare, whilst varied in style and delivery, is generally characterized by scientific expertise and influenced by professional history and culture. Time and resource constraints often lead to transactional, rather than transformational, experiences (Britto et al. 2018; Budrionis and Bellika 2016; Nelson et al. 2016). As patients and carers became more involved in the work of the NIHR CLAHRC Northwest London programme, we recognized limitations in this traditional approach, and the nature and qualities of our learning spaces changed over time. We share four examples: (a) the use of open space technology at events; (b) the move to an inclusive Improvement Leader Fellowship; (c) collaborative learning events; and (d) the development of the Exchange Network.

Open Space Technology: Sharing Power

In the first two years of funding, NIHR CLAHRC Northwest London held events focused on PPI. These followed a conventional approach with invited speakers and limited discussion opportunities which became frustrating for all parties. One participant suggested using Open Space Technology (Owen 2008) as an alternative approach. The approach is designed to support groups to self-organize around a specified theme to tackle complex issues in a time limited period. It means identifying a theme that a diverse group of people can relate to and inviting them to spend time exploring related issues in order to generate new insight and fresh ideas. Working with facilitators from the Participation Agency, we tested Open Space Technology. Instead of NIHR CLAHRC Northwest London controlling or feeling responsible for an agenda, participants were invited to explore themes posed as a question at two events in 2011 and 2012. Participants designed the agenda during the event, self-organized around issues raised on the agenda, and reported their reflections, ideas, knowledge, and actions by the end of each event. A democratic process completed each event by enabling all participants to vote on the most important ideas or actions that emerge for further attention. The practice of co-production was promoted by one participant in our 2011 Open Space Event and was validated through the voting process. The experience of participating in a different group dynamic suspended familiar hierarchy temporarily and enabled more diverse insight to emerge. The use of Open Space Technology revealed a shared appetite in our community connections to work more creatively. As a result of this experience, our style shifted from 'telling' and operating as 'experts' to one which 'asks' more questions and seeks broader expertise.

Improvement Leader Fellowship

The Improvement Leader Fellowship programme was launched in 2010 to build capacity in improvement science with our organizational partners. Nine cohorts have completed the programme since 2010 in Northwest London. The year-long fellowships developed leadership skills for quality improvement (QI) through a work-based project (12–15 multidisciplinary fellows each year, including patients) (Myron et al. 2018). Participants from the 'Effective Patient and Community Representative' programme challenged us to open the fellowship to patients, carers, and service users from 2012. Over 55 improvement initiatives and 118 individual fellows were supported over nine years of the Northwest London programme. One of the core criteria and common features of the fellowship is 'in person' learning sessions, which enable shared learning on QI approaches and evidence-based interventions and include collaborative shared learning where the patient perspective is a key contribution.

The fellowship is designed to be a participatory space (Renedo and Marston 2015b) where professionals and patients' knowledge both shape and are shaped by the participatory spaces created by the fellowship. It is a novel empirical case as it is designed for patients and healthcare professionals to learn together. The fellowship is modelled on collaborative learning theory, which suggests that social interaction is an integral part of learning, and multiple perspectives strengthen this process. Participants on the fellowship programme are drawn from varied backgrounds. They include patients and different professional groups with diverse research interests and educational attainment. The fellowship is unique, in that it is the only programme to our knowledge that engages and integrates patients as well as professionals in joint educational development. In part three, you can read reflections from some of the patient and service user fellows.

Collaborative Learning

The experience of delivering the 'Effective Patient and Community Representative' programme and testing Open Space Technology reinforced our ethos of collaboration, especially in learning. A collaborative approach to learning emphasizes the role social interaction plays in cognitive development and effective learning (Vygotsky 1997). Learners benefit from understanding a range of perspectives on real-world problems which are best developed through interactions and experience rather than didactic modes of teaching (Reeves et al. 2017).

In healthcare, the features of collaborative learning include small group work, peer problem solving discussions (Marsick et al. 1999), and learning within a 'real-world' context (Barkley et al. 2004) where the role of faculty is to facilitate rather than 'teach'. The patient perspective is key in understanding the real-world problems faced and the real-world context. Knowledge exchanges are not static but are shaped by an individual's professional and personal priorities, drawing on a range of 'knowledges' and past experiences to inform decisions in healthcare practice (Dixon-Woods 2018).

A key feature of quality improvement initiatives is facilitating dialogue between groups from different backgrounds (Busari et al. 2017) and a collaborative learning approach encourages shared learning between groups (Anderson et al. 2017). This learning involves both the 'technical' (e.g. learning tools such as process mapping and Plan-Do-Study-Act cycles) and the 'social' (e.g. influencing, problem solving, and empathy) skills of quality improvement needed to create and sustain improvements (Godfrey 2013; Lucas and Nacer 2015).

As part of the NIHR CLAHRC Northwest London programme remit to build capacity, we create frequent opportunities for our improvement community to connect, share learning, and collaborate. The improvement collaborative events feature a combination of plenary and breakout sessions and involve attendees from different professional groups. Patient inclusion in such groups brings a richness and reality to the discussion, enabling participants to understand the real-world context in a more effective way. Thirty-five events have been held between 2009 and 2018, with 1384 unique individuals attending from different backgrounds, including healthcare professionals (67 per cent), researchers (15 per cent), and patients and carers (6 per cent). Attendees reported gaining and subsequently using QI knowledge and that peer-to-peer learning about QI methods and opportunities to meet new people afforded by the events were beneficial to improvement work. Collaborative learning approaches through a series of events not only support the development of QI skills, particularly those relating to relationship building and behaviour change, but also support the development of a community and wider network. Patients, carers, and service users are essential to that network.

The Exchange Network

The Exchange Network emerged from dissatisfaction with tokenistic engagement and involvement practice across healthcare experienced and witnessed by a group of patients, carers, researchers, and team members at NIHR CLAHRC Northwest London. There was a desire to create a shared learning space. Open Space Technology (Owen 2008) was the catalyst which changed the nature of conversations and enabled co-production to be promoted and championed by service user Alison Cameron. The value of co-production is often championed by individuals with experience of being let down by a healthcare system that is perceived as reluctant to see the person in the patient with skills, experience, and attributes to support improvement in care. The Exchange Network emerged in late 2013 to address this concern. A small group of patients, carers, service users, and members of the NIHR CLAHRC Northwest London team convened to explore and shape ideas that could be co-designed and tested in practice. The aim and objectives of the Exchange Network emerged through question-based enquiry with support from a third-party facilitator.

Aim and Objectives of the Exchange Network

Aim

To co-design an inclusive network, underpinned by principles of co-production for shared learning in involvement, improvement, and research

Objectives

(1) Eliminate tokenistic practice
(2) Create a space that fosters mutual trust
(3) Model effective dialogue and shared learning
(4) Notice and respond to power differentials
(5) Provide peer support
(6) Connect patients, carers, clinicians and researchers, and others with interest in involvement, improvement, and research
(7) Identify and create inclusive opportunities for personal development
(8) Influence the practice of involvement, improvement, and research

The Exchange Network developed iteratively in line with the principles underpinning improvement at NIHR CLAHRC Northwest London (Reed et al. 2018). The defining features of the Exchange Network emerged from a combination of testing a structure and process in practice.

Defining Features of the Exchange Network

- The Exchange Network gathers in a community venue, not an institutional setting
- It is co-facilitated by two members, ideally with different backgrounds
- The day opens with introductions by first name and not by title
- The discipline of dialogue underpinned by the ladder of inference (Argyris 1982; Ross 1994) guides all interaction between the network—asking open questions, resisting judgement, checking assumptions, and reflecting on personal beliefs and feelings to help self and others
- Asking for and offering help with an issue or task in the spirit of shared learning
- Engaging with action learning (Revans 1982) to advance personal reflection and expand potential course of action
- Offering and receiving peer support and engaging with networking
- Time: the Exchange Network meets for five hours four times a year

The Exchange Network has sustained for five years and grown from 13 to 68 members. No previous experience or skills are required of members.

The inclusion criteria require just two commitments from participants which are mutually identified with prospective members before they join their first meeting: a desire to learn with people from different backgrounds and expressed comfort with emergent rather than concrete learning. The meetings offer a framework for further co-design and collaborative effort. Tokenism is resisted. Mutual trust is built through the careful preparation and explanation of what will happen and how and continuous reflection by all participants. The role of co-facilitation is critical to achieve this and is constantly monitored to ensure trust is maintained, without which the quality of conversations and interactions would be compromised. Difficulties are attended to in the moment or immediately after the meeting. The Exchange Network tests the possibility of co-designing a democratic learning space that fosters mutual trust in the process (Filipe et al. 2017; Matthews and Papoulias 2019).

Lesson 3. Testing Frameworks in Practice

There is a proliferation of toolkits and guides about PPI. Whilst there are policy and legal incentives to involve patients in quality improvement, making it happen in practice can be challenging. The example in this section describes the use of a framework to take a deliberative approach in co-designing the roles that services users played in an improvement project. The mortality of people with serious mental illness (SMI), such as schizophrenia and bipolar disorder, is greater than the general population, accounting for a 15- to 20-year difference in the UK and representing one of the most significant health inequalities in society (Chang et al. 2011; Miller and Bauer 2014). This has been attributed to the increased prevalence and impact of respiratory, cardiovascular, and endocrine disorders. Whilst the underlying causes are not fully understood, they are associated with potentially modifiable risk factors linked to the environment and lifestyle.

In order to address this issue, a QI project was established within an acute mental health setting, supported by NIHR CLAHRC Northwest London, to design and implement a physical health pathway. The multi-professional team was led by a consultant psychiatrist and consultant psychologist who recruited a number of service users to the team to provide

Table 6.1 4 Pi framework

Principles	Clear and shared principles and values
Purpose	Agreed purpose of involvement linked to the improvement or research of services and patient experience
Presence	Involvement of patients at multiple levels and stages of an initiative
Process	Communication and support to ensure engagement with patients, carers, and patients
Impact	Assessment of the effect of involvement on both the individuals and the initiative

Source: Faulkner et al. (2015)

input and insight into the potential solutions that the team developed. Many approaches have been developed and promoted for the involvement of patients in the design, delivery, and improvement of services and applied health research. Despite the dissemination of such approaches to involvement, their application in QI, especially related to the impact of involvement, has rarely been reported (Mockford et al. 2012). Whilst it might be said there is no right way of engaging patients, frameworks and approaches are available to support the process. At NIHR CLAHRC Northwest London, the 4Pi framework (Table 6.1) was adopted as one such approach to be tested and to guide the involvement of patients in QI projects (Faulkner et al. 2015).

The 4Pi framework should inform the development of a plain English 'involvement proposal' and 'role descriptions' for patients, which sets the tone for early discussion with, and recruitment of, patients into the QI or applied research team. The involvement proposal and role description together addressed each of the 4Pi concepts, as follows:

Principles: Throughout the development and planning of the project, there should be clear commitments from senior members of the team to involvement of patients in a meaningful way. This could be with any number of (or all) aspects of the project including development, co-design of interventions and their subsequent implementation or the dissemination of learning. It helps to be clear about these principles, even if a precise plan isn't developed, as this may allow a more flexible way of working and support emergent opportunities for the whole team to be involved in decisions about the process.

Purpose: The team should be clear about the range of experiences, skills, and knowledge required by the project and ensure these are relevant to the everyday experience of patients and staff. Involving patients as equal members of the QI or research team is intended to achieve a more nuanced understanding of service user's experience by identifying groups and individuals not usually involved in this type of work to appreciate alternative explanations, interpretations, ideas, and perspectives. For many staff, this could be the first time they will have worked with patients as partners and could create a unique space where patients, healthcare professionals, researchers/QI specialists can work together.

Presence: The presence of patients may not be solely at the level of the project steering committee as advisors but may also include working directly alongside healthcare professionals/researchers to co-design interventions and/or support implementation. All team members, including patients, should be provided with clear aims of the project, if not involved in developing them, along with meeting schedules and details of responsibilities, expectations, and time commitments to ensure the presence and contribution of all those involved were clear and well-thought out. This ensures that all members of the team have sufficient information and assurance that the processes are accessible, transparent, and adaptable to support effective and meaningful involvement.

Process: Patients, like all project team members, should be invited to participate in regular team meetings and workshops, where a range of participatory methods should be used to provide a voice to all those present. The use of participatory approaches to involving staff and patients are intended to ensure the voices of all stakeholders are considered, to benefit the project, but also intended to provide skills and opportunities for patients to engage with healthcare improvement.

Impact: The involvement of patients in the project should have a direct impact on the project itself, according to the stage and level of involvement. This might depend also on the engagement of patients and staff in the success of the various participatory methods and their ability to empower those involved. However, impact may also be seen at individual level, on the patients that were involved and/or the staff that have had the unique opportunity to work alongside these patients.

At the individual level, staff expressed the impact that involvement of service users had had on them:

> *Involving service users in our project has been critical. As well as improving the outputs and outcomes of the project, their presence has had a real personal impact. Meeting with people who have used our services not as patients, but as colleagues has been genuinely thought provoking, helping to focus our thinking on end benefits to people using our services. It has also been really rewarding to see how the process has been beneficial to service user colleagues—personally for us as team members and leaders, but also in terms of knowing that we have played a part in supporting the development of people who will go on to contribute to other healthcare projects and quality improvement initiatives. And it has helped to bring a more 'human' feel to the project overall—where we have all been able to leave our professional roles and hierarchies at the door and work constructively together.*

Further detail about the use of 4Pi in this project is reported by Green and colleagues (Green et al. 2016). In part three, you will read a range of personal reflections about the contributions patients and service users bring to the improvement of care and healthcare organizations.

Personal Reflections of Involvement for Improvement

The striking aspect of our learning since 2009 is the value of collaborative relationships which develop over time. The exchange of insight, knowledge, and experience has enriched our programme. In this section, we respond to the challenge posed by Professor Bill Lucas to use 'The Habits of an Improver' as a framework to explore new ways of learning about improvement (Lucas and Nacer 2015). We propose that patients, carers, and service users possess many of the improvement attributes identified including the mathematical and scientific habits and skills to build learning power. We suggest that these attributes are mislaid, dismissed, or discarded through bureaucratic processes and tokenistic practice. Publishers, for example the British Medical Journal, are pioneering a more inclusive approach to the dissemination of research and scientific enquiry. Here, we invite new voices to our chapter. They share their reflections, either directly or in partnership with chapter co-authors. We organize the section by grouping the reflections under four of the five main habits of an improver (see the following textbox). We suggest that each of these individuals possess all five habits, and we group stories to share a snapshot of insight. All contributors exhibit resilience in their personal circumstances and in encounters with the healthcare system, when seeking to promote improvement.

The Habits of Improvers

1. Creativity
2. Influencing
3. Learning
4. Systems thinking
5. Resilience

Source: Adapted from Lucas and Nacer (2015)

Creativity: Jean Straus

Jean is an improvement leader fellow who draws on her professional background in education and her experience of sudden hearing loss to raise awareness of this condition in the healthcare system. She promotes the use of visual formats and innovative participatory approaches, for example hackathons, to generate better insight and empathy between people.

I became involved in improvement work as a result of developing an isolating condition, idiopathic sudden sensorineural hearing loss. In medicine and research, I found little to help me understand what I had to live with. In my search for knowledge I gradually became aware of greater issues, of being a patient, having hearing loss, deafness, tinnitus, and age.

I realised by sharing my experience I might be able to help others. I went from having dizzy spells and getting hearing aids, to writing book reviews for the magazine of the charity Action on Hearing Loss, to giving talks to Rotary and other groups about hearing loss and speaking to and blogging for the MRC (Medical Research Council). I was invited to represent the patient view on a James Lind Alliance steering group on research priorities for mild to moderate hearing loss. Awarded a NIHR CLAHRC Northwest London Improvement Leader Fellowship, I began focusing on the challenge of hearing loss in care homes.

What does all this mean, to healthcare and to me? I have been given platforms where I can raise often-ignored hearing loss issues within the context of health care. I have discovered and supported numerous related healthcare issues, such as hearing loss in acute wards, acoustics in hospitals and care homes, ageism, dementia and hearing loss, mental health and hearing loss, tinnitus, and lately patient involvement in healthcare.

Age 76, I am affiliated with researchers and clinicians in multiple fields, known to them, published by them and able to call upon them. They call on me too, to give talks about who I am and what I have learned. The Fellowship has given me options of becoming involved and having a voice. The Exchange network has given me regular opportunities for exchanging ideas and working through dilemmas. The collaborative events have given me a larger community and the stimulating possibility of learning about work I never could have known existed. The methodologies and systems training by NIHR CLAHRC Northwest London have given me discipline and an understanding of how little one individual can do, and yet how much she can change just by trying. I've learned that in improvement projects, one starts with something small and builds on it in small increments. I like to think I exemplify the same process.

Creativity: Laura E. Fischer

Laura experienced extreme personal trauma. Here she offers a glimpse of her insight. Laura is an Improvement Leader Fellow who uses film and non-verbal body-based approaches to convey the limitations of established methods to promote healing and to explore the possibilities of alternative approaches. She rightly challenges the label of 'patient' involvement.

When I heard of NIHR CLAHRC Northwest London, my work on psychological trauma had just begun to develop and take varied and tangible forms—I was yet to discover where exactly it would lead me, and little did I realise that the Improvement Leader Fellowship would be a key determinant in this. After years of struggle, battling complex Post-Traumatic Stress Disorder and severe depression following events of extreme interpersonal violence which propelled me into a dual reality where past and present blurred, living turned into survival, and home regularly gave way to hospital, I had gone far enough in my healing journey and was ready to open it to others. I stepped on a TEDx stage and, for the first time, publicly shared my story and used it as an opportunity to open a dialogue about trauma—today's most pervasive and unspoken public health threat. The limitations I experienced in therapy also pushed me to research the neuroscience of trauma and the way in which creative practices could appropriately reactivate the parts of the brain that are damaged by traumatic experiences, and how, based on this, new methods could be designed to improve our current treatments. I moved beyond the conceptual and began to develop a survivor-led body-based creative practice for the processing and communication of traumatic memories. It was clear to me that drastic changes were due in our approach to healing. NIHR CLAHRC Northwest London understood this and entrusted me with a fellowship.

Whilst I had not yet fully grasped the work of NIHR CLAHRC Northwest London and neither had they mine, our values were in line and we clearly shared the motivation to shift things for the better. The most powerful and beautiful aspect of our year together was that not only these values carried us through and the motivation continued to grow, but the relationship we created between faculty and fellows nurtured and expanded both our individual and collective approaches and formed but one whole movement of genuine and passionate improvement work. With time, we withdrew of the labels that separated us and allowed a blank canvas of diverse minds to challenge and inspire one another. My unconventional art and science background and my personal experience of trauma were valued, my disruptive and creative ideas were welcomed and even sought out, and eventually, through and with NIHR CLAHRC Northwest London, I became an active Improvement Leader. In addition to projects, I spoke at several events and conferences across the UK and beyond, from breakout sessions to keynote speaker—most importantly, I felt validated in my confidence to speak openly, without fear to tackle topics which some wish not to discuss, and with complete honesty. In other words, I became someone whose wild interdisciplinary work people may still not quite fully grasp, but that brings a certain productive disruption that many, like NIHR CLAHRC Northwest London, understand is due.

There are many other survivors, too, who are extremely keen on contributing in their own unique and powerful way. Their experiences, like my own, are not ones justly captured under the label of 'patient' or 'service user'. They are not passive, they have survived what no manual could ever rightly capture—they are leaders; leaders of growth and leaders of positive change in a culture in dire need to be challenged. Their experience is their insight, and their insight is our asset.

Influencing: Sandra Jayacodi with Stuart Green

Sandra plays an important role in promoting the physical health of people with serious mental illness. She is an improvement leader fellow. With this experience, she revisited the country of her birth to advocate for better mental health care. She was invited to the Malaysian Health Ministry and to be a plenary speaker at the International Society for Quality in Health Care (ISQua) 2018 International Conference in Kuala Lumpur. Here she describes her influence in the SHINE (Green et al. 2018) project described in part two.

Being part of the project, the team took on board what the service users were saying, for example, when I first became a member of SHINE, I was quite shy, I brought in a booklet from the British Heart Foundation called 'Everyday Triumphs—Mental Health Service Users', and this was accepted and included in the physical health information pack for patients. This gave me a lot of confidence that I could make a difference. I also suggested that the results of the patient's physical health assessment information should be given to them, as it belongs to them. This led to the development of the patient held physical health booklet, which we co-designed with healthcare professionals. All the feedback I gave was taken on board, and I felt yes, there was quite a lot of influence from that perspective. As a service user, I felt that being involved in the project has given me more confidence to work with professionals now. Also, when I go out and disseminate information about the project, from a service user perspective, people seem to pay a lot more attention and engage more, especially when I presented at the board of directors about the project. If the project didn't have service users, they wouldn't have the passion from the patients' perspective but also, the project itself has helped me understand my own continuous battle with my physical health, it's because of my involvement in the project I have been able to maintain my weight. Finally, I'd say it's important to not only recognise the input and involvement of service users but also provide support for them, when necessary.

Influencing: Adrian Brown and Justin Baker

Adrian Brown is a nurse specializing in the care of people with addiction and alcohol dependency. Justin Baker is in recovery for alcohol dependency. Here Adrian shares his reflections about the influential conversations with Justin when they worked together on a project to improve the care for people admitted to an acute general hospital with alcohol dependency.

Our project focused on an issue for hospital patients that is often poorly understood by the two main clinical groups that will be called upon to support those patients. People who are alcohol dependent are more likely to attend Emergency Departments and to be admitted to hospital than average for their age group. Addiction is seen by many as a mental health issue, but the withdrawal symptoms require physical health treatment. Add to this, the too common opinion that alcohol problems are 'self-inflicted'. In setting up this project, our team listened to in-patients treated for withdrawals and people in recovery at the local addiction services.

It was not easy to engage people in direct feedback at this difficult time, so focus groups at the local community services often revealed more about the negative experiences. Several themes emerged from those people: 'some staff attitudes are negative', 'most staff are compassionate but don't recognise the symptoms', 'we don't feel that we deserve to be in hospital'. The NIHR CLAHRC Northwest London [Exchange] network of people with experience of care was an inspiration. People who did not have experience of alcohol dependence understood that it's not always easy to become an 'expert by experience' but they had ideas and encouraged us to continue telling patients about the project.

At one of the community focus groups, the project lead was approached by one of the people who had been treated in our hospitals—Justin. He said that he had nearly died due to acute pancreatitis, but the support and treatment of the Trust's gastroenterology nurses and medical colleagues—right up to the consultants—had encouraged him to get into rehab. Justin is now sober and helping people by being a peer mentor in the recovery programmes. He was keen to contribute, by telling his story as part of our training, and agreed to take part in our project groups.

What Justin brought to the meetings was a perspective none of us had—what it is like to be on the receiving end of judgemental attitudes, of frightening symptoms and the compassion of nurses and doctors caring for them. What it is like to see people give up on you, but to be given a chance by a hospital team. We had no hesitation in involving Justin as a member of the quality improvement project team, with equal status to the clinical experts, the experienced nurses, and the hospital managers. He asked us questions that challenged our clinical familiarity and moved us towards a process that is understandable to all participants—ward staff AND patients. If only all systems projects were able to involve someone who knows first-hand what the benefits of improvement can be.

Learning: Jenny Trite with Stuart Green

Jenny is a service user and experienced contributor to improvement and research. Drawing from personal experience and as an important member of the SHINE team, she reflects with Stuart Green on the very particular acquisition of new skills in improvement and what she has learned about herself in this process.

When I joined the SHINE project team I didn't have any experience in quality improvement but I had been involved in many research projects over the years. In the SHINE project, we all started out the same, learning together about quality improvement and designing the project, this is the first time I've really felt an 'equal' part of a team and as such have learnt so much about the process. After this experience, I don't know who or what I'm representing anymore …. I've definitely changed and to be truthful I'm not sure where I fit in anymore! The 'system' isn't really geared up for people like me who do not enter through the 'normal' pathways. Whilst being part of the project was a great opportunity and I learnt so much about myself and working with others opportunities for the future are less certain.

Learning: Howard Bluston

Howard brings professional and personal experiences to support and advocate for people with Inflammatory Bowel Disease (IBD). He speaks at events with patients and professionals and is a member of the team that won the 2018 NIHR CLAHRC Northwest London Brian Turley Award for Patient and Carer Involvement and received a Highly Commended at the 2018 BMJ Awards.

My views are based on personal experience, that all patients, whatever their condition, have a unique aspect and special variation on their state of health. However, they also have rich experience of life, from all types of background—working and social environments—to be able to contribute significantly to the 'patient journey'.

There must be an effective partnership, for meaningful improvement, between all parties—the professionals (consultants, NHS staff, and academic liaisons) and patients, plus others within the health system.

Patients, particularly working adults, have limited time to contribute to the team work required to make the patient journey improvements truly effective. Special attention is needed to care for the physical and psychological situations in paediatrics and adolescents.

It has been said that much information is incomprehensible or badly-written, so health literacy is an important factor in improving communication. Much is complex for the public to understand readily, but the intelligence of the ordinary person must not be underestimated either—a happy medium must be found.

However, the initiative lies with the NHS staff. There has to be a leadership team who have defined roles, and who communicate with each other as well as with patients. Constant evaluation is necessary at all stages of the journey.

All this is just words, I know. What is tangible for me is that I've been an intrinsic part of the St Mark's Patient Centred IBD Care Model project over the last two years, to use 'Patient co-production to improve the quality of care and experience for IBD outpatients'. Our Patient Panel supplied two members, including yours truly. Dr Naila Arebi has been a great leader, with Dr Rishi Forfaria and other participants, including academic analysts and a local GP.

It has been salutary that we patients have been treated as equals, and been an integral part of the project. So all involved have learned so much, and will continue to learn and strive for improvement in the patient pathway. I have enjoyed thoroughly liaising with so many wonderful people for such a major scheme. Patient involvement, in all its forms, is here to stay!

Learning: Richard M Ballerand

Richard has a background in finance and military service and is an experienced strategic contributor. His reflections amplify the personal learning required and acquired through challenging personal circumstances and new opportunities.

My personal journey has been an interesting one. Until the late nineties, I had parallel military and civilian career paths. However, sustaining a Traumatic Brain Injury and other injuries after being run-over by a hit-and-run driver, I did not submit my doctoral thesis in psychology and resigned my commission as a reserve military liaison officer. I underwent years of rehabilitation, surgeries, and medication, managing to regain much of what I had lost. This necessitated my working part-time, leading to my involvement as trustee in several think-tanks and charities over the following fifteen years. From 2013 I often acted as carer and/or care-coordinator with my and my partner's ageing parents—two of whom had dementia with multiple co-morbidities—becoming increasingly involved with the British, French, and American healthcare systems.

I met Dr Rowan Myron on a Lay Partner course. She suggested I apply for an Improvement Leader Fellowship at NIHR CLAHRC Northwest London. I did so, was interviewed via *Skype from the US, and was accepted for the 2017–18 cohort. That was to be a challenging year, flying back and forth to the US, staying several months dealing with a parent's complex issues. Fortunately work could be done remotely, making use of NIHR CLAHRC Northwest London's excellent QI4U eLearning modules, with early morning Skype and telephone meetings. All staff were very helpful, particularly my mentor, Dr Catherine French, and our clinical lead, Dr Paul Sullivan.*

This led to several lay expert appointments; for example, NHS England's London Clinical Senate, NIHR's Health Technology Assessment committee, and NICE's Technology Appraisal Committee. I act as Central Commissioning Facility (CCF) public reviewer, BMJ patient reviewer, and serve on NHS trust advisory bodies.

What motivates me is being able to work with passionate people to achieve something beneficial for the wider community: helping in a small way to bring about positive change within our NHS. In the past, I had worked in extremely competitive sectors and found it refreshing to work with cooperative groups—which can be more productive as well as more virtuous. During my fellowship, I was able to learn from inspirational staff and fellows—including another patient fellow and nine clinical fellows. I joined the NIHR CLAHRC Northwest London Exchange Network led by Rachel Matthews and participated in its inspiringly collaborative away-days where I explored issues with stimulating individuals from a range of clinical, patient, and managerial backgrounds—learning that vulnerability provides the opportunity to grow and bring about both personal and organizational transformation. The programme is superbly facilitated and well supported.

I wholeheartedly recommend that people become more involved at all levels (NIHR CLAHRC Northwest London is excellent at advancing this) and engage in the ongoing process of gradual but iterative improvement. The improvement journey can be frustrating at times. However, with gradually implemented, measurable changes, and recursive feedback, I believe that it is definitely the best way to move forward.

Systems Thinking

In this section, we summarize the contributions of three people who are associated with NIHR CLAHRC Northwest London from early on. Their input is valued because they work with the 'complex inter-relationships, connections and dependencies' (Lucas and Nacer 2015) and are able to see beyond isolated components of the health system.

Ron Grant with Dionne Matthew

Ron is an improvement leader fellow who promotes health at his local hospital. Ron developed influential connections at national level through this work. He was instrumental in promoting community engagement for a project focused on improving the awareness of atrial fibrillation (irregular heartbeat) as a cause of stroke and to encourage people to be screened.

We provide information for heart patients. We formed what we call a Cardiovascular Alliance which is heart, stroke, and diabetes. We are giving out information, reassuring some of the patients, especially those who have had some kind of procedure done or are about to have a procedure. We talk about healthy lifestyle, the kind of diet that they should be on, what changes in their diet they can make to improve their health, exercise, that kind of thing. All our volunteers get trained as health champions, they can go on any other courses they want, like the Expert Patient course.

As the CEO of the Cardiovascular Alliance and the Upbeat Heart Help desk, I suppose I'm the one that monitors everything, I keep all the accounts, do a lot of the work myself for the group. I'm a member of the Clinical Cardiovascular Network in Hounslow (Borough of London) which with clini-

cians, consultants, and general practitioners. We have raised issues, for example, the patient's right to say no to certain medication and if I take responsibility for saying I'm not going to take a particular medication then that's my choice, I shouldn't be forced by a clinician or consultant, and they found it difficult that there could be a comeback on them. I have been on BBC Radio discussing heart health and in a film about the AliveCor device (for checking heart rate) and its use.

We are appreciated for what we do and the way we go about doing it. We have credibility and that is something that I am very hot on, you've got to be credible, you've got to be professional because at the end of the day that comes back to me.

Maurice Hoffman with Rachel Matthews

Maurice Hoffman is a lay adviser in the Early Years Theme steering group at NIHR CLAHRC Northwest London. With a professional background in research, Maurice brings wide experience of working across different public service organizations. He worked in local government initiating and conducting social and population research. He became an Office for Standards in Education (OFSTED) Lay Inspector then retrained as a secondary school teacher of Health and Social Care and Business. In 2008, Maurice was appointed to NHS National Research Ethics Service (Brent) reviewing over 500 applications in ten years. Maurice supports the Patient Research Forum at his local NHS trust. He has experience and insight into health and care services from commissioning and delivery through to monitoring, as well as the research process.

I get involved because I want a continually improving world-class NHS. I enjoy learning new things and generating ideas. I like to make a difference and to be recognised for the contributions I make. I attend many conferences networking with participants, receive downloads from organizations and follow up interesting news. I keep myself up to date.

I value my relationship with the team and the wider community at NIHR CLAHRC Northwest London because they are welcoming to new people. There are regular free opportunities to meet with clinicians, researchers, managers and other service users where we learn together. I receive and contribute to peer support through the Exchange Network.

Through my association with NIHR CLAHRC Northwest London I've seen at first hand that it is fully recognised that improving healthcare in a practical way can only be done with the active involvement of patients and the community at every stage of every project. I believe that NIHR CLAHRC Northwest London has shown through its work, ethos and achievements to be an effective, responsive, creative, and caring organization.

Fran Husson with Susan Barber

Fran contributed to several health service improvement projects to enhance patient safety by improving methods and incidence of medication reviews for patients who are prescribed a high number of medicines, with associated risks of adverse drug reactions and preventable hospital admissions.

Fran's involvement in service improvement projects took the form of regular participation in project team meetings working closely with pharmacists and using quality improvement methods, for example, process mapping and Plan-Do-Study-Act cycles. Achievements include improved uptake of reviews and avoidance of unsafe medicines practices in hospitals in Northwest London.

Fran was an influential member of a team of patients and healthcare professionals that developed a hand-held passport size booklet, My Medication Passport (MMP) (Barber et al. 2014; Jubraj and Blair 2015). MMP acts as an aide memoire and supports communication between patients, carers, and healthcare professionals about medicines taken; medicines changed; reasons for changes; other information such as allergies; use of medical aides; record of medical appointments; and special needs.

Fran has become an active agent in her own healthcare and an expert in the potential for the improvement of supported self-care. One example is her interest in and being an advocate for digital tools, such as the Personal Health Record (PHR), enabling active partnership between healthcare professionals and patients to manage treatment and monitoring of long-term conditions.

Fran was winner of the prestigious 'Inspirational Partner Award for Societal Engagement' 2018, for individuals or teams outside Imperial

College London who have made outstanding contributions for her work with the Health Protection Research Unit (HPRU).

Conclusion

Patients, carers, and service users are essential to the transformation of care. In addition to their interaction with health services, they bring unique stories shaped through life experience. The effective practice of patient and public involvement is necessary to the provision of future healthcare. It needs conditions which provide space and time for people to learn and lead together. Transformation of care and health organizations relies on a compelling strategic vision *and* leaders willing and able to support patients and professionals to work closely together.

Our experience of working together enriched the transformation and improvement opportunities in our applied health research programme. The shared emergent and experiential learning enabled us to evolve abstract ideas, translate policy rhetoric into real work, and move away from tokenism. Transformation requires us to embrace the possibilities of inclusive partnership. Advances in science and technology have delivered many benefits in terms of diagnosis and treatment. New developments must recognize and harness the collective intelligence generated through effective connections. We encourage and promote dialogue and practice to embrace the learning that lies ahead. Involvement is, and should be, dynamic, mutually informative, and enlightening. As Cherelle reminds us, 'It's your job, but this is my life'.

Acknowledgements The contributors wish to thank all those in the wider CLAHRC Northwest London community and across the UK who have contributed to the advancement of patient and public engagement and involvement in applied health research, especially Alison Cameron who opened our eyes to co-production and the Exchange Network Co-Design Group: Alison Baker, Alison Cameron, Cherelle Augustine, Ganesh Sathyamoorthy, Jane McGrath, Jenny Trite, Liz Evans, Meerat Kaur, Nicola Kingston, and Nordia James. We mention Margaret Turley for her dedication to championing people with learning disabilities who with Fran Husson masterminded 'My Medication Passport'; Stan Papoulias and Savi Hensman from NIHR CLAHRC South London for their generous intellectual and peer support. We thank Derek Bell (Director, CLAHRC Northwest London), Julie Reed, and the NIHR CLAHRC Northwest London team, London School of Hygiene and Tropical Medicine research partners, Cicely Marston, Alicia Renedo, Angela Filipe, and Sam Miles. Thanks to Simon Denegri, Jocelyn Cornwell, Samira Ben Omar, Christine Mead, David Gilbert, Mark Doughty, Roma Iskander, Sheila Marsh, Maryrose Tarpey, Helen Hayes, Steven Towndrow, Sandra Howgate, and Lloyd Pestell. Particular thanks to Neil Stillman for his contribution to final revisions, proof reading, and citation support.

Disclaimer This article presents independent research supported by/in part funded by the National Institute for Health Research (NIHR) under the Collaboration for Leadership in Applied Health Research and Care (CLAHRC) programme for Northwest London. The views expressed in this publication are those of the author(s) and not necessarily those of the NHS, the NIHR, or the Department of Health and Social Care.

References

Acheson, D. 1998. *Inequalities in health: Report of an independent inquiry*. Acheson Report, London.

Anderson, E.S., R. Gray, and K. Price. 2017. Patient safety and interprofessional education: A report of key issues from two interprofessional workshops. *Journal of Interprofessional Care* 31 (2): 154–163. https://doi.org/10.1080/13561820.2016.1261816.

Argyris, C. 1982. The executive mind and double-loop learning. *Organizational Dynamics* 11 (2): 5–22.

Barber, S., K. Thakkar, V. Marvin, B.D. Franklin, and D. Bell. 2014. Evaluation of my medication passport: A patient-completed aide-memoire designed by patients, for patients, to help towards medicines optimisation. *BMJ Open* 4 (8): e005608. https://doi.org/10.1136/bmjopen-2014-005608.

Barkley, E.F., K.P. Cross, and C.H. Major. 2004. *Collaborative learning techniques: A handbook for college faculty*. San Francisco: Jossey-Bass.

Barnes, M., and P. Cotterell, eds. 2012. *Critical perspectives on user involvement*. Bristol: Policy Press.

Batalden, P. 2018. Getting more health from healthcare: Quality improvement must acknowledge patient coproduction—An essay by Paul Batalden. *BMJ Clinical Research* 362: k3617.

Batalden, M., P. Batalden, P. Margolis, M. Seid, G. Armstrong, L. Opipari-Arrigan, and H. Hartung. 2016. Coproduction of healthcare service. *BMJ Quality and Safety* 25 (7): 509–517. https://doi.org/10.1136/bmjqs-2015-004315.

Beresford, P. 2019. Austerity is denying patients and care service users a voice. *The Guardian*.

Beresford, P., and F. Branfield. 2012. *"Building solidarity, ensuring diversity: Lessons from service users' and disabled people's movements", critical perspectives on user involvement*. Bristol: Policy Press.

Berwick, D.M. 2016. Era 3 for medicine and health care. *JAMA* 315 (13): 1329–1330. https://doi.org/10.1001/jama.2016.1509.

Black, D. (Chair). 1980. *Report of the working group on inequalities in health*. Black Report, London.

Boivin, A., K. Currie, B. Fervers, J. Gracia, M. James, C. Marshall, C. Sakala, S. Sanger, J. Strid, V. Thomas, T. van der Weijden, R. Grol, and J. Burgers. 2010. Patient and public involvement in clinical guidelines: International experiences and future perspectives. *Quality & Safety in Health Care* 19 (5): e22. https://doi.org/10.1136/qshc.2009.034835.

Britto, M.T., S.C. Fuller, H.C. Kaplan, U. Kotagal, C. Lannon, P.A. Margolis, S.E. Muething, P.J. Schoettker, and M. Seid. 2018. Using a network organisational architecture to support the development of learning healthcare systems. *BMJ Quality and Safety* 27 (11): 937–946. https://doi.org/10.1136/bmjqs-2017-007219.

Budrionis, A., and J.G. Bellika. 2016. The learning healthcare system: Where are we now? A systematic review. *Journal of Biomedical Informatics* 64: 87–92. https://doi.org/10.1016/j.jbi.2016.09.018.

Busari, J.O., F.M. Moll, and A.J. Duits. 2017. Understanding the impact of interprofessional collaboration on the quality of care: A case report from a small-scale resource limited health care environment. *Journal of Multidisciplinary Healthcare* 10: 227–234. https://doi.org/10.2147/jmdh.S140042.

Carman, K.L., P. Dardess, M. Maurer, S. Sofaer, K. Adams, C. Bechtel, and J. Sweeney. 2013. Patient and family engagement: A framework for understanding the elements and developing interventions and policies. *Health Affairs (Millwood)* 32 (2): 223–231. https://doi.org/10.1377/hlthaff.2012.1133.

Chang, C.K., R.D. Hayes, G. Perera, M.T.M. Broadbent, A.C. Fernandes, W.E. Lee, M. Hotopf, and R. Stewart. 2011. Life expectancy at birth for people with serious mental illness and other major disorders from a secondary mental health care case register in London. *PLoS One* 6 (5): e19590. https://doi.org/10.1371/journal.pone.0019590.

Chita, S., C. Mead, and M. Fernando. 2012. Long-term conditions: A few words on self-management. *Health Service Journal* 122 (6312): 28.

Clarke, J., J. Waring, and S. Timmons. 2018. The challenge of inclusive coproduction: The importance of situated rituals and emotional inclusivity in the coproduction of health research projects. *Social Policy & Administration* 53 (2): 1–16.

Cochrane, A.L. 1972. *Effectiveness and efficiency: Random reflections on health services*. London: Nuffield Provincial Hospitals Trust.

Community Health Council. n.d. *The board of community health councils in wales*. http://www.wales.nhs.uk/sitesplus/899/home. Accessed 4 Oct 2018.

Cooksey, D. 2006. *A review of UK health research funding (Cooksey review)*. London: HMSO.

Coulter, A. 2001. The future. In *Evidence-based patient choice*, ed. A. Edwards and G.J. Elwyn. Oxford: Oxford University Press.

———. 2011. *Engaging patients in healthcare*. Maidenhead: Open University Press.

Darling, M., and C. Parry. n.d. *Emergent learning: Taking "learning from experience" to a new level*. https://thesystemsthinker.com/emergent-learning-taking-learning-from-experience-to-a-new-level/. Accessed 21 Jan 2019.

deBronkart, D. 2018. The patient's voice in the emerging era of participatory medicine. *International Journal of Psychiatry in Medicine* 53 (5–6): 350–360. https://doi.org/10.1177/0091217418791461.

Denegri, S. 2019. Missing in action—Public involvement and the #NHSLongTermPlan. *Simon Denegri's Lay Review*. https://simondenegri.com/2019/01/11/missing-in-action-public-involvement-and-the-nhslong termplan/.

Department of Health. 1991. *The patient's charter*. London.

———. 2000. *The NHS plan: A plan for investment, a plan for reform*. London.

———. 2009. *The NHS constitution for England*. London: HMSO.

Department of Health Northern Ireland. n.d. *Personal and public involvement (PPI)*. https://www.health-ni.gov.uk/topics/safety-and-quality-standards/personal-and-public-involvement-ppi. Accessed 4 Oct 2018.

Dixon-Woods, M. 2018. *Improving quality and safety in health care*. London: Harveian Oration 2018, Royal College of Physicians.

Evans, D. 2014. Patient and public involvement in research in the English NHS: A documentary analysis of the complex interplay of evidence and policy. *Evidence & Policy* 10 (3): 361–377. https://doi.org/10.1332/174426413X662770.

Farmer, J., C. Bigby, H. Davis, K. Carlisle, A. Kenny, and R. Huysmans. 2018. The state of health services partnering with consumers: Evidence from an online survey of Australian health services. *BMC Health Services Research* 18 (1): 628. https://doi.org/10.1186/s12913-018-3433-y.

Faulkner, A., D. Crepaz-Keay, J. Kalathil, S. Yiannoullou, F. Singer, N. James, R. Griffiths, E. Perry, D. Forde, and J. Kallevik. 2015. *Involvement for influence: 4Pi national involvement standards*. London.

Filipe, A., A. Renedo, and C. Marston. 2017. The co-production of what? Knowledge, values, and social relations in health care. *PLoS Biology* 15 (5): e2001403. https://doi.org/10.1371/journal.pbio.2001403.

Francis, R. (Chair). 2013. *Report of the Mid Staffordshire NHS Foundation Trust public inquiry executive summary*. London.

Gibson, A., J. Welsman, and N. Britten. 2017. Evaluating patient and public involvement in health research: From theoretical model to practical workshop. *Health Expectations* 20 (5): 826–835. https://doi.org/10.1111/hex.12486.

Gilbert, D. 2018. Rethinking engagement. *BJPsych Bulletin* 29: 1–4.

Godfrey, M.M. 2013. *Improvement capability at the front lines of healthcare: Helping through leading and coaching*. PhD Thesis, School of Health Sciences, University of Jönköping, University of Jönköping, Sweden.

Green, S.A., L. Evans, R. Matthews, S. Jayacodi, J. Trite, A. Manickam, R. Evered, J. Green, J. Williams, E. Beveridge, C. Parker, and B. Tiplady. 2016. Service user engagement in quality improvement: Applying the national involvement standards. *Journal of Mental Health Training Education and Practice* 11 (5): 279–285. https://doi.org/10.1108/jmhtep-02-2016-0011.

Green, S., E. Beveridge, L. Evans, J. Trite, S. Jayacodi, R. Evered, C. Parker, L. Polledri, E. Tabb, J. Green, A. Manickam, J. Williams, R. Deere, and B. Tiplady. 2018. Implementing guidelines on physical health in the acute mental health setting: A quality improvement approach. *International Journal of Mental Health Systems* 12 (1): 1. https://doi.org/10.1186/s13033-018-0179-1.

Greer, S. 2008. Devolution and health policy in the UK. *Eurohealth* 14 (4): 22.

Hallsor, S. 2017. A comparison of the early responses to AIDS in the UK and the US. *Journal of the Royal Medical Society* 24 (1). https://doi.org/10.2218/resmedica.v24i1.1558.

Healthwatch. n.d. *What we do*. https://www.healthwatch.co.uk/what-we-do. Accessed 4 Oct 2018.

Hickey, G. 2018. Co-production from proposal to paper: Share power in five ways. *Nature Comment* 562: 29–30.
Hogg, C.N. 2007. Patient and public involvement: What next for the NHS? *Health Expectations* 10 (2): 129–138. https://doi.org/10.1111/j.1369-7625.2006.00427.x.
Illich, I. 1975. The medicalization of life. *Journal of Medical Ethics* 1 (2): 73–77.
INVOLVE. n.d. About INVOLVE. http://www.invo.org.uk/about-involve/.
Jubraj, B., and M. Blair. 2015. Use of a medication passport in a disabled child seen across many care settings. *BMJ Case Reports*. doi: https://doi.org/10.1136/bcr-2014-208033.
Kennedy, I. 2001. *Learning from Bristol: The report of the public inquiry into children's heart surgery at the Bristol Royal Infirmary 1984–1995*. London: HMSO.
Klein, R. 2010. *The new politics of the NHS: From creation to reinvention*. 6th ed. Oxford: Radcliffe Publishing.
Lucas, B., and H. Nacer. 2015. *The habits of an improver: Thinking about learning for improvement in health care*. London: The Health Foundation.
Madden, M., and E. Speed. 2017. Beware zombies and unicorns: Toward critical patient and public involvement in health research in a neoliberal context. *Frontiers in Sociology* 2: 7. https://doi.org/10.3389/fsoc.2017.00007.
Malby, B., and M. Anderson-Wallace. 2017. *Networks in healthcare: Managing complex relationships*. Bradford: Emerald Group Publishing.
Manganiello, M., and M. Anderson. 2011. *Back to basics: HIV/AIDS advocacy as a model for catalyzing change*. Washington, DC.
Marsick, V.J., M. Volpe, and K.E. Watkins. 1999. Theory and practice of informal learning in the knowledge era. *Advances in Developing Human Resources* 1 (3): 80–95. https://doi.org/10.1177/152342239900100309.
Martin, G.P. 2009. Public and user participation in public service delivery: Tensions in policy and practice. *Sociology Compass* 3 (2): 310–326. https://doi.org/10.1111/j.1751-9020.2009.00200.x.
Matthews, R., and C. Papoulias. 2019. Toward co-productive learning? The exchange network as experimental space. *Frontiers in Sociology* 4: 36. https://doi.org/10.3389/fsoc.2019.00036.
McKeown, T. 1976. *The role of medicine: Dream, mirage, or Nemesis?* London: Nuffield Provincial Hospitals Trust.
Miller, C., and M.S. Bauer. 2014. Excess mortality in bipolar disorders. *Current Psychiatry Reports* 16 (11): 499. https://doi.org/10.1007/s11920-014-0499-z.

Mockford, C., S. Staniszewska, F. Griffiths, and S. Herron-Marx. 2012. The impact of patient and public involvement on UK NHS health care: A systematic review. *International Journal for Quality in Health Care* 24 (1): 28–38. https://doi.org/10.1093/intqhc/mzr066.

Myron, R., C. French, P. Sullivan, G. Sathyamoorthy, J. Barlow, and L. Pomeroy. 2018. Professionals learning together with patients: An exploratory study of a collaborative learning fellowship programme for healthcare improvement. *Journal of Interprofessional Care* 32 (3): 257–265. https://doi.org/10.1080/13561820.2017.1392935.

National Institute for Health Research. 2015. *Going the Extra Mile: Improving the nation's health and wellbeing through public involvement in research*. London.

———. 2016. *Briefing document: Collaborations for leadership in applied Health Research and care (CLAHRCs) (v.9)*. London: NIHR.

Nelson, E.C., M. Dixon-Woods, P.B. Batalden, K. Homa, A.D. Van Citters, T.S. Morgan, E. Eftimovska, E.S. Fisher, J. Ovretveit, W. Harrison, C. Lind, and S. Lindblad. 2016. Patient focused registries can improve health, care, and science. *BMJ* 354: i3319. https://doi.org/10.1136/bmj.i3319.

NHS England. 2014. *Five year forward view*.

———. 2019. *The NHS long term plan*.

Nuffield Trust. n.d. *NHS timeline*. Nuffield Trust. http://nhstimeline.nuffieldtrust.org.uk/. Accessed 1 Nov 2018.

Ocloo, J., and R. Matthews. 2016. From tokenism to empowerment: Progressing patient and public involvement in healthcare improvement. *BMJ Quality and Safety* 25 (8): 626–632. https://doi.org/10.1136/bmjqs-2015-004839.

Owen, H. 2008. *Open space technology: A user's guide*. 3rd ed. San Francisco: Berrett-Koehler Publishers.

Percy Commission. 1957. *Report of the Royal Commission on the law relating to mental illness and mental deficiency 1954–1957 (Cmnd 169)*. London.

Pereira, P, and N. Creary. 2018. *Q: The journey so far*. London.

Reed, J.E., C. Howe, C. Doyle, and D. Bell. 2018. Successful healthcare improvements from translating evidence in complex systems (SHIFT-evidence): Simple rules to guide practice and research. *International Journal for Quality in Health Care* 31 (3): 238–244.

Reeves, S., F. Pelone, R. Harrison, J. Goldman, and M. Zwarenstein. 2017. Interprofessional collaboration to improve professional practice and healthcare outcomes. *Cochrane Database of Systematic Reviews* (6). https://doi.org/10.1002/14651858.CD000072.pub3.

Renedo, A., and C. Marston. 2015a. Developing patient-centred care: An ethnographic study of patient perceptions and influence on quality improvement. *BMC Health Services Research* 15 (1): 122. https://doi.org/10.1186/s12913-015-0770-y.

———. 2015b. Spaces for citizen involvement in healthcare: An ethnographic study. *Sociology* 49 (3): 488–504. https://doi.org/10.1177/0038038514544208.

Revans, R.W. 1982. What is action learning? *Journal of Management Development* 1 (3): 64–75.

Ross, R. 1994. The ladder of inference. In *The fifth discipline fieldbook: strategies and tools for building a learning organization*, 242–246. London: Nicholas Brealey Publishing.

Schramme, T., ed. 2015. *New perspectives on paternalism and health care*. Basel: Springer International Publishing.

Scottish Health Council. n.d. What we do. http://www.scottishhealthcouncil.org/about_us/what_we_do/what_we_do.aspx#.W7YigntKi70. Accessed 4 Oct 2018.

Seale, B. 2016. *Patients as partners: Building collaborative relationships among professionals, patients, carers and communities*. London.

Skrabanek, P. 1994. *The death of humane medicine*. London: The Social Affairs Unit.

Staniszewska, S., S. Denegri, R. Matthews, and V. Monique. 2018. Reviewing progress in public involvement in NIHR research: Developing and implementing a new vision for the future. *BMJ Open* 8 (7): e017124.

Terrence Higgins Trust. n.d. How it all began. https://www.tht.org.uk/our-work/about-our-charity/our-history/how-it-all-began. Accessed 13 Nov 2018.

Tritter, J.Q., and A. McCallum. 2006. The snakes and ladders of user involvement: Moving beyond Arnstein. *Health Policy* 76 (2): 156–168. https://doi.org/10.1016/j.healthpol.2005.05.008.

Vygotsky, L.S. 1997. *The historical meaning of the crisis in psychology: A methodological investigation. In the collected works of L. S. Vygotsky. Vol. 3. Problems of the theory and history of psychology*. New York: Plenum.

Wicks, P., T. Richards, S. Denegri, and F. Godlee. 2018. Patients' roles and rights in research. *BMJ* 362: k3193. https://doi.org/10.1136/bmj.k3193.

Wiig, S., M. Storm, K. Aase, M.T. Gjestsen, M. Solheim, S. Harthug, G. Robert, N. Fulop, and Quaser team. 2013. Investigating the use of patient involvement and patient experience in quality improvement in Norway: Rhetoric or reality? *BMC Health Services Research* 13 (1): 206. https://doi.org/10.1186/1472-6963-13-206.

7

Partnering with Patients for Change and Improvement: An Australian Perspective

Jeffrey Braithwaite, Kate Churruca, Leanne Wells, Frances Rapport, Tony Lawson, Paula Arro, and Jo Watson

Introduction

Australia has a comprehensive health system operating within a federated political system. There are split responsibilities between the Commonwealth (Federal) government, the states and territories, and local providers. About two-thirds of the system is publicly funded and

J. Braithwaite (✉) • K. Churruca • F. Rapport
Centre for Healthcare Resilience and Implementation Science, Macquarie University, North Ryde, NSW, Australia
e-mail: Jeffrey.braithwaite@mq.edu.au; kate.churruca@mq.edu.au; Frances.rapport@mq.edu.au

L. Wells • T. Lawson • J. Watson
Consumers Health Forum of Australia, Deakin, ACT, Australia
e-mail: L.Wells@chf.org.au

P. Arro
Brisbane North Primary Health Network (PHN), Brisbane, QLD, Australia
e-mail: Paula.arro@brisbanenorthphn.org.au

M.-P. Pomey et al. (eds.), *Patient Engagement*, Organizational Behaviour in Healthcare,
https://doi.org/10.1007/978-3-030-14101-1_7

one-third is private, with the latter predominantly funded through health insurance monies or out-of-pocket expenses (Australian Institute of Health and Welfare 2018). Australia's population of 25 million is spread across a large continent of over 7.692 million kilometres^2, but most people live in cities. As a consequence, care providers are disproportionally located in these urban conurbations.

Australia spends 10.3 per cent of GDP on healthcare, amounting to AUD$170.4 billion (USD$124.99, €107.45 billion) (Australian Institute of Health and Welfare 2017). It has more than one million personnel in the health workforce engaged in direct care or indirectly, including 101,070 doctors, 369,790 nurses and midwives, 29,591 physiotherapists, 29,163 psychologists, and 16,549 dentists (Australian Institute of Health and Welfare 2018). Life expectancy for people born in 2016, at 80.4 years for males and 84.6 years for females, is in the top third of all countries. It is one of the higher performing health systems internationally on many dimensions according to the Commonwealth Fund (Schneider et al. 2017). The Commonwealth Fund's 2017 Mirror, Mirror report, assessing 11 high-income countries according to multiple criteria including equity, health outcomes and access, ranks Australia number two, behind the UK which was ranked first, and, in descending order following Australia are The Netherlands, New Zealand, Norway, and Switzerland (Schneider et al. 2017). Additional selected key data is provided in the following textbox.

Selected Key Data

On a typical day, there are 850 babies born, 440 people die, 380 are diagnosed with cancer, 170 people have a heart attack, 100 people have a stroke and 1300 people are hospitalized due to an injury (Australian Institute of Health and Welfare 2018). Australia spends AUD$467 million on healthcare each day; there are 406,000 visits to a general practitioner (GP); 777,000 pharmacy prescriptions filled; 21,400 presentations made to emergency departments; 6,000 elective surgeries performed; and 26,000 community mental health consultations occur.

Although Australia has a largely young and relatively fit population, and smoking is at a very low level by international standards (only 14.5 per cent of the population smoke daily), there are relatively high levels of coronary heart disease, diabetes, dementia, and Alzheimer's disease, suicide, and musculoskeletal disease, and Australia ranks high in the proportion of people (almost two-thirds, 63 per cent) who are overweight or obese (Australian Institute of Health and Welfare 2018). The Australian public has a strong inclination that their healthcare preferences should inform the priorities of services provided (Wiseman et al. 2003).

Patients in the Care System

It has often been said that patients are the only actors in healthcare that see and experience the whole system. Surgeons, physicians, anaesthetists, GPs, community nurses, local pharmacists, pathologists, radiologists, ward-based nurses, psychologists, physiotherapists, speech pathologists, occupational therapists, and all the other providers of care; each see every patient episodically, during a particular stage of their care needs. It is certainly the case that health teams spend quite a while with some individuals or cohorts of patients, caring for or treating them, especially those with chronic conditions or in residential aged care settings. But the only constant across the healthcare journey is the patient.

It follows that those best able to make observations about the health system and how it can be improved, and the people with the most knowledge of both the system and their own condition, are patients. Logically, then, we should be tapping into this knowledge if we are going to improve how the care system can be mobilized to provide more benefits to patients over time.

What is remarkable is how relatively recent in the history of health systems that idea is. In past eras, far less involvement of and consultation with patients occurred than was preferable. Almost as striking is the fact that we have not made the progress we would like in systematically incorporating patient knowledge into thinking about how to deliver better care in the present and how to use such knowledge to improve and transform the system over time. This chapter takes this radical idea—that patients should be at the heart of decisions in healthcare and at the very least be in equal partnership with health professionals, managers, and policymakers—and discusses the extent to which patients in Australia are actually being involved as collaborators in the continuous improvement of healthcare. It also demonstrates some of the key ways that this goal is being actualized and provides some pointers for the future.

Frameworks for Patient Involvement

Patient involvement is becoming more widely accepted as a fulcrum in the transformation of healthcare systems (Wells 2018). In a healthcare system where patients can be overlooked if traditional service-centric cultures and roles amongst providers and policymakers predominate, frameworks have been developed through which we can conceive and aim to implement forms of patient involvement across each level: policy, programme, service, and research. One of the most widely recognized is the International Association for Public Participant's Spectrum of Engagement (IAP2). Designed to help determine the level of participation using a scale from "inform" to "empower", IAP2 can be applied to research involvement and the wider health system (International Association for Public Participation Australasia 2016). Similarly, the Wellcome Trust's Public Engagement Onion model illustrates different activities and methods of engagement across a series of layers from "understanding" through to "making decisions" (Wellcome Trust 2011).

Models of patient involvement are moving beyond simply seeking patient feedback, with greater emphasis on the experience of patients and staff when interacting with a health service. Bate and Robert (2006) illustrate this notion across a continuum of patient influence spanning from "complaining" to "experience-based co-design". Against this background canvass of international ideas, the Consumers Health Forum (CHF) of Australia has developed a toolkit, Real People, Real Data (RPRD) to assist health services, policymakers, and organizations to gather, analyse, and use patient stories, bringing forward consumer experience into evidence-based decision-making to help improve healthcare (Consumers Health Forum of Australia 2015).

The Australian health system is undergoing a cultural shift, then, towards patient-centred care with co-design forming a key component

(Chamberlain and Partridge 2017). Co-design is a growing strand of research and practice whereby patients and providers—often alongside managers, commissioners, and policymakers—partner to review, plan, and implement new or improve existing services (New South Wales Agency for Clinical Innovation (ACI) 2015). Infusing the system with a patient perspective and doing this work collaboratively (the "co" in co-design) is a very powerful model (Dawda and Knight 2017; Robert et al. 2015).

While this concept has been applied across many industries for decades, the co-design model was underutilized within the health sector until relatively recently. A key event occurred in 2006 when co-design was piloted in the UK at the Head and Neck Cancer Service of the Luton and Dunstable University Hospital (Boyd et al. 2012). Since then, innovations and variations on this theme have gained momentum and have led to the development of evidence-based co-design (EBCD) resources, tools, education, and training programmes with the purpose of bringing together consumers and clinical leaders in collaborative arrangements (Boyd et al. 2012).

In 2017, an EBCD toolkit for Australia was developed with support from CHF and the Australian Healthcare and Hospitals Association (AHHA), utilizing existing resources from the UK and New Zealand, contextualized for Australian health services through Australian case studies (Dawda and Knight 2017). Developing consumers and clinical leaders who work together in partnership is aimed at transforming the health system and embedding more integral patient-centred care.

More recently, CHF has embarked on a collaboration with the King's Fund UK, four Australian Primary Health Networks (PHNs), and the Australian Commission on Safety and Quality in Health Care (ACSQHC) to conduct a national trial of Collaborative Pairs. Collaborative Pairs is a promising programme for taking patient and consumer involvement to the next level. The trial aims to break down cultural barriers, power imbalances, and information asymmetry prevailing between those receiving and those delivering healthcare, by moving beyond a "them and us" relationship to one where power, leadership, and ownership are shared (Consumers Health Forum of Australia 2017). Pairs consist of a consumer leader and a clinician or health service provider looking to find new ways of harnessing the role of consumers as agents of change.

Further afield, drawing on international experience, our colleague in Canada co-editing this volume, Professor Marie-Pascale Pomey, has written about partnership models in the context of Quebec. The Quebec model, which is also influencing thinking in Australia, not only includes collaboration with patients but is supported by inter-professional collaboration amongst healthcare professionals who are providing the care and helping structure patient and consumer engagement in a more encompassing manner (Pomey and Lebel 2016).

Back in Australia, research underpinning greater levels of health literacy is progressing. Smith et al. (2009), alongside UK colleagues, examined patient involvement in decision making at the point-of-care delivery among various groups with differing levels of health literacy. They randomly selected 250 members of the University of Sydney's alumni network and interviewed 73 of them. As might be expected, members of the cohort had different levels of health literacy. Smith et al. (2009) showed how distinguishable groups, particularly those with differing levels of education, perceived their involvement in decisions about healthcare in markedly different ways. Those with higher education levels were more likely to see their goal as sharing decisions with their health practitioners. Those with lower levels of education were more likely to regard their involvement in terms of providing their consent to the recommendation of their doctor, albeit they saw that the responsibility for the final decision rested with them. This latter group was less likely to consider alternative choices. Regardless of educational background or levels of health literacy, all participants wanted respect from their practitioners and the clinical encounter and were very keen to be "listened to, understood, and supported" (Smith et al. 2009 p. 1811). It seems to us that this, at the very least, is what we might expect from an effective health system—for patients to be listened to, understood, and supported.

If that is the baseline expectation of a health system, however, we want to go further in this chapter. We will show studies and provide case examples and perspectives from patient and consumer representatives, on ways that patients have been or are being involved in providing their knowledge, experience, and expertise across Australia in different contexts and circumstances with a goal of changing and improving the system that serves them. It is to this task that we now turn. In the next section, we present some recent Australian research by way of providing context and following that we adduce examples that map to three levels of the Australian health system: clinical, organizational, and policy.

Partnering with Patients: Engagement, Involvement, Participation, and Co-production

We know progressively more about partnering with Australian patients and consumers than we did in the past and how to leverage the knowledge this group provides for the benefit of both patients and the systems that care for them. Increasingly, there is research advancing the knowledge base (Sarrami-Foroushani et al. 2014a, b). CHF, as the leading body for patients and consumers of care, publishes a monthly journal, *Health Voices*, with opinion pieces, authoritative editorial contributions, and research on how consumers are being represented and playing a role at macro (e.g., policy), meso (e.g., in organizations and institutions) and micro (e.g., with health teams, practices, and delivery vehicles) levels, designed to show how instrumental and evocative patients' input is, and can be, in shaping the system which cares for them (Wells 2016).

We are learning more about the multi-faceted roles that patients can play. These include patient advocate, co-designer of services, a voice in narrowing health inequalities, community representative, provider of knowledge to policymakers and managers, shared decision maker, political activist, carer, and concerned family member. All of these and many others are roles that patients play in Australia, and they fall along a continuum of patient engagement from consultation, through to involvement, and to full partnership through shared leadership of programmes or parts of the system (Ocloo and Matthews 2016). Some of these approaches to patient engagement have been the subject of studies and research.

Wiley et al. (2014), for example, examined the views of young Australian adults with Type 1 diabetes, asking 150 surveyed participants and 33 in-focus groups about their experiences with clinician-led diabetes education. While most participants were satisfied with their education, the vast majority (96.7 per cent) wanted more self-education opportunities.

In another study, Nathan and colleagues (2013) investigated the activities of community participation coordinators in Western Sydney, New South Wales. Field data included 42 hours of observations, and in-depth interviews with 10 community representatives, 19 staff members and seven coordinators. They uncovered four roles for community participation: building skills and confidence in self and others; engaging others in agendas for action; helping community representatives to navigate the system; and advocating their contributions or potential contributions to staff and services (Nathan et al. 2013). In the sections that follow, we examine how roles of patient and consumer involvement have successfully affected the clinical, organizational, and policy levels of healthcare in Australia.

The Clinical Level: Consumer Representative Involvement in Health Service Organization Accreditation

Despite some localized examples such as the research reported above, prior to 2013 the involvement of patients as advisers for improving and monitoring quality and safety at the clinical level in acute care settings in Australia was rudimentary and not systemic. In 2013, Australia adopted the National Safety and Quality Health Service (NSQHS) standards, developed by the ACSQHC through a widespread consultation across stakeholder groups (Braithwaite et al. 2018; Greenfield et al. 2016). The NSQHS standards aim to improve the quality of health service provision in Australia and provide a nationally consistent statement of the level of care consumers can expect from health service organizations (HSOs). These standards are used to assess HSOs for accreditation every 3–4 years.

The first two standards relate squarely to the role of patients—in HSO governance, clinical governance, and improvement. This recognizes the growing evidence that partnerships between HSOs, health professionals, patients, families, and carers can lead to enhancements in healthcare quality and outcomes by increasing safety, cost effectiveness, and patient and family satisfaction (Australian Commission on Quality and Safety in

Health Care 2017a). The ACSQHC had responded to consumer consultation in the development of the standards, during which there was a strong call for assessing HSOs on how patients and patient insights are integrated into governance systems to maintain and enhance the reliability and quality of patient care and improve patient outcomes. Additionally, there was a desire for assessment of how leaders of HSOs implement systems to support partnering with patients, carers, and other consumers to improve safety and quality of care.

The introduction of the NSQHS standards changed the game for HSOs. To attain accreditation, Australian HSOs must now demonstrate how patients are involved at the clinical level through governance systems and how they partner with consumers in making decisions for service planning, developing models of care, measuring service, and evaluating systems of care. This has stimulated significant shifts in HSO culture and practice. While there is scope for further improvement and increased maturity, these initiatives provide demonstrable evidence that patients are increasingly and systemically being involved in governance, clinical governance, and in shaping consumer partnership programmes and initiatives within HSOs (Freeman et al. 2014; Nathan et al. 2014).

Australia has also seen the emergence of consumer involvement in the surveyor workforce that accredits HSOs. There has been a growth in the number of consumer surveyors—surveyors who have developed expertise and experience around consumer involvement in health—and at least one surveyor on most surveys of HSOs has this skill set (Australian Council on Healthcare Standards 2018). Some accreditation agencies have recognized the merit of, and actively developed a pool of, consumer surveyors to concentrate on the achievement of this NSQHS standard. Notwithstanding this, recruitment, retention, and management of a quality surveyor workforce is a challenge for accreditation agencies. Unlike in the USA and Canada, the accreditation workforce in Australia has traditionally relied more heavily on volunteers than paid personnel though there is now a trend towards the payment of honorariums to those participating as consumer surveyors.

Consistency among surveyors is an important factor in the legitimacy of surveyors; the concept of inter-rater reliability plays a key role in survey outcomes (Greenfield et al. 2009). Factors influencing consistency among surveyors include their style, objectivity, understanding of the context, flexibility, as well as the degree of interpretation required to assess compliance with a standard based on rationale, evidence, and observations (Greenfield et al. 2008). Most surveyors undertake two associated but different tasks—verifying that a standard or recommendation is met and advising on continuous improvement strategies. The process places much emphasis on verification of documentation, but many surveyors also use informal conversations as a source of evidence, particularly conversations with consumers and patients.

The burden of complying with standards may well fall as quality improvement mechanisms become embedded in the culture of HSOs—or at least, that is the theory. However, there is a way to go. For example, it has been observed in some HSOs that consumers are not sufficiently engaged in clinical governance activities because it has been reported that senior clinicians are not ready for this to occur. While it has also been observed that consumers have been involved in service planning and performance assessment, it can be fragmented and appears as "busy work" with no joined-up or logical reporting lines or outcomes.

All in all, the NSQHS standards have laid significant foundations for patient and consumer involvement and, importantly, have been shaped and administered with the input of consumer leaders. They compel Australian HSOs to involve consumers in their governance and quality improvement systems, processes, and initiatives, and they have spurred an emergent new workforce centred on the consumer surveyor. Consumer involvement in both administering and embedding the standards is therefore on an improvement trajectory.

We have learned through this process that education for clinical leaders in the principles of partnering with consumers and the value consumers can bring to governance and quality improvement initiatives is a must-do across Australian HSOs. If well designed, such education will assist with receptiveness and readiness to embrace these initiatives. Localized education for experienced consumer advocates in improvement science and methodology should also be envisaged and steps might be taken to further develop and formally recognize and mandate the role of the consumer surveyor system wide. Translational measures such as these should accompany the second version of the NSQHS standards, which is in operation from 1 January 2019 and features strengthened standards pertaining to consumer involvement in governance and quality improvement initiatives and a heightened emphasis on health literacy to encourage HSOs to communicate with patients in ways that support effective partnerships.

The Organizational Level: Involving Patients in Primary Health Commissioning and Delivery

Australian Primary Health Networks (PHNs) are a regional web of 31 organizations responsible across Australia for commissioning services such as primary mental health and alcohol and other drug treatment services in response to local needs (see Fig. 7.1). Commissioning allows PHNs to devote limited resources to health and community care

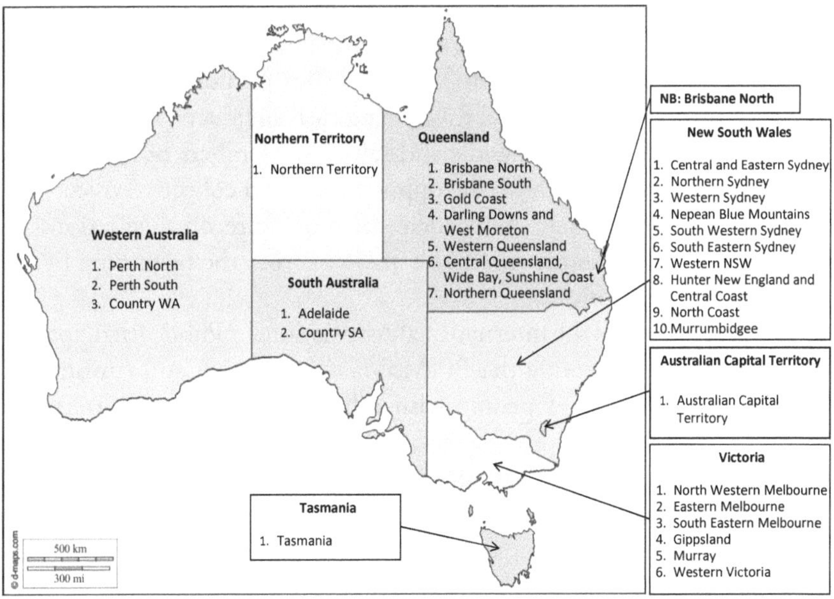

Fig. 7.1 Australia's 31 Primary Health Networks. (Source: Adapted from Department of Health (2015a), map taken from https://d-maps.com/carte.php?num_car=25129&lang=en)

interventions with the aim of improving the health system and delivering better consumer outcomes.

By way of example, Brisbane North PHN serves the North Brisbane and Moreton Bay region of south east Queensland, a predominantly metropolitan region with a population of almost one million residents (Brisbane North PHN 2018a). The PHN has indicated its commitment to collaborative partnerships with consumers and carers at each stage of the commissioning cycle. In one initiative, the PHN employed a consumer and carer participation coordinator to support the organization's mental health activities and broader sector development. It also originated a peer participation project to develop a regional framework aimed at increasing participation of people experiencing mental health issues in the development, implementation, and evaluation of services. The need for a framework was identified through forums involving service providers as well as specific consumer and carer forums.

Based on this framework, a key activity undertaken in the PHN was the establishment of a network of people with a lived experience of mental health issues: the Peer Participation in Mental Health Services (PPIMS) Network (Brisbane North PHN 2018b). The purpose of the PPIMS Network is to work collaboratively and for members to participate actively in mental health systems and reforms. Members of the network agreed that they want to have the opportunity for a collective voice; support other people to actively participate; provide recommendations on how the system can improve; and be involved from the beginning in any co-design opportunities.

The PHN adopted the International Association for Public Participation (IAP2) Spectrum to guide the PPIMS' *modus operandi* and continue to increase participation of people with a lived experience (International Association for Public Participation Australasia 2016). The PPIMS Network is now recognized across the levels of the governance structure for PHN-commissioned services. Through the Network, people with a lived experience have been involved in the co-design of procurement activities, variously as members of governance groups, project advisory groups, recruitment panels and tender panels, or as participants in discussion workshops. Notably, the PPIMS Network has been involved in the development of a five-year regional plan for mental health and alcohol and other drug treatment services. It advised on what an integrated system should look like for people with lived experience of mental health issues, how the sector would know if the system was meeting the needs of people, and the principles that should guide the direction. This work is ongoing.

As a result, people with lived experience, the PHN, and the local hospital and health service (as co-sponsors of the plan) have agreed on shared objectives over the next five years. Through the PPIMS, people with lived experience of mental health issues have led change in clear and demonstrable ways, working to strengthen and diversify a collective voice to drive service improvement activity; made available training and capacity building for others; actively participated in planning, delivery, and evaluation; established and sustained a region-wide approach to participation; advocated for peer workforce development; and expanded and diversified the lived experience workforce across all levels of employment in the sector.

The PPIMS Network and associated activities have been recognized at the national level as best practice. In mid-2018, the Commonwealth Department of Health invited Brisbane North PHN to chair a National PHN Mental Health Lived Experience Engagement Network to share resources, learnings, and practices with other PHNs across Australia. This includes monthly meetings with other PHNs; a stocktake of PHN lived experience engagement across Australia; establishment of a central point to situate resources, tools, templates, and research; and identification and sharing of best practice case studies to inform and support PHNs.

The Policy Level: Improving Access to Pharmaceutical Medicines Nationally

The Pharmaceutical Benefits Scheme (PBS) sits as a cornerstone policy initiative of the Australian healthcare system, enabling Australian citizens to access pharmaceutical medicines through government subsidized prescriptions. Affordable and equitable access to medicine for the community is enshrined in the National Medicines Policy of Australia (Department of Health and Ageing 2000) and these are principles that

Australian patient networks and the health consumer movement have strongly supported.

Since its introduction in 1948, the PBS has evolved and developed, not only in volume and expenditure but also in the way it has been positioned within the system; it is arguably the most visible and valued feature of healthcare accessed by consumers. Specific policy reform and advocacy efforts have been a focus of many patient and community groups which, over the decades, have pushed strongly for ensuring access to new drugs and treatments, through a PBS listing for specific medicines, as well as influencing drug approval processes and health system reviews.

Consumer engagement with the development of reforms and policy related to the PBS are varied and complex. The presence of a patient representative on the PBS, whose perspective is focused on access to new medicines and therapies for patient communities, is paramount. For the health consumer representative expected to participate on behalf of the community and represent their views and perspectives, there will often be diverse viewpoints to consider and wider accountability to a formal consumer body. Formal consumer representation has usually been coordinated and provided through peak consumer bodies, such as the CHF, or for specific sectors or disease groups as relevant.

Successive federal governments have, over time, initiated significant changes to policy in the PBS, leading to a more general acceptance that the consumer or patient perspective needs to be referenced and visible in its activities and decision making. The fundamental premise of this involvement is that the PBS is ultimately about delivering health outcomes to the community and thus a strong consumer voice is needed in its deliberations and decisions.

Historically, an early example of patient and consumer involvement in PBS reform came in the 1990s, when the Australian government adopted recommendations from a review of the Therapeutic Goods Administration (TGA, the peak body responsible for carrying out assessment and monitoring to ensure therapeutic goods meet an acceptable standard) that considered the future of drug evaluation arrangements. Activism and leadership among HIV-AIDS community groups was often cited as contributing to the initiation of the review and the outcomes it delivered.

The Baume Review (Baume 1991) and early TGA reforms were delivered on the basis of this strong community effort to see clinical trials and special access arrangements restructured to better respond to AIDS patients who were desperate to access experimental drugs, before their registration and subsequent listings on the PBS. Other outcomes also included the ministerial appointments of consumer representatives to bodies such as the Australian Drug Evaluation Committee (ADEC) and the Pharmaceutical Benefits Advisory Committee (PBAC).

The advocacy, representation, and intellectual participation of patients and health consumer advocates such as this has underpinned the evolution of the PBS system and its framing as one of the primary pillars of Australian healthcare. The strategic policy debates and development of new features for the scheme over the decades have required not only this participation but also the inherent imprimatur of the community to satisfy the fundamental principle that the PBS is protected for Australians now and into the future. Consequently, Australian patients have ensured that their interests and voices are the critical aspect of the National Medicines Policy and are embedded in its framework into the future.

As recognition of the value and need for consumer representation—in the PBS and more generally in policy development—became more established over time, the Commonwealth Government has formally supported and increasingly recognized the CHF as the national health consumer association with coordination and consultative responsibilities for the membership of patient organizations and health consumer groups from the states and territories. From this base, members of the CHF have become engaged with many Commonwealth processes across the health system and have been in the past, and continue to be, called on to fill representative positions, as well as becoming more collectively focused on points of the system where policy influence and input can be best placed. The measure of health consumer involvement has not just rested on the notion of appointments and a seat at the table but also the calibre of that representation for articulating meaningful policy inputs that make the health system increasingly more responsive to, and accountable to, patients.

Australian patient groups have responded and are now invested significantly in ensuring that their representatives are well-informed and able to contribute in a rigorous and consistent manner to policy debates and reform changes. Few people doubt that the health sector is a complex political landscape and the mobilization of patient groups through health consumer advocacy at the macro level has been decisive in realizing many of the most pivotal changes. Government policies for adoption of new technologies, introduction of new arrangements for public health surveillance, and redirections of health financing are areas where the support of Australian patient groups and the health consumer movement have been sought or strong opposition against a proposal has been recognized in these developments. Notable examples include input into the Biosimilar Awareness Initiative (Department of Health 2015b), the Australian National Preventive Health Agency (Australian Government 2014), and the push for abandoning a policy of consumer co-payments in general practice (Stankevicius 2014). While patient and consumer involvement in PBS reform has been a flagship activity, it is only one of many prominent examples of their contribution to Australian healthcare policy.

What Can We Learn from These Examples?

The case study and research examples we have provided in this chapter—of consumer and patient involvement, engagement, and co-production in Australian healthcare development and delivery—offer wider lessons for the value that consumer contributions can bring, at clinical, organizational, and policy levels. The examples illustrate how consumers and patients can affect positive changes to medical policy, access to treatment and drugs, drug approval processes, accreditation, quality and safety, decision making, and health systems' reviews. Consumer engagement can be impactful in, for example, supporting survey accreditation (Braithwaite et al. 2018; Greenfield et al. 2016), and we know from systematic reviews on the topic that patient engagement can help with getting a wide range of research projects successfully off the ground (Domecq et al. 2014; Sarrami-Foroushani et al. 2014b). In respect of research, there is ample evidence that including consumers in studies early on can enhance patient enrolment and decrease patient attrition (Domecq et al. 2014; Oliver et al. 2004).

In turn, according to The Picker Institute in the UK and Planetree in the USA, consumer engagement can ensure a more person-centred approach to care (Frampton et al. 2008). Person-centred care initiatives have been shown to indicate the intentions of others, such as healthcare professionals or policy developers to share knowledge and understanding with members of the public and healthcare consumers to effect developments in healthcare systems (Domecq et al. 2014).

As to the future, to ensure consumer engagement is widely embraced and increasingly embedded in healthcare services and systems in Australia, we now need to actively work towards a more systematic approach to patient involvement, in terms of: (1) health and medical policy initiatives, (2) drug developments, (3) technology adoption, (4) service delivery, (5) medical and health services research design, and (6) outcome translation. This needs not only to take account of the latest government healthcare changes and reforms and build on the national and international initiatives, some of which we have documented in this chapter, but also to recognize in the future, further potential for involving the general public as they access healthcare services.

Beginning to map the spectrum of consumer engagement approaches in the real world of Australian care provision would be a good starting point: from setting the agenda for consumer engagement, to conducting research where consumers are actively involved, to implementing research findings that inform practice with consumers as key "purveyors of change" (Rapport et al. 2017). This would also have significant benefits for reworking of systems to match patient need and would ensure that increased attention is given to building resilience into our health care systems (Braithwaite e al. 2017; Hollnagel et al. 2013; 2019; Wears et al. 2015), including the delivery of high-quality, safe, and effective care.

Is There a Limit to Patient Engagement?

Despite the progress made and the successes we have discussed, we must be realistic in appreciating the limits to the place of patients and consumers in healthcare decision making, policy, planning, and care provision. We know from international healthcare experience that patient and consumer engagement and involvement brings with it social, systems, cultural, and financial benefits. Improvements emanating from consumer and patient involvement can be felt at the healthcare system level, the organizational level, and the individual patient level (Domecq et al. 2014; Ham and Murray 2018; Sarrami-Foroushani et al. 2014a).

However, we strike a word of warning against tokenistic consumer and patient engagement. Just because there are policies for engagement—and involvement of patients and consumers in PHNs, HSOs, and peak bodies—does not mean there is thoroughgoing involvement, where consumer and patient expertise is at the heart of the system, and they are heard and valued, and can share in decision making (Ocloo and Matthews 2016). When taken seriously, through national strategic planning, the consumer voice can be a powerful mechanism for change, raising standards of care, and ensuring research questions are addressed holistically. Informed patients can drive appropriate standards of care in line with patient expectations. We also know that the more involved patient can inform the kind of healthcare service the general public wants, one that supports not only their physical health but also their mental health and emotional well-being, so that people are more likely to function as valuable members of society.

The cases in this chapter indicate that while there is no foreseeable ceiling to patient engagement, there is nevertheless some way to go before Australia includes the consumer voice in a systematic, universally organized fashion. If we can achieve this, patients and consumers can become involved in range of national platforms, including health boards, advisory panels, steering groups, statutory health bodies, policy consortia and research grant awarding committees. At the moment, this level of involvement is piecemeal, but when it becomes more inculcated and habituated, we could expect to see normalization of consumer participation, leading to more fully informed and engaged Australian public.

For this agenda to be realized, Australia, despite its progress, might do well to take a leaf out of other countries' books about the potential for consumers to design their own public fora, such as the Patient Public Involvement (PPI) Group in the UK (The King's Fund 2018). This will ensure further gains such that consumers and patients are more than passive advisers but are active partners in building relationships with healthcare professionals. Kitson et al. (2012) have indicated that full involvement matters: consumers want to feel active within the context where care is being delivered, working at the coalface. The Picker Institute and Planetree's 2008 principles of patient-centred care are as relevant now as when they were written, underpinned by seven key dimensions, including "respect for patients' values and expressed needs", and "active involvement of family and friends". Together these dimensions and others like them have the potential to engender more in-depth and extensive patient-centred care driven by patient engagement. This will not only reduce levels of patient vulnerability but also lead to greater patient empowerment and perhaps whole-family buy-in (Frampton et al. 2008).

So, there is increasing evidence to support the value of patient and consumer involvement in healthcare services, policy, and research (Bombard et al. 2018). We have provided some instructive, illustrative examples of this in the Australian context. However, the potential for making this involvement even more successful is influenced by a number of factors, including the practices of clinicians on the front lines of care; the differing backgrounds, attitudes, beliefs and knowledge of patients, clinicians, and managers; the policies, practices, and organizational cultures of HSOs; the support for progress in policy and government circles; and, more broadly, funding support and altering societal norms regarding involvement (Davis et al. 2007; Sarrami-Foroushani et al. 2014a; World Health Organization 2016).

Barriers identified in the Australian context include those related to resourcing (lack of infrastructure, skills, or confidence), and stigma, language, and cultural differences (Sarrami-Foroushani et al. 2014a). For example, healthcare professionals may value patient input into HSOs and care delivery in a consultative capacity, but believe that they should not ultimately make decisions (Gagliardi et al. 2008). With increasing adoption of models of patient and consumer involvement in Australia, and at various levels of the caring system, traditional beliefs such as these may be challenged, though. Nathan and her colleagues (2006), for example, showed that 12 months following the appointment of consumer representatives to a range of committees involved in governance and service delivery, the attitudes of other committee members, particularly clinicians, had become more positive towards community participation.

Therefore, as patient and consumer involvement becomes increasingly normalized and legitimized—such as in policies, by leadership, and through appointment of specific roles (Liang et al. 2018)—and as the evidence-base supporting its value increases, some of these cultural and attitudinal barriers are likely to diminish (Boivin et al. 2010). An active approach to reducing barriers to involvement will remain an important matter: for example, by continuously educating healthcare professionals and other stakeholders about the value of patient involvement and training them to be involved in such partnerships (Liang et al. 2018). Another issue that may need to be addressed into the future, and among both consumers and other stakeholders, is the expectation that consumer input is, and should be, truly "representative". That is, in their recent Australian study, Scholz et al. (2018) found a common assumption that consumers are responsible for representing their whole community; this assumption can have potentially negative implications, as they argue it "perpetuates a power imbalance and further marginalises consumers" (p. 2).

For patient and consumer representatives, too, appropriate training and support, as well as reimbursement of their time and payment for their expertise, may assist in overcoming some of the financial and organizational barriers to their contribution (Boivin et al. 2010). Other enablers of patient and consumer involvement include institutional and leadership commitment to the process and from the outset of any initiative; respectful communication and practices related to health literacy; a mix of formal and informal methods of interaction; provision of tools and explicit policies to support and empower patients; and utilization of innovative approaches to include patients and consumers, including meeting them in environments outside where services are delivered (Bombard et al. 2018; Liang et al. 2018; Ocloo and Matthews 2016). The need for an active approach to patient and consumer involvement in Australia is explicit in the model we have developed, which outlines eight stages of implementation (Fig. 7.2).

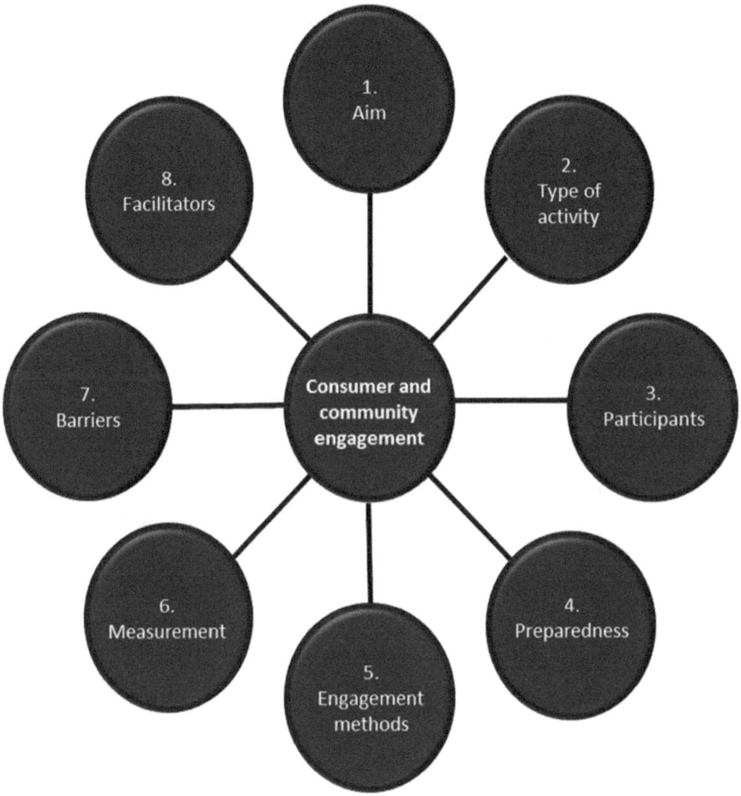

Fig. 7.2 An eight-stage model of implementing patient and consumer involvement. (Source: Adapted from Sarrami-Foroushani et al. 2014a)

The Future: Implementing Further Patient and Consumer Involvement in Australia

In essence, patient and consumer involvement in healthcare at macro-, meso-, and micro-levels demonstrably confers many benefits, including potential reductions in hospital admissions, increased accountability and quality in HSOs, improved efficiency and the justified delivery of outcomes to patients that they want, and value (Bombard et al. 2018). In the Australian context, specifically, there is growing evidence for the valuable contributions patients and consumers can make to care delivery, the design of services and healthcare policies. Furthermore, there is increasing acknowledgement of the potential of these roles among other stakeholders (Nathan et al. 2011).

For over 30 years, CHF has been representing the interests of all Australian health consumers and during this time, the role of the health consumer has shifted considerably (Consumers Health Forum of Australia 2016). Now extending beyond simply engaging patients in their own care, the role of the consumer is moving towards a partnership approach across the levels of the health system (Parsons et al. 2010). Amongst many examples of this in the Australian context are the Partnering with Consumers Standard from the NSQHS Standards (Australian Commission on Quality and Safety in Health Care 2017b) and the Partnering with Patients programme, established by the New South Wales Clinical Excellence Commission and adopted by the state's local health districts (Clinical Excellence Commission 2017). Both are designed to support the inclusion of patients, family, and carers as part of the care team to promote safety and quality.

Finally, even though we have been optimistic in our reporting here, a chasm remains in some domains, settings and parts of the health sector between rhetoric and practice. The challenge moving forward is not only to maintain and improve consumer participation across the levels of the system but also to shift the regard for consumers as "users and choosers" to the "makers and shapers" of policy, practice, and system development (Janamian et al. 2016). It is not enough to simply advance the challenges, but the task is to continue the progress and take further genuine steps to involve patients at all levels in the system. Politicians, funders, policymakers, and practitioners alike have an obligation to not only formally acknowledge the merit of patient involvement in health system change and improvement but also to invest in building the capacity of the system to work to its best effect by drawing on their insights, as well as investing in patient leadership skills.

Conclusion

We can draw some lessons and observations from Australia's experience of partnering with patients and consumers in terms of recommendations for change and improvement for other countries. Our concluding comments bring these lessons together under a policy–system–service schema.

Perhaps surprisingly, Australia lacks an explicit, high-level policy commitment that signals the role consumers can play in shaping health policy and services in the same way that the UK's National Health Service (NHS) Five-Year Forward View committed to "a new relationship with patients" (National Health Service England 2014). However, it has nevertheless become increasingly common practice for consumer advocates to participate in significant policy debates and reform changes. This is evident in patient and consumer involvement in decisions in major national schemes such as the PBS and National Medicines Policy and the Primary Health Care Advisory Group which resulted in an Australian pilot of a patient-centred healthcare home model of care. The role played by the CHF over more than three decades, as a national peak Australian healthcare consumer organization with support through the Health Peak and Advisory Bodies Programme and its forerunners, is also an indicator of how important the consumer voice is to national policy discourse.

At a systemic level, we have adduced evidence of multiple promising initiatives that seem to signal recognition of the value being added by patient and consumer involvement in healthcare. National service standards command patient involvement in HSO governance and safety and quality improvements and for HSOs to be accredited against these. Our peak research body, the National Health and Medical Research Council (NHMRC), in a joint statement with the CHF advocates for consumer involvement in research (National Health and Medical Research Council and Consumers Health Forum 2016). Similarly, official guidance for PHNs requires them to have consumer involvement in their formal governance arrangements, necessitating, as a minimum, a Community Advisory Committee sitting alongside Clinical Councils to their PHN Boards. PHNs and their hospital counterparts, Local Health Districts and Networks, are well placed to be incubators of accelerated consumer and community engagement practice into the future.

In services, at the point-of-care delivery, there is a myriad of professional standards and codes of conduct that also require clinicians to regard patients as partners in care. Such standards and codes are enabled by emergent initiatives such as Choosing Wisely Australia, which aim to encourage conversations between providers and consumers about improving care quality by eliminating unnecessary, sometimes harmful, procedures (NPS MedicineWise 2016). The future of further Australian consumer and patient involvement is not guaranteed, and its shape and form are not as clear as they could be, but it is hard to see how progress will be arrested and even harder to see how stakeholders across the system will fail to capitalize on the platform of activities that have been contributed. We remain challenged by the amount of work ahead of us, but greatly encouraged by the successes we have had to date.

References

Australian Commission on Quality and Safety in Health Care. 2017a. *Factsheet 2: Partnering with consumers*. Sydney: ACSQHC.

———. 2017b. *National safety and quality health service standards*. 2nd ed. Sydney: ACSQHC.

Australian Council on Healthcare Standards. 2018. *What is accreditation?* https://www.achs.org.au/about-us/what-we-do/what-is-accreditation/. Accessed 30 Aug.

Australian Government. 2014. *Australian national preventive health agency*. https://www.directory.gov.au/portfolios/health/australian-national-preventive-health-agency. Accessed 13 Aug.

Australian Institute of Health and Welfare. 2017. Health expenditure Australia 2015–2016. In *In Health and welfare expenditure series*. Canberra: AIHW.

———. 2018. *Australia's health 2018*. Canberra: AIHW.

Bate, Paul, and Glenn Robert. 2006. Experience-based design: From redesigning the system around the patient to co-designing services with the patient. *BMJ Quality & Safety* 15 (5): 307–310.

Baume, Peter. 1991. *A question of balance: Report on the future of drug evaluations in Australia*. Canberra: Australian Government Publishing Service.

Boivin, Antoine, Kay Currie, Béatrice Fervers, Javier Gracia, Marian James, Catherine Marshall, Carol Sakala, Sylvia Sanger, Judi Strid, Victoria Thomas, Trudy van der Weijden, Richard Grol, and Jako Burgers. 2010. Patient and public involvement in clinical guidelines: International experiences and future perspectives. *Quality and Safety in Health Care* 19 (5): e22–e22. https://doi.org/10.1136/qshc.2009.034835.

Bombard, Yvonne, G. Ross Baker, Elaina Orlando, Carol Fancott, Pooja Bhatia, Selina Casalino, Kanecy Onate, Jean-Louis Denis, and Marie-Pascale Pomey. 2018. Engaging patients to improve quality of care: A systematic review. *Implementation Science* 13 (1): 98. https://doi.org/10.1186/s13012-018-0784-z.

Boyd, Hilary, Stephen McKernon, Bernie Mullin, and Andrew Old. 2012. Improving healthcare through the use of co-design. *The New Zealand Medical Journal* 125 (1357): 76–87.

Braithwaite, Jeffrey, Robert L. Wears, and Erik Hollnagel, eds. 2017. *Resilient health care: Reconciling work-as-imagined and work-as-done*. Vol. III. Boca Raton, FL: Taylor & Francis.

Braithwaite, Jeffrey, Kate Churruca, Janet C. Long, Louise A. Ellis, and Jessica Herkes. 2018. When complexity science meets implementation science: A theoretical and empirical analysis of systems change. *BMC Medicine* 16 (1): 63. https://doi.org/10.1186/s12916-018-1057-z.

Brisbane North PHN. 2018a. *About us*. https://www.brisbanenorthphn.org.au/page/about/.

———. 2018b. *Recovery: Mental health, suicide prevention, alcohol and other drugs news from your PHN*. http://www.brisbanenorthphn.org.au/content/Document/MHAOD_Recovery_newsletter_June%202018_FINAL_lowres.pdf.

Chamberlain, Paul, and Rebecca Partridge. 2017. Co-designing co-design: Shifting the culture of practice in healthcare. *The Design Journal* 20 (sup1): S2010–S2021.

Clinical Excellence Commission. 2017. *Person-centred care*. http://www.cec.health.nsw.gov.au/quality-improvement/people-and-culture/person-centred-care. Accessed 6 Aug.

Consumers Health Forum of Australia. 2015. *The real people real data toolkit*. https://chf.org.au/sites/default/files/docs/rprdtoolkit.pdf. Accessed 8 Aug.

———. 2016. *About CHF*. https://chf.org.au/about-chf. Accessed 8 Aug.

———. 2017. *Collaborative Pairs Australia*. https://chf.org.au/collaborative-pairs. Accessed 6 Aug.

Davis, Rachel E., Rosamond Jacklin, Nick Sevdalis, and Charles A. Vincent. 2007. Patient involvement in patient safety: What factors influence patient participation and engagement? *Health Expectations* 10 (3): 259–267. https://doi.org/10.1111/j.1369-7625.2007.00450.x.

Dawda, P., and A. Knight. 2017. *Experience based co-design—A toolkit for Australia*. Deakin West, ACT: Prestantia Health, Consumers Health Forum of Australia and Australian Healthcare and Hospitals Association.

Department of Health. 2015a. *Australia primary health networks*. Australian Government. http://www.health.gov.au/internet/main/publishing.nsf/Content/phn-maps-aust. Accessed 27 Aug.

———. 2015b. *Biosimilar awareness initiative*. Australian Government. http://www.health.gov.au/internet/main/publishing.nsf/Content/biosimilar-awareness-initiative. Accessed 22 Aug.

Department of Health and Ageing. 2000. *National medicines policy*. Canberra, ACT: Australian Government.

Domecq, Juan Pablo, Gabriela Prutsky, Tarig Elraiyah, Zhen Wang, Mohammed Nabhan, Nathan Shippee, Juan Pablo Brito, Kasey Boehmer, Rim Hasan, Belal Firwana, Patricia Erwin, David Eton, Jeff Sloan, Victor Montori, Noor Asi, Abd Moain Abu Dabrh, and Mohammad Hassan Murad. 2014. Patient engagement in research: A systematic review. *BMC Health Services Research* 14 (1): 89. https://doi.org/10.1186/1472-6963-14-89.

Frampton, Susan, Sara Guastello, Carrie Brady, Maria Hale, Sheryl M. Horowitz, Susan Bennett Smith, and Susan Stone. 2008. *Patient-centered care improvement guide*. Derby, CT: Planetree, Inc. and Picker Institute.

Freeman, Toby, Frances E. Baum, Gwyneth M. Jolley, Angela Lawless, Tahnia Edwards, Sara Javanparast, and Anna Ziersch. 2014. Service providers' views of community participation at six Australian primary healthcare services: Scope for empowerment and challenges to implementation. *The International Journal of Health Planning and Management* 31 (1): E1–E21. https://doi.org/10.1002/hpm.2253.

Gagliardi, Anna R., Louise Lemieux-Charles, Adalsteinn D. Brown, Terrence Sullivan, and Vivek Goel. 2008. Barriers to patient involvement in health service planning and evaluation: An exploratory study. *Patient Education and Counseling* 70 (2): 234–241. https://doi.org/10.1016/j.pec.2007.09.009.

Greenfield, David, Jeffrey Braithwaite, and Marjorie Pawsey. 2008. Health care accreditation surveyor styles typology. *International Journal of Health Care Quality Assurance* 21 (5): 435–443. https://doi.org/10.1108/09526860810890422.

Greenfield, David, Marjorie Pawsey, Justine Naylor, and Jeffrey Braithwaite. 2009. Are accreditation surveys reliable? *International Journal of Health Care Quality Assurance* 22 (2): 105–116. https://doi.org/10.1108/09526860910944601.

Greenfield, David, Anne Hogden, Reece Hinchcliff, Virginia Mumford, Marjorie Pawsey, Deborah Debono, Johanna I. Westbrook, and Jeffrey Braithwaite. 2016. The impact of national accreditation reform on survey reliability: A 2-year investigation of survey coordinators' perspectives. *Journal of Evaluation in Clinical Practice* 22 (5): 662–667. https://doi.org/10.1111/jep.12512.

Ham, C, and R Murray. 2018. *The NHS ten year plan: How should the extra funding be spent?*. The King's Fund. https://www.kingsfund.org.uk/publications/nhs-10-year-plan.

Hollnagel, Erik, Jeffrey Braithwaite, and Robert L. Wears, eds. 2013. *Resilient health care*. Farnham, Surrey: Ashgate Publishing, Ltd.

———, eds. 2019. *Delivering resilient health care*. London: Routledge.

International Association for Public Participation Australasia. 2016. IAP2's public participation spectrum. https://www.iap2.org.au/Tenant/C0000004/00000001/files/IAP2_Public_Participation_Spectrum.pdf. Accessed 8 Aug.

Janamian, Tina, Lisa Crossland, and Leanne Wells. 2016. On the road to value co-creation in health care: The role of consumers in defining the destination, planning the journey and sharing the drive. *The Medical Journal of Australia* 204 (7): 12.

Kitson, Alison, Amy Marshall, Katherine Bassett, and Kathryn Zeitz. 2012. What are the core elements of patient-centred care? A narrative review and synthesis of the literature from health policy, medicine and nursing. *Journal of Advanced Nursing* 69 (1): 4–15. https://doi.org/10.1111/j.1365-2648.2012.06064.x.

Liang, Laurel, Albina Cako, Robin Urquhart, Sharon E. Straus, Walter P. Wodchis, G. Ross Baker, and Anna R. Gagliardi. 2018. Patient engagement in hospital health service planning and improvement: a scoping review. *BMJ Open* 8 (1): e018263. https://doi.org/10.1136/bmjopen-2017-018263.

Nathan, Sally, Elizabeth Harris, Ben Harris-Roxas, and Lynn Kemp. 2006. Health service staff attitudes to community representatives on committees. *Journal of Health Organization and Management* 20 (6): 551–559. https://doi.org/10.1108/14777260610702299.

Nathan, Sally, Lynda Johnston, and Jeffrey Braithwaite. 2011. The role of community representatives on health service committees: Staff expectations vs. reality. *Health Expectations* 14 (3): 272–284.

Nathan, Sally, Jeffrey Braithwaite, and Niamh Stephenson. 2013. Facilitating the action of community representatives in a health service: The role of a community participation coordinator. *BMC Health Services Research* 13 (1): 154. https://doi.org/10.1186/1472-6963-13-154.

Nathan, Sally, Niamh Stephenson, and Jeffrey Braithwaite. 2014. Sidestepping questions of legitimacy: How community representatives manoeuvre to effect change in a health service. *Health* 18 (1): 23–40. https://doi.org/10.1177/1363459312473617.

National Health Service England. 2014. Five year forward view. https://www.england.nhs.uk/wp-content/uploads/2014/10/5yfv-web.pdf.

National Health and Medical Research Council, and Consumers Health Forum. 2016. *Statement on consumer and community involvement in health and medical research*. https://www.nhmrc.gov.au/guidelines-publications/s01.

New South Wales Agency for Clinical Innovation (ACI). 2015. *Patient experience and consumer engagement: A framework for action*. Chatswood, NSW: ACI.

NPS MedicineWise. 2016. *Choosing wisely Australia*. http://www.choosingwisely.org.au/about-choosing-wisely-australia.

Ocloo, Josephine, and Rachel Matthews. 2016. From tokenism to empowerment: Progressing patient and public involvement in healthcare improvement. *BMJ Quality & Safety* 25 (8): 626–632. https://doi.org/10.1136/bmjqs-2015-004839.

Oliver, Sandy, L. Clarke-Jones, R. Rees, R. Milne, P. Buchanan, J. Gabbay, G. Gyte, A. Oakley, and K. Stein. 2004. *Involving consumers in research and development agenda setting for the NHS: Developing an evidence-based approach*. Tonbridge Wells: Gray Publishing.

Parsons, Suzanne, Anna Winterbottom, Peter Cross, and Don Redding. 2010. *The quality of patient engagement and involvement in primary care*. London: The King's Fund.

Pomey, Marie-Pascale, and Paule Lebel. 2016. Patient engagement: The Quebec path*. *HealthcarePapers* 16 (2): 80–85.

Rapport, Frances, Jeffrey Braithwaite, Rebecca Mitchell, Johanna Westbrook, and Kate Churruca. 2017. Transitional care in a federated landscape. In *Researching quality in care transitions: international perspectives*, 179–200. Cham: Palgrave Macmillan.

Robert, Glenn, Jocelyn Cornwell, Louise Locock, Arnie Purushotham, Gordon Sturmey, and Melanie Gager. 2015. Patients and staff as codesigners of healthcare services. *BMJ* 350: g7714. https://doi.org/10.1136/bmj.g7714.

Sarrami-Foroushani, Pooria, Joanne Travaglia, Deborah Debono, and Jeffrey Braithwaite. 2014a. Implementing strategies in consumer and community engagement in health care: Results of a large-scale, scoping meta-review. *BMC Health Services Research* 14 (1): 402.

———. 2014b. Key concepts in consumer and community engagement: A scoping meta-review. *BMC Health Services Research* 14 (1): 250.

Schneider, Eric C., Dana O. Sarnak, David Squires, Arnav Shah, and Michelle M. Doy. 2017. *Mirror, mirror 2017: International comparison reflects flaws and opportunities for better US health care*. New York, NY: The Commonwealth Fund.

Scholz, Brett, Julia Bocking, Michelle Banfield, Chris Platania-Phung, and Brenda Happell. 2018. "Coming from a different place": Partnerships between consumers and health services for system change. *Journal of Clinical Nursing* 27 (19–20): 3622–3629. https://doi.org/10.1111/jocn.14520.

Smith, Sian K., Ann Dixon, Lyndal Trevena, Don Nutbeam, and Kirsten J. McCaffery. 2009. Exploring patient involvement in healthcare decision making across different education and functional health literacy groups. *Social Science & Medicine* 69 (12): 1805–1812. https://doi.org/10.1016/j.socscimed.2009.09.056.

Stankevicius, Adam. 2014. Consumers and copayments: Implications for health and Medicare. *The Medical Journal of Australia* 200 (9): 517–518. https://doi.org/10.5694/mja14.00421.

The King's Fund. 2018. *Our work on the role of patients and the public in health and care and service design*. The King's Fund. https://www.kingsfund.org.uk/topics/patient-involvement.

Wears, Robert L., Erik Hollnagel, and Jeffrey Braithwaite, eds. 2015. *Resilient health care: The resilience of everyday clinical work*. Vol. II. Farnham, Surrey: Ashgate Publishing, Ltd.

Wellcome Trust. 2011. *Community engagement–under the microscope*. London: Wellcome Trust.

Wells, Leanne. 2016. Patient first—Innovation in consumer-centred care. *Health Voices: Journal of the Consumers Health Forum of Australia* 17: 1–2.

———. 2018. The paradox of consumer-centred care. In *Australian healthcare and hospitals association: The health advocate*, April 13. https://ahha.asn.au/system/files/docs/publications/apr2018_tha_web_final.pdf.

Wiley, Janice, Mary Westbrook, Janet Long, Jerry R. Greenfield, Richard O. Day, and Jeffrey Braithwaite. 2014. Diabetes education: The experiences of young adults with type 1 diabetes. *Diabetes Therapy* 5 (1): 299–321. https://doi.org/10.1007/s13300-014-0056-0.

Wiseman, V., G. Mooney, G. Berry, and K.C. Tang. 2003. Involving the general public in priority setting: Experiences from Australia. *Social Science & Medicine* 56 (5): 1001–1012. https://doi.org/10.1016/S0277-9536(02)00091-6.

World Health Organization. 2016. *Patient engagement: Technical series on safer primary care*. Geneva: World Health Organization.

8

The Engagement Conundrum of French Users

Véronique Ghadi, Luigi Flora, Pascal Jarno, and Hélyette Lelievre

Introduction

In France, the state is primarily responsible for steering and regulating the health system. It acts as the guarantor of public interest and protector of population health at central and regional levels through decentralized Regional Health Agencies called *Agences régionales de santé* (ARS). Each region's ARS is a unique health authority (state + social insurance), inde-

V. Ghadi (✉)
Haue Autorité de Santé, Paris, France
e-mail: v.ghadi@has-sante.fr

L. Flora
University of Côte d'Azur, Nice, France
e-mail: ginologic@free.fr

P. Jarno • H. Lelievre
CHU de Rennes, Rennes, France
e-mail: Pascal.JARNO@chu-rennes.fr

M.-P. Pomey et al. (eds.), *Patient Engagement*, Organizational Behaviour in Healthcare,
https://doi.org/10.1007/978-3-030-14101-1_8

pendent of local elected representatives (Regional Council [*Conseil Régional*]). At the territorial level, responsibilities are shared with care providers, while an insurance system—which includes a compulsory health insurance scheme (for employers and employees)—finances the health system. Social insurance finances two-thirds of health expenditure, the state and local authorities finance about one-fifth, while private funding covers 15 per cent (DREES 2017). Health expenditure in France amounted to 271 billion euros in 2017 (DREES 2017) or 11.8 per cent of country's GDP.

The French population consists of 67 million inhabitants spread across a 550,000 km^2 territory, of which three-quarters live in urban areas. They are served by 226,000 physicians, 661,000 nurses, 88,000 massage-physiotherapists, 23,000 midwives distributed across the territory, within practices or hospitals, working as employees or under fee-for-service arrangements (DREES 2017). With one of the top high-performing health systems in the world in terms of access to care (almost 100 per cent of its population is covered), France's overall health indicators are positive and, relative to OECD Countries, it boasts the lowest user fee burden and one of the highest life expectancy rates (79.2 for men and 85.5 for women) (OECD 2017). That said, male mortality remains relatively high (HCSP 2017). Death rates in general are decreasing, regardless of the cause of death, and this is particularly true for cancers, despite increased incidence due to improved diagnoses and the impact of screening. While life expectancy in France is particularly high, premature mortality (linked to risk behaviour such as alcohol consumption, smoking, suicide, road accidents, etc.) is higher relative to other OECD countries (HCSP 2017). This could very well indicate lack of prevention. Moreover, mortality inequalities are particularly notable and persistent between men and women, among territories, and among social groups. This situation led health authorities to focus on two recent texts (the National Health Strategy in 2016 and *Ma santé* 2022 in 2018) with more emphasis on prevention and the involvement of patients and their representatives.

Like other Western countries throughout the twentieth century, France was struck by the emergence and affirmation of users seeking a rightful place within the health system, mainly through the mobilization of community organizations (Pomey and Ghadi 2009).

The French model of user involvement is characterized by a strict national regulatory framework which applies identically across the territory. In addition to a solid structure for community organizations, designated user representatives are present in institutional bodies at regional and national levels. That said, the goal of changing care practices and the organization of care in daily life is yet to be achieved, given that the impact of community involvement was mainly felt at governance levels of the health system and its institutions. The remaining challenge is to integrate the experiential knowledge that patients draw from care experiences and organizational procedures and to promote shared decision-making for treatments and diagnostic procedures, in other words all elements that affect people's daily lives. To take on this challenge, the model of democracy in healthcare has been evolving, not only to mobilize new actors in the creation of modalities, which can be adapted to as many people as possible, but also to move towards Health Democracy as reminded by the Minister of Health in September 2018 (*Ministère des Solidarités et de la Santé* [Ministry of Solidarity and Health] 2018).

After a brief overview of user mobilization history in France, including the description of the country's current health system, the following section will present positive lessons and limits drawn from health organizations, the national agency in charge of care quality and safety (*la Haute Autorité de Santé* [French National Authority for Health]) and the relationship between health professionals and patients as part of therapeutic education development. The chapter will end with concrete user–professional co-construction examples which illustrate changes that are in progress.

Democratic Impetus: Mobilizing Community Organizations to Defend Rights

User mobilization in healthcare is nothing new. As in other countries, user mobilization manifests itself via support between patients in parallel with professional and organizational interventions and a structured supply of care and support by directly concerned users or their relatives. User mobilization, partly invisible to professionals, took on a new dimension with user engagement in HIV during the mid-1980s.

From the creation of Alcoholics Anonymous in the early twentieth century (1934), to the extension of the first recovery movement in mental health based on mutual assistance interactions, information sharing and training between patients (1937), peer training eventually came about (Jouet et al. 2010) with the implementation of self-, co- and eco-training processes (Pineau 1989).

In France, the influence of community organizations is deep-rooted and decisive in social and medico-social sectors which support people in precarious situations and the protection of children. The medico-social sector concerns services and institutions which support elderly people in situations of dependency and people with disabilities. In the health sector, particularly, mobilization around AIDS in the 1980s marked a crucial step in recognizing the place of community organizations in public and scientific discourse.

Indeed, in the medico-social sector, a structure for the supply of care and support surfaced between the two world wars. At that time, the state entrusted parent or disability groups with the task of managing structures for people with disabilities. Community organizations, such as the *Association Française des Familles* (AFF, [French Association for Families]) or the *Union Nationale des Associations de parents et amis de personnes déficientes intellectuelles* (UNAPEI, [National Association of Groups representing Parents and Friends of People with Intellectual Disabilities]), were created in a hybrid form, associating directly concerned people with professional organizations. This cohabitation led community organizations to regularly question their positioning, more specifically the balance between their "users" and "professionals" components. This form of co-management accelerated with the establishment of the welfare state model after 1945 and led to a permanent dialogue which culminated in a 1975 law on the adaptation of society to people living with handicaps.

On the other hand, in the health sector, it was not until the 1990s—and the tainted blood scandal—that HIV/AIDS community organizations mobilized politically to demand recognition of individual and collective rights of healthcare users. The HIV/AIDS pandemic added a fourth axis to the professional relational triangle of user health: (1) mutual assistance, (2) information sharing, (3) training and (4) involvement of concerned people in decision-making. This fourth axis developed, thanks to patient mobilization conducted through effective advocacy and taking full advantage of what is coined as the "Information Society" (Flora 2012, p. 81).

Furthermore, this resulted in citizen mobilization in the form of *États généraux de la Santé* (States-General, or General Assemblies for Health) which were forums where citizens and professionals met to discuss specific pathologies. The first meetings concerned HIV/AIDS in 1990, rare diseases in 1995 and cancer in 1998.

As of 1995, this process turned into a structure built around the creation of an association which united all user community groups, also known as the *Collectif inter-associatif sur la santé* (*CISS*, [Inter-Associative Health Collective]). Initially created out of 15 community groups in 1996, the CISS gradually opened its doors to more members and currently comprises more than 40 community organizations (link website http://www.france-assos-sante.org/). The specificity of the CISS is its capacity to bring together organizations representing patients, people with disabilities, consumers and families. The collective gradually became an interlocutor with public authorities to partake in early reflections on user representation in health organizations. That same year, the role of the CISS was recognized in a law meant to modernize the health system.

Meanwhile, France was dealing with health scandals such as the tainted blood scandal (Fillion 2005) or the sports clinic case (Carriburu 2009) in which many people had contracted nosocomial infections. These high-profile cases led victims' associations to organize and question the organization of services and professional practices which, evidently, did not guarantee satisfactory levels of patient safety. Due to their inability to prevent incidents or accidents, confidence in public authorities and health professionals was deeply shaken and questioned.

In 1999, the General Assemblies for Health (*États généraux de la Santé*) provided an opportunity for users to highlight their expectations in terms of information, support and participation in choices of direct concern and reflects a time of know-how transmission beyond mere pathological aspects and the search for common ground. As a result, the prime minister at the time committed to drafting a law on patient rights. In this context, the CISS became a key player and participated in drafting the law, which was published in March 4, 2002. This law firstly deals with the recognition of individual rights, such as rights to information, respecting dignity and refusing care. It also endorses the health democracy model by introducing the obligation to include user representatives at governance levels of the health system and health institutions. It follows another law, published on January 2, 2002, which laid the foundation for creating individual and collective participation spaces in medico-social institutions. On the one hand, this law enables individualized projects which compel professionals to start working from a patient's life projects and expectations. On the other hand, the Social Life Council (*Conseil de la vie sociale*) was created to structure and integrate user participation in daily life and collective decisions within health organizations. The Social Life Council is a place for debate and exchange among representatives elected by residents, relatives and professionals of the health organization or service. This first impetus given by the law of January 2002 was reinforced by the February 11, 2005 law regarding equal opportunities and citizenship for people with disabilities.

Thus, in France, the law of March 4, 2002 on patient rights and health system quality has clearly introduced a process redefining the place of patients relative to their own care. It also strengthens health democracy by mobilizing citizens as users with the right to speak, or as of user group representatives with an approved presence in various strata of governance within health organizations and, more broadly, the health system. In health organizations, this materializes though user representatives now being part of executive boards (board of directors, etc.); the creation of a commission for user relations and care quality with an advisory role; the integration of user representatives into other specialized committees such as Nosocomial Infection Control Committees and Pain Control Committees.

In 2014, at the request of the health minister, a user representation assessment was conducted, and proposals were pushed to further user participation (Compagnon et Ghadi 2014). However, findings concomitantly demonstrated how user representatives lacked access to healthcare professionals and patients, as well as no true participation in decision-making, which ultimately highlighted the non-transformation of care practices and the absence of care being organized through user involvement. Moreover, some proposals were reintroduced in the January 26,

2016 Health System Modernisation Act, such as expanding the missions of user representatives in various aspects of care quality and patient safety (i.e. the need to strengthen the users' place in the certification process of health organizations; participation in the reporting or analysis of serious undesirable events) and the incentive for organizations to produce user projects aimed at reinforcing collaboration with users and groups around priority topics. First and foremost, these topics must be considered as priorities by users, which include mistreatment prevention, information, organization of care for people with disabilities. The modernization act also changed the name of the community organization collective (CISS) by creating a national association of "approved community organizations" in health, named *France Asso Santé* (FAS). In continuity with the CISS, *France Asso Santé* now counts 76 national community organizations.

Therefore, France currently has a model which allows the imposition of users at almost all levels of the healthcare system. At the national level, users participate in the National Conference of Health and Autonomy (*Conférence nationale de santé et de l'autonomie*) as well as in the French National Authority for Health (*Haute Autorité de Santé* [HAS]). At the regional level, they participate at the supervisory board of regional health agencies and the regional health conference. And finally, they participate at the institutional level as well (see above).

However, the legal recognition of user representation—and more recently, the creation of a national association of approved health groups (FAS) as a main interlocutor financed by public authorities—led user participation to be often limited to technocratic activities, distant from actual care provision (Martinent 2017). Also, the question remains as to whether this recognition contributed, on the one hand, to transforming practices and organizations while, on the other hand, considering the point of view and experiences of users.

Building Real User Participation Beyond the Notion of Rights

In French-style health democracy, the focus has mainly been on defending "rights" and "representation" of community groups within governance but much less on patient "participation" or "engagement" at the individual level and in direct patient care. This observation can be illustrated not only by the way their involvement in the *Haute Autorité de Santé* (HAS)—the health agency responsible for care quality and safety—has been set up but also through the way projects related to therapeutic education in healthcare organizations were established.

From Isolated Initiatives to a Structured Approach of User Integration in HAS Duties

The HAS holds two main missions. The first one focuses on improving care quality, which includes preparing recommendations for good practice, producing quality indicators and accreditation. The second one regards the evaluation of health technologies, including drugs.

The HAS was involved very early in integrating user representatives (from regional health agency-approved community organizations) into most of its committees, with the exception of regulated committees, at least not until legal texts were modified in 2015. For example, users were integrated into commissions that assess drugs and health devices. From the outset, the HAS granted them expert status, with their own prerogatives and obligations, and appointed them individually for their expertise and affiliation to approved community organizations. They were compensated in the same way as other experts and were subject to declaring conflicts of interest and honouring the confidentiality of information shared during committees or working groups.

That said, with regard to the definition of the HAS (2012) strategy and orientations, or the development of its duties, it is important to nuance the participation levels of users and their representatives:

- User integration into HAS working groups and processes has been uneven across directorates. For example, the Directorate for the Improvement of the Quality of Care has been more active in this regard than the one in charge of assessing health products and technologies. Beyond cultural differences, this integration gap can be explained by time constraints to which the latter directorate is subject in order to respond to marketing requests for new drugs or devices. In addition, user participation was limited to one or two representatives taking part in working groups. Therefore, their contribution turned out to be less visible.
- The appointment, by the Health Minister, of a representative of patient groups to the highest governance instance of the HAS, known as the HAS College (*Collège de la HAS*), only occurred in 2017.

But beyond a quantitative aspect, HAS professionals were intrigued by user involvement methods and research results. With support from directors, project managers who were sensible of the issue began exchanging information about their practices, thus uncovering heterogeneity not only in way users were engaged but also in terms of methods and moments chosen for their involvement. This led to a survey of all project managers, which highlighted:

- An uneven culture within the institution, mixed feelings about the interest in user engagement pertaining to HAS duties, and confusion in terms of project manager expectations regarding users, which contributed to misunderstandings.
- Project managers did not feel the necessity of having a variety of user profiles to match user skills with project needs and expectations: for example, not waiting for political or strategic input from patients outside of patient groups or, conversely, not expecting community group leaders to share personal experience.

These observations led to a number of questions: what place should be given to user perspectives with regard to HAS duties and for what purposes? Under which circumstances should users be called upon? At what point in the implementation process should users be integrated? What methods should be set up to collect user perspectives?

To address these shortcomings, a few initiatives were put in place to bring about more dynamic participation from users and their representatives:

- A lexicon, which includes fact sheets, was written in order to propose different modes of user engagement and to better match method selection with desired objectives. In other words, the challenge is to evolve from just having one or two users sitting in a working group (overwhelmingly composed of professionals) to embracing methods such as interviews, focus groups or citizen juries.
- A questionnaire was developed and proposed to interested community organizations to participate in drug/health technology medico-economic assessments run by the directorate in charge of those specific areas. Calls for contributions were regularly shared on social networks (Twitter, LinkedIn, Facebook ...). Collected user feedback is incorporated into the assessment file (alongside the expert report) and discussed within committees responsible for issuing opinions.
- To strengthen partnership between users and health professionals, a User Space is being created within the directorate responsible for improving the quality of care.
- In addition, HAS invited applications for the creation of a Council for User Engagement in order to involve more patients and users in its work.

The work of these two directorates feeds the ongoing strategic project of the HAS, of which one pillar focuses on strengthening user engagement within HAS duties as well as equipping all involved professionals and health system users with ways to integrate users into their work at both collective and individual levels. In fact, in 2017, results from a citizen workshop were presented at the HAS Annual Symposium (*Colloque annuel de la HAS*) about the relevance of care (HAS 2015).

From Defending Rights to Improving the Organization of Care and Services in Institutions

The purpose behind having user representatives in healthcare institutions was to objectify and value their point of view in order to influence organizational modalities and clinical practices. First, this resulted in the presence of user representatives in political bodies (supervisory board, equivalent to boards of directors), technical bodies (such as the Committee Against Healthcare-Associated Infections (*Comité de Lutte contre les Infections Associées aux Soins* [CLIAS]), the Food–Nutrition Liaison Committee (*Comité de Liaison Alimentation Nutrition* [*CLAN*]) or the Pain Control Committee (*Comité de Lutte contre la Douleur* [*CLUD*]), as well as in a "user-dedicated body". Initially, this body was termed the Conciliation Commission, then the Committee on User Relations and the Quality of Care, before finally being named the Users Commission (UC) (*commission des usagers* [*CDU*]).

The UC's aim is to increase users' share of voice and to integrate them into decision-making in order to defend their rights. Gradually, the commission's role grew to ensure the consideration of user complaints as information sources, which could lead to quality improvements in care and services. The UC also takes part in various committees within health organizations (e.g. Committee Against Healthcare-Associated Infections, Food–Nutrition Liaison Committee, Pain Control Committee) or working groups.

Moreover, since 2014, as part of the certification process of health organizations, UCs are compulsorily consulted by experts during site visits, and 80 per cent of UCs participate in the development of the *Compte Qualité* (Quality Account), which is a document that summarizes the analysis and prioritization of care-related risks in health organizations as well as implemented measures. The *Compte Qualité* is sent to the HAS six months prior to on-site visits by experts. Such institutional-level participation recognizes the expertise of users and their representatives in risk assessment and implementation of measures for bettering quality and safety in care and services.

Even if the exact number remains unknown, between 6000 and 7000, user representatives from approved patient groups currently provide time, train themselves, learn to interact with managers and health professionals not only to assert their rights as users (patients, relatives or potential patients) but also to improve the quality and safety of care and services.

Unfortunately, user representatives still lack high social visibility. In fact, their existence and mission remain poorly known by the general public, patients or health professionals. While there is a legal obligation to develop "health democracy", user representatives remain in the shadows. A report even indicates mistrust between professionals and user representatives (Compagnon and Ghadi 2014). Furthermore, their legitimacy is still not established, and the processing of UC letters of protest and complaints remains dissatisfying. Although user representatives are expected to read those letters for analysis, some health organizations limit access to them, that is, late deliveries—delivery once matters are already resolved; summaries in EXCEL tables—thus truncating the user's full account of events; summaries of main causes—even though letters often contain multiple malfunctions that could eventually lead to complaints.

Additionally, direct access to user testimonials is also limited. For example, very few requests are made to meet directly with users to learn more about their experience, to allow users to meet with user representatives, or to invite users to mediation interviews when addressing user complaints.

In sum, few initiatives are currently organized to promote user representatives access to professionals—and even users—at the clinical level. Meanwhile, a certain number of user representatives believe that their connection to community organizations is sufficient to legitimize their position and knowledge at organizational levels. As a result, for years, the participation of many user representatives has been limited to commissions, away from clinical practice. Incidentally, they seem better known and recognized by directors of health institutions than by physicians or other health professionals. Moreover, user representatives are not well-known to the general population which ends up left with little recourse. Some user representatives struggle to move away from meeting rooms, while others encounter real resistance when trying to participate at clinical levels.

A recent study examined this situation and proposed several recommendations to strengthen the involvement of user representatives (PREPS RUPIN 2017):

- Train and integrate user representatives in commissions and get them to take part in all work stages (preliminary study of documents, exchanges with professionals and participation in the development, planning and implementation of measures);
- Encourage user representative retention in health organizations to increase their long-term involvement;
- Promote their role and function within organizations by highlighting their connections to community groups; and
- Encourage co-construction between health professionals and users (Compagnon and Ghadi 2014) to provide a "fresh perspective" on themes concerning the quality and safety of care (cf. 3rd part).

For the time being, measures to promote greater user participation (in accordance with the 2016 law) have been implemented, such as the users' commission, for which institutions are recommended to appoint a user as chair. The commission's capacities have also been extended to include serious adverse event monitoring or soliciting yet-to-be-approved community groups. This allows users to expand their organizational influence beyond the issue of rights and therefore influence general internal policy as well as quality and patient safety policy. The 2016 law also provides for the possibility of building user projects within organizational projects in order to include themes that are deemed as priorities by users, such as abuse prevention, access to information, or organizing care to improve access for people with disabilities. In other words, the patient engagement model is evolving from a rights-based approach to a co-construction approach to finding solutions for the betterment of the health system.

Therefore, one of the challenges ahead consists in successfully articulating the "representative approach" of health democracy—which is still in its adolescence (17 years have passed since the 2002 law!)—alongside the "participative approach" geared towards individual users such as expert patients, patient trainers and resource patients born from the therapeutic education movement.

In Focus: User Houses (Maisons des usagers) in Mental Health or Oncology

"User Houses" emerged as a particular form of user participation in the operations of health organizations. The first User House was born in 1995 from the initiative of a militant healthcare worker who sought to develop democracy in healthcare institutions. During a public meeting, she invited neighbourhood residents to voice their expectations regarding their local hospital. More than one hundred people, including neighbours, community group volunteers and professionals, met for discussion. The outcome of this meeting was a User House, as facilities offered by the hospital's director turned into a space of welcome, listening, guidance, and debate for all. In 2001, when the hospital moved and merged with two other hospitals—in what was intended to be the flagship of the AP-HP University Hospital Centre (Assistance Publique—Hopitaux de Paris)—the User House followed and relocated at the heart of the new premises.

In 2002, as part of a hospital project, the University Hospital of Nantes opened a User House after organising a citizens' jury. Again, this project relied on cohabitation between citizens and community organizations. In 2003, the Sainte Anne Hospital Centre, specialised in psychiatry, opened its own User House to promote information access to patients and their relatives. As a community-based residency practice, meetings took place every afternoon of the week. The User House was built on modalities clearly aimed at inter-community group dynamics for the benefit of patients and the respect of their rights.

In support of User Houses, the Ministry of Health published a circular on December 26, 2006 which encouraged health organizations to multiply such initiatives while laying down principles and operating methods for the creation of User Houses or User Spaces. Since then, User Houses have increased in number and exist in more than one hundred health organizations. The dynamics, however, often remain difficult as user engagement varies depending on management support, the number of community organizations, commitment by professionals, and physical location. Moreover, dynamics related to care quality policy in health organizations often require more work as well. Some User Houses have begun to leave health organizations to move closer to the people.

A national federation of User Houses was created in 2014.

Therapeutic Education: From Red Tape to Greater Stakeholder Inclusion

In 2009, the Hospital, Patients, Health and Territory Act (*Hôpital, Patients, Santé et Territoire* [*HPST*]) provided a new framework for the participation of patients living with one or several chronic diseases. Indeed, in Article 84 pertaining to Therapeutic Education for Patients (TEP), the act encourages professionals to grant a new role to patients by strengthening their autonomy.

When drafting the act, the secretary general of the CISS and former president of the AIDES community organization, Christian Saout, stressed the importance of involving user groups in the therapeutic support of patients in collaboration with physicians. However, the drafted article, which was adopted by parliamentarians, ended up not being published in the official gazette, thus preventing its implementation.

To circumvent this limitation, other initiatives emerged such as the creation of Patient Universities within faculties of medicine in Paris, Marseille and Grenoble, as well as TEP training programmes open to patients and delivered in various formats (Flora 2013a).

That said, due to the funding mechanism in place, the programmes' hospital-centred structure, a limited public health culture and the lack of trained professionals in patient participation, TEP training programmes turned out to be too hospital centric. In fact, these programmes fail to take interest in the patients' living environment (contrary to the spirit of Article 84) and do not include real involvement from patients and their representatives. Simply put: all TEP programmes are devoid of patients.

Although TEP was thought to be emancipatory for patients, it mostly mobilized healthcare professionals who mainly worked on improving patient compliance. Rather than strengthening patient autonomy, professionals searched for ways to convince patients to follow prescribed treatments instead. A huge contributing factor to this is the fact that TEP remains within the hospital realm.

Nonetheless, despite these flaws, a movement is now in motion. The number of TEP programmes has multiplied depending on different modalities, and patient integration in programmes—as expert patients, patient trainers in targeted educational initiatives or even as resource patients—continues to grow progressively, though in varying degrees across the territory. Steadily, TEP programme funding from sources other than hospitals have led to the creation of programmes closer to patients' needs and expectations which, despite a ten-year delay, finally tap into with the spirit of the HPHT Act, as illustrated in the next section. For example, the programme carried by "La Maison des Citoyens" of Rennes (collective of almost 50 associations) which obtained in 2017 a financing of the Regional Agency of Health for a programme outside the hospital, no specialty (all chronic diseases), on non-therapeutic topics.

A Second Wind Towards New Practices

Apart from the legislative context created since 2002, in addition to advances brought about by user representation and its limits, several initiatives were conducted officially or experimentally. Thus, new patient manifestations, alongside user representatives (by way of user community organizations), have been recognized since the 2000s, socializing their knowledge and playing a role beyond their own care within the different strata of the health system. These manifestations propose new forms of collaboration build upon the notion of peer emulation found in TEP.

User Representatives Depart for Institutional Bodies: Towards New Forms of Collaboration and New Methods

Learning Co-construction in the FORAP-HAS Working Group on "Well-Treatment"

In 2010, following the inclusion of a criterion on "well-treatment" (*bien-traitance*) in the Federation of Regional and Territorial Bodies for the

Improvement of Health Practices and Organisations (*Fédération des Organismes Régionaux et territoriaux pour l'Amélioration des Pratiques et organisations en santé* [FORAP]), the Federation and the HAS decided to create a special work group to address the issue. This working group first produced a guide and a set of tools to encourage the mobilization of health organizations. The guide promotes partnership with users as a fundamental characteristic of "well-treatment". In 2012, the guide and tools were distributed to professionals and health organizations via the HAS and regional bodies (HAS 2012).

Two years after the guide's implementation, the working group conducted a usage assessment which highlighted increased "well-treatment" awareness within organizations and usage mainly among paramedical professionals. However, paradoxically, users seemed to be excluded from measures taken to address the issue. These mixed results led the working group to revise its objectives and working methods (HAS 2015). Thus, the group insisted on the need to: (1) take into account the voice of patients and accompanied people to avoid situations of mistreatment and infringement upon the quality of care and patient safety, (2) working with patient groups and user representatives to implement a "well-treatment" policy and (3) make health professionals understand that it is nonsensical to work on issues of mistreatment and "well-treatment"—and more broadly, care safety and quality—without the target population (users).

Accordingly, there was a willingness to refocus the working group's efforts on greater user engagement and true co-construction for deliverables, all of which took place via three measures:

1. The national working group welcomed five health system users, involving them in all phases of reflection and deployment. Indeed, initially, the group did not include user or patient representatives. This rectification revealed that the working group's deliverables were too technical and that tools were not adapted to users' needs. Therefore, measures were taken to encourage the adoption of a culture conducive to co-construction.
2. Regional and territorial bodies integrated patients into working committees for the Improvement of Practices, in consultation with the

regional branches of the CISS/FAS. Two regions in France (Brittany and Pays de la Loire) have already set up such initiatives, while other regions are following suit as measures to provide better quality and safer care and to identify a user who could join the national working group.

3. A collection of short videos was produced to present: (a) "real" abuse situations with testimonials from different actors, professionals and users; (b) a joint analysis of causes that led to the abuse situation and (c) a joint definition of improvement measures. Each regional body currently identifies at least one situation and produces a short video.

As a scientific agency, beyond its participation in the national working group and internal changes for user and patient participation (see paragraph 2a), the HAS organizes events to (1) promote user participation in care safety and quality and (2) make it a central theme in France. The HAS 2016 Colloquium on "Patient Dynamics: Innovating and Measuring" highlighted ongoing research on patient engagement contributions at all levels of the system. Further, as part of the National Programme for Patient Safety (*Programme National Sécurité Patient* [PNSP]) with regard to patient engagement in patient safety (DGOS 2016), a seminar organized by the Health Ministry and the HAS (2016) unearthed potential ways to reinforce the patient's role as a co-actor in care safety.

Creation of Joint User–Professional Committees

As mentioned previously, when the role of user representatives is strictly limited to sitting-in institutional bodies and committees, their impact is somewhat limited. Confining them in those roles keeps them away from clinical and organizational issues, despite attempts to involve them in the preparation of accreditation visits. In order to escape this unproductive situation, two initiatives have appeared: (1) the formation of joint "user–professional committees" which create new partnership spaces and closer relationships between professionals, patients and user representatives and

(2) the recruitment of patients to take part in user–professional committees. In this case, recruited patients are not user representatives. Instead, they come from community groups which have ongoing agreements with health organizations. This allows expansion of the user recruitment pool.

To help illustrate these new forms of patient/user involvement, the following section will present two examples: one example from a health organization and another one from a Regional and Territorial Body for the Improvement of Health Practices and Organizations.

The Rennes University Hospital

At the time, the national context seemed favourable. On the one hand, the National Programme for Patient Safety (PNSP) and the FORAP-HAP working group for patient engagement in care quality were in effect. On the other hand, meetings with members of the Nursing Commission (*Commission des soins infirmiers*), representatives of the users commission and patient groups were taking place, which created a context where collective engagement between professionals and users became necessary.

Consequently, in 2016, the Rennes University Hospital set up a joint committee comprising 20 professionals and 20 user/community group representatives. This newly created joint committee had three specific objectives:

- Create a space for reflection and exchange
- Begin a partnership between users and health professionals around the issue of patient pathways;
- Define measures that would encourage user/community group involvement in processes designed to improve the quality and safety of care, as well as the promotion of patient rights

After a first meeting, expectations from both users and professionals were gathered, and the decision was made to set up five working groups in charge of:

- The Patient Pathway Charter
- Patient Rights: trustworthy person and anticipated directives
- Patient Discharge
- Organizing visits for people accompanying children
- The patient's environment

Given the current orientations of the Ministry of Health, the Regional Health Agencies and the HAS, joint committees address the need to create a collective dynamic between users and professionals to improve health pathways and patient care quality. Joint committees revisit interactions between actors and define new alliances, the time between users/patients and clinicians rather than between user representatives and directors.

Thus, for instance, the Patient Discharge working group connects health managers and representatives from various services and patient organizations. Through meetings, they eventually learn how to work together, allowing them to develop common objectives based on existing best practices while proposing new individualized methods that involve patients and their relatives. In connection with the nursing directorate, the working group formalizes its recommendations and engages user–professional duos to raise awareness about these recommendations among different departments.

Brittany's Regional Body: The Coordination Group for Improving Practices of Health Professionals in Brittany (CAPPS Bretagne)

Beyond the participation of CAPPS professionals in various national initiatives (PNSP seminar, FORAP-HAS working group, HAS strategic reflection, HAS colloquium, etc.), for many years already, users and professionals have been interacting to address issues of care, safety and quality.

At the governance level, two *CISS Bretagne* user representatives sit on *CAPPS Bretagne*'s scientific council. In addition, the regular exchanges with CISS Bretagne translate to regular presentations to its board of directors. And lastly, CAPPS intervenes at the *CISS Bretagne* general assembly for matters regarding care quality and safety.

At a national level, three user representatives from Brittany participate in the FORAP-HAS national working group, and at a local level, two representatives sit on a follow-up committee for care-related harm notification training.

In terms of concrete activities, patients participate in the organization of special science days (2007, 2011, 2016); the production forum-theatre training programmes on healthcare-acquired infection management (2008–2012) and in the working group responsible for establishing and following up on care-related harm notification training (2015–2018).

With regard to research, patients are engaged in research projects revolving around user representative involvement (2008, 2012), the place of patients and caregivers in chronic disease management (2014), and usage assessments of "well-treatment" tools developed by the HAS-FORAP group (2015–2018).

Moreover, *CAPPS Bretagne*, in affiliation with *CISS Bretagne*, offers support to professionals in health and medico-social organizations across the region to encourage the involvement of users and their representatives in various initiatives related to the promotion of care safety and quality (beyond patient rights). Operationally speaking, this means setting up and coordinating a regional working group comprising users and professionals from *CAPPS Bretagne* and *CISS Bretagne*; making an inventory of existing procedures in the region's health organizations; promoting the pooling of existing tools and approaches for the involvement of users and their representatives in quality and safety approaches (such as identification of positive experiences); continuing existing measures ("well-treatment", participation in the HAS-FORAP national working group, etc.); offering training for professionals, users and their representatives; organizing a user-themed annual science day showcasing users as actors of their own safety; creating a directory of user representatives and community organizations.

Last but not least, the operating principle remains identical to the one which guided all of regional efforts over the past ten years, namely, the co-construction of objectives and interventions by users and professionals, including implementation and assessment phases. To achieve this,

CAPPS Bretagne added to its team a part-time project manager hired from a community organization. The objective was to integrate a "user" dimension to all projects (changing attitudes) and promote partnerships with all actors of the health system.

Beyond Links with User Representatives: User Partnerships Built Closer to Care

Patient involvement can include various elements. For instance, supporting other patients through care such as in therapeutic education or psychological support; improving care quality and safety, training or participating in research activities. Driven by actors in the field (i.e. users and health professionals within their respective organizations such as community groups, learned societies, institutes, committees), patient involvement often takes shape through various local interventions often undertaken by professionals from within a service or even in the context of singular physician–patient relationships. Mostly informal, these new forms of collaboration are rarely known to the rest of the organization, which raises the question of their visibility. Collaborations can be born either from healthcare professional initiatives or from patient group initiatives as evidenced by the two following examples.

Emerging Practices Coupled with Expectations from Professionals

Based on an assumption that many patient engagement experiences are little-known, a study was conducted in two university hospital centres in western France. The main objective was to take stock of initiatives that involved patients and their representatives to promote them and stimulate new projects.

The first learning from this study was the strong participation of professionals (over 550 respondents) and their relative enthusiasm towards the topic (more than 1000 patient partnership initiatives were reported). Nearly three out of four initiatives focused on care provision or support, mainly participation in therapeutic education programmes or care, quality and safety improvement activities (mostly the assessments of practices and organizational arrangements). One-third of these initiatives was framed by a charter or a mission statement. In almost half of the cases, participating patients came from patient groups and they underwent training in 10 per cent of cases.

Furthermore, the study highlighted a number of enabling factors that explained such levels of participation: health organizations which had a dedicated transversal unit for more than ten years showed more involved patients in therapeutic education programmes; health organizations with a joint user–professional committee reported more care, quality and safety initiatives; the perception of professionals towards the relevance of this partnership; community group engagement and the recognition of "patient representative" status; time allotted for proceedings; health professionals' knowledge and training on patient expectations. In sum, this study not only revealed true willingness from professionals but also a need to properly equip them to facilitate the development of these innovative approaches.

More Peer Helpers

In the field of peer education for people living with chronic diseases, the example of the French Association of Diabetics (*Association Française des diabétiques* [AFD]) is significant both in terms of measures taken and its lack of recognition from other actors of the French health system. In 2005, the association, which has a solid knowledge base stemming from its helpline for people living with diabetes, decided through its board of directors to launch a training programme given by expert patients. Their goal was to act within the community, closer to the living environments of people living with the disease.

To design the training programme, the AFD turned to an association specialized in TEP, the French Association for Therapeutic Education and Development (AFDET), and to the first research laboratory specialized in therapeutic education and medical pedagogy at the University of Bobigny-Paris XIII directed by Rémy Gagnayre and Jean-François

D'Ivernois, opened in 1978 to promote patient education and therapeutic education for patients (TEP). This first attempt at scientific collaboration failed on the grounds that, in patient education, medical knowledge must prevail and training must be delivered by physicians. Therefore, as decided by its board, the AFD sought help from a specialist in popular education, which led to the creation of training modules.

It was not until 2010, once professor Brigitte Sandrin-Berthon (2008) took charge of the French Association for Therapeutic Education and Development (*Association Française pour le Développement de l'Enseignement Technique* [AFDET]), that true scientific collaboration occurred. Hence, the training programme's contents were assessed by peers (people living with diabetes) and built upon knowledge from both patients and physicians through shared learning. Also, it was based on years of work performed by the AFD, namely, keywords drawn from most frequently asked questions on the AFD helpline. Since 2015, there are ten modules on pathology and the environment, supplemented by a day of extended active volunteering and a five-day TEP training in a classroom, under the co-responsibility of AFD and AFDET. This original programme helped train thousands of expert patients.

Remarkably, this programme leverages a wealth of community organizations and is significant considering what is being organized in terms of peer education in France. Currently, due to internet-enabled access to information, many patients socialize their experiences and knowledge beyond collective movements, particularly institutionalized health agency-approved community organizations. For instance, since the 1990s (1994), there are Addiction Counsellors who welcome and supervise rehabilitation patients and draw their expertise from their own experience with addition (Flora 2015a, pp. 347–356). Also, since 2012, university-trained Peer Mediators in mental health (Flora 2013b) evolve within mobile teams to tend to peers or within Mutual Help Groups (*Groupes d'entraide mutuelle* [GEM]) in accordance with the WHO Regional Office for Europe (WHO/Europe) mental health collaboration centre framework.

In short, the peer support movement has developed through solidary—even commercial—endeavours to coach other patients using university training for TEP or coaching. The creators of *Hospitalidée* are a telling example. Based on their hospitalization experience, they propose a peer evaluation of the hospitality capabilities of health organizations. Although some new forms of intervention may liken to businesses rather than community groups, they still offer solutions to patients or propose new organizational methods that may impact the health system (Flora 2013b).

The Rise of User Teachers: New Forms of User Involvement for Training and Research Purposes

User Involvement for Training Purposes

For several years now, users have been sporadically involved in sessions dealing with patient rights or health democracy issues, mainly for nursing or managerial training. During those sessions, user representatives are invited to present and explain the ins and outs of the laws for which they fought. More recently, users have been included in physician and paramedic training programmes centring on the care giver–receiver relationship. They intervene frequently by way of testimonials to emphasize relationship issues and share their disease experience with professionals.

As a result of individual initiatives, patient interventions exist in nursing schools since 1992, in the faculty of medicine at Diderot University since 1995 and that of University of Paris-Sud (Paris XI) since 1997 (Jouet et al. 2010; Flora, 2012, pp. 43–47 et 76–103).

As of the second decade of the twenty-first century, thanks to work completed by researchers (Jouet and Flora 2010), these interventions have been a subject of reflection for several academic pedagogy teams:

- Programme for 4th year medical students from the Pierre and Marie Curie Faculty of Medicine initiated and renewed every year by the deans and vice deans (Flora 2012, pp. 216–219).
- Programme for all 3rd year students of the Faculty of Medicine Claude Bernard Lyon-Est at the initiative of a philosopher faculty researcher; renewed every year since 2012; developed within the framework of Patient ACTors in Medicine Education (*Patients ACTeurs de*

l'Enseignement en Médecine [PACTEM]) combining an initiative in two faculties of medicine—one in Lyon and the other in Saint-Etienne (Lechopier and Granier 2017).

- Graduate courses on the care relationship at Paris-Est Créteil Val-de-Marne University (Paris XII) conducted by a user–professional duo.
- Coursework for General Medicine Interns at Paris XIII University (University of Paris North), systematically conducted by a physician–patient duo (Gross et al. 2017a, b); based on a reflexive approach inspired by a similar initiative in Montreal (Flora 2012, 2015b; Compagnon and Ghadi 2014; Flora et al. 2016). The model was a remarkable success with medical teachers and gradually convinced the students as well. These initiatives piqued the interest of other universities as a network is currently under construction. With the goal of integrating patient trainers earlier into medical education, a medical thesis recently investigated the feasibility of implementing the Montreal model throughout the medical curriculum of a French medical school (Charoy-Brejon 2016).

Along those lines, in 2016, a report published by a working group under the Institute for Health Democracy (*Institut Pour la Démocratie en Santé* [IPDS]) referenced all initiatives in France (de Singly and Gaillaget 2017).

In December 2017, a seminar was organized following discussions between professionals and users involved in training programmes for the social, health and medico-social sectors. Entitled "Let's combine our knowledge" (*Associons nos savoirs*), this seminar demonstrated the extent of existing initiatives. As part of ongoing efforts, a participatory initiative is underway with the aim of producing a text to which all organizations involved in initial and continuing education within those three sectors, including the National Agency for Continuing Professional Development, are invited to subscribe. The goal is to make user engagement an essential part of healthcare professional training and a crucial criterion for training quality and funding.

Clearly, the issue is to make interventions evolve from users merely expressing their individual experiences to users positioned as full-fledged trainers, defining educational objectives and contributing knowledge that differs from that of professionals. Reported experiences showcased alternative pedagogical modalities which support user participation. This new way of intervening bolsters action from users on issues of care and patient support that extend far beyond the defence of rights.

Within the broader scope of health sciences and social work, continuing education currently benefits the most from patient involvement. As of 2018, initiatives have multiplied with three patient universities opened in recent years (Paris, Aix, Marseille and Grenoble) and two more about to be launched (Lyon, Toulouse). Among more heterogeneous practices, some TEP training programmes train professionals (health, psychosocial), patients and relatives (as caregivers) together. In addition to patient universities, academic courses have also been created, which are open to patients, relatives and user association members, similar to training courses in the field of addictions where users are trained alongside health and psychosocial professionals (Paris XI).

Another initiative, created and launched a few years ago by a citizens group, pushes the concept even further. It organizes civic education events in the form of ethical debates combining art (cinema at first) and current major health issues, which resulted in ethical questioning beyond closed circles of medical students. The Faculty of Medicine of Nice Sophia Antipolis currently grants "credits" when students participate in public debates. In 2018, a university degree (UD) on the Art of Care, which comprises seminars on Narrative Medicine, was offered to medical students, practicing health science professionals, patients and relatives. Different modules are grouped under the same concept of "Care UniverCity" (*UniverCité du Soin*) (Benattar and Flora 2018).

User Involvement for Research Purposes

Regarding research, several examples illustrate the essential role of users as key interlocutors with researchers. For example, since the end of the twentieth century, members of a group originally composed of five HIV/AIDS community organizations—referred to as TRT-5 (Therapeutic Research and Treatment 5 [*Traitement Recherche Thérapeutique 5*])—have been involved in all research commissions, in addition to being featured in the organizational chart of the National Research Agency on AIDS and Hepatitis. This agency is the world's third largest producer of HIV research publications.

Another example comes from the telethon of the French Association of Myopathy (*Association française de Myopathie* [AFM]) whose donations allowed the creation of the association's own pharmaceutical laboratory to supplement drug offerings against rare diseases. Moreover, the AFM is the initiator of a European community group network, Eurordis, and the Orphanet Internet platform, integrated into the National Institute of Health and Medical Research (*Institut National de la Santé et de la Recherche Médicale* [INSERM]).

Based on these examples, in early 2003, INSERM set up the Patient Group Think Tank (*Groupe de Réflexion Avec les Associations de Malades* [GRAM]), a name chosen with patient groups. The idea was to create collaborations between patient groups and researchers and to be cognizant of each party's expectations while trying to identify common expectations. As a reflection of that, the GRAM is currently managed by a collective of ten user representatives from approved community organizations, five researchers and five administrators. However, a recent study indicated that researchers still show reluctance towards this type of collaboration, highlighting antagonism between patient groups, their subjectivity and the expected objectivity of science. Although researchers with actual collaboration experience generally tend to be supportive of the think tank …

Conclusion

While the experiential knowledge of patients and users has become a social fact (Durkheim 1894) internationally (Flora 2012; Jouet 2013, 2014; Flora et al. 2014), their recognition in France still remains a work in progress. As presented through this chapter, the voice of users was brought to the fore at a regulatory level via a 2002 framework law and then a general law on TEP in 2009. Additionally, this chapter described the process by which multiple experiences mobilized various forms of experiential knowledge from users/patients. This mobilization led to forms of co-construction and even partnerships.

That said, the challenge now lies in the health system's capacity to allow widespread use of such knowledge in partnership settings (Duflo 2009, 2010; Suàrez-Herrera 2010) with stable elements which guarantee homogeneity and quality and flexibility which enables ownership. Drawing lessons from collective partnership experiences would help federate all the actors gradually (i.e. health professionals and users) and support progress for the benefit of all.

The process for mobilizing the voice and knowledge of patients–users would be a major contribution to the health system's restructuring (or that of the French social model in general) especially to grasp its complexity (Morin 1977; Mintzberg 1982). Indeed, our societies and health systems must face several deep transformations: epidemiologically, due to the explosion of patients living with at least one chronic disease (Borges Da Silva 2015; Grimaldi et al. 2017); generationally, with ageing populations; organizationally, with the redistribution of power relations (Ghadiri et al. 2017); and finally, the 4th industrial revolution driven by the world going digital (Schwab 2017). The mobilization of patient voices and knowledge and their translation into applicable knowledge for co-construction, collaboration and partnership will contribute to the management of these transformations. Also, their knowledge will enable us to break new grounds in the process of patient–user appreciation, consideration and engagement.

However, the emergence of this new modality of collaboration between users and professionals should not rule out what was the strength of the French model, namely, the structured representation of user representatives. The risk would be to substitute one by another while the challenge is to jointly strengthen the action of some by that of others.

If we look at the evolution of user representatives, we can be surprised at the shift in their position as bearers of a direct democracy towards representative democracy. Their establishment in 1996, and their reinforcement in 2002, was part of the process of challenging representative democracy and aimed at strengthening mechanisms of direct democracy. Twenty years later, the action of user representatives is questioned, as embodying a form of representative democracy that is heavily questioned today far beyond the health system. The inability of the directorates to have facilitated access to the users of the establishment, the necessary and often fecund alliance with the quality management led to situate them on the side of the technocratic and managerial logic, away from the nursing logic who touches the users much more directly.

The articulation with these new forms of participation is then an opportunity to achieve a mature system of user engagement in the health system: users with patient support functions, peer support, collaboration with health professionals as close as possible to the care that coordinates their actions with those of the users registered in the governance of the institutions and the health system. The latter will guarantee the exercise of the former, who in return will help legitimize the representatives of the users by providing them with the field material, namely, the daily experience of the patients. In addition, the gradual commitment of users in actions closer to the realization of care will lead some to engage in representation actions, thus broadening the base of user representatives and renewing their action methods.

It is on this condition and because the users will then be located at all levels of the system that the expected cultural revolution can be made … it has besides begun.

Acknowledgement The authors would like to thank the members of the HAS-FORAP group on wellness and the members of the "users-professionals" group of CAPPS Bretagne.

References

Benattar, J.-M., and L. Flora. 2018. Culture du Soin. La Stradda, N° 296 du 25 juin au 25 juillet 2018, p. 49.

Borges Da Silva, G. 2015. Maladies chroniques: vers un changement paradigmatique des soins. Santé publique, Vol. 27, janv.-fev., S1, pp. 9–11.

Carriburu, D. 2009. Les infections nosocomiales: un risque collectif en cours de normalisation?, Sciences sociales et santé, Vol. 27, N°4, 2009/12, pp. 43–71.

Charoy-Brejon C. 2016. *Le patient formateur dans un enseignement de l'approche centrée patient à la faculté de médecine de l'UPEC, projet exploratoire*. Thèse de

médecine, spécialité de médecine générale, Faculté de médecine de Créteil, Université Paris est, Créteil.
Compagnon, C., and V. Ghadi. 2014. L'an II de la démocratie sanitaire.
De Singly C., et J. Gaillaguet. 2017. Enquête—Contribution à un état des lieux de la démocratie en santé dans les instituts de formations en soins infirmiers et dans les facultés de médecine, p. 60.
Direction générale de l'offre de soins (DGOS). 2016. Promouvoir le patient co-acteur de sa sécurité: enjeux et perspectives. Séminaire du vendredi 18 novembre 2016 organisé dans le cadre du Programme national pour la sécurité des patients 2013–2017. https://solidarites-sante.gouv.fr/IMG/pdf/actes_du_seminaire_promouvoir_le_patient_co-acteur_18nov2016.pdf.
DREES les dépenses de santé en 2017, Résultats des compte de la santé 2018, 224 p.
Duflo, E. 2009. Cours santé 1 & 2, collège de France, accessible à l'adresse Internet: www.college-deFrance.fr/site/esther-dufflo/course-2009-01-19-17h00.htm; www.college-deFrance.fr/site/esther-dufflo/course-2009-01-19-18h00.htm.
———. 2010. *La politique de l'autonomie. Lutter contre la pauvreté, tome 2*. Paris: Le seuil/république des idées.
Durkheim, E. 1894. «Qu'est-ce qu'un fait social?» dans les règles de la méthode sociologique. Felix Alcan, Paris: Presses universitaires de France, 1ère édition.
EHPAD. p. 25.
Fillion, E. 2005. Que font les scandales? La médecine de l'hémophilie à l'épreuve du sang contaminé. Politix, 2005/3, N°71, pp. 191–214.
Flora, L. 2012. Le patient formateur: élaboration théorique et pratique d'un nouveau métier de la santé. Thèse de doctorat de sciences sociales, spécialité « Sciences de l'éducation », Université Vincennes Saint Denis—Paris 8, campus Condorcet.
———. 2013a. Savoirs expérientiels des malades, pratiques collaboratives avec les professionnels de santé: état des lieux. *Education permanente* 195: 59–72.
———. 2013b. Des patients en formation avec des professionnels de santé en faculté de médecine: un nouveau paradigme à l'aube de la loi HPST?. Le bulletin juridique du praticien hospitalier, éditions Les études hospitalières, N° 154, janvier 2013, Dossier pp. 1–4.
———. 2015. *Plateformes numérique et approches digitales Qu'est ce qui se construit pour, avec et par des patients en France?* Conférence de Montréal, Québec au centre de recherche du centre hospitalo-universitaire de Montréal [CRCHUM] sous le titre Regards croisés France/Québec: co-construction en

partenariat avec les patients et les citoyens dans le système de santé, la formation et la recherche, les 24–25 novembre 2015.

———. 2015a. *Le patient formateur: nouveau métier de la santé? Comment les savoirs expérientiels de l'ensemble des acteurs de santé peuvent relever les défis de nos systèmes de santé*, 347–358. Sarrebruck: Presses Académiques Francophones.

———. 2015b. *Un référentiel de compétences de patient: pour quoi faire? Du savoir expérientiel des malades à un référentiel de compétences intégré: l'exemple du modèle de Montréal*. Sarrebruck: Presses Académiques Francophones.

Flora, L., E. Jouet, and O. Las Vergnas. 2014. *Contribution à la cartographie des publications établissant le fait social des malades*, 235–236. Paris: Archives contemporaines.

Flora, L., A. Berkesse, A. Payot, V. Dumez, and P. Karazivan. 2016. L'application d'un modèle intégré de partenariat patient dans la formation des professionnels de la santé: vers un nouveau paradigme humaniste et éthique de co-construction des savoirs en santé. *Le Journal International de Bioéthique et d'éthique des sciences* 27 (1): 59–72.

Ghadiri, D.-P.S., L. Flora, and M.-P. Pomey. 2017. Le virage patient partenaire de soins au Québec. Reconfiguration de l'exercice du pouvoir médical et luttes de nouvelles subjectivités. In La participation des patients (Dir. Hervé C., Jean-Stanton M. Mamzer M.-F.). Paris Dalloz, pp. 25–36.

Grimaldi, A., et al. 2017. *Les Maladies chroniques—vers la troisième médecine*. Paris: Odile Jacob.

Gross, O., Y. Ruelle, T. Sannié, C.-A. Khau, and R. Gagnayre. 2017a. L'utilité des patients enseignants dans la formation initiale des médecins généralistes. *Education Santé Société* 3.

Gross, O., Y. Ruelle, T. Sannié, C.-A. Khau, C. Marchand, A. Mercier, T. Cartier, and R. Gagnayre. 2017b. Un département universitaire de médecine générale au défi de la démocratie en santé: la formation d'internes de médecine générale par des patients-enseignants. *Revue française des affaires sociales* 1: 62–78.

HAS. 2012. Le déploiement de la bientraitance—Guide à destination des professionnels en établissements de santé et Ehpad; groupe FORAP-HAS bientraitance, p. 47.

———. 2015. « État des lieux 18 mois après la sortie du guide et des outils: « Promouvoir la bientraitance en établissement de santé et.

———. 2016. La Dynamique Patient Innover et Mesurer. Colloque HAS, paris, 16-novembre 2016. https://www.has-sante.fr/portail/jcms/c_2672110/fr/colloque-has-la-dynamique-patient-innover-et-mesurer-paris-16-novembre-2016.

HCSP. 2017. Stratégie nationale de santé, Constribution du Haut Cosneil de la santé publique, 189 p.

Jarno, P., and Quelier, C. 2017. Le Représentant des Usagers dans la Prévention des Infections Nosocomiales (RUPIN): quelles modalités pour un soutien adapté à son implication dans le nouveau contexte institutionnel?. Rapport final PREPS. Service d'Epidémiologie et de Santé Publique, CHU de Rennes, 51 pages.

Jouet, E. 2013. Faire de sa maladie un apprentissage: l'exemple du projet EMILIA. *Education permanente* 195: 73–84.

———. 2014. *La reconnaissance des savoirs des malades: de l'émergence au fait social*, 9–20. Paris: Archives contemporaines.

Jouet, E., and L. Flora (coord.). 2010. *Usagers-Experts: la part du savoir des malades dans le système de santé, N°58/59, Pratiques de formation: Analyses.* Université Paris 8.

Jouet, Emmanuelle, Luigi Flora, and Olivier Las Vergnas. 2010. Construction et reconnaissance des savoirs expérientiels des patients. *Pratiques de Formation – Analyses* 58/59: 13–94.

Lechopier, N., and B. Granier. 2017. Patiente expérience. Savoirs expérientiels et épistémologie de la formation médicale, HAL-Archives ouvertes. https://halshs.archives-ouvertes.fr/halshs-01521725.

Martinent, E. 2017. la démocratie sanitaire, entre participation(s) et représentation (s). In *La participation des patients*, 63–104. Paris: Editions Dalloz.

Ministère des Solidarités et de la Santé. 2018. *Ma santé 2022: un engagement collectif—dossier de presse*. Paris. p. 52.

Mintzberg, H. 1982. *Structure et dynamique des organisations*. Paris: Éditions d'Organisation.

Morin, E. 1977. La méthode 1, la nature. Paris: Le Seuil.

OECD Health at glance 2017, OECD Indicators, OECD Publishing Paris.

Pineau, G. 1989. La formation expérientielle entre auto, éco et co-formation. In *Éducation Permanente*, Courtois B. (dir. pub.), n°100–101, pp. 23–30.

Pomey, M.-P., and V. Ghadi. 2009. La participation des usagers au fonctionnement des établissements de santé: une dynamique encore à construire. *Santé, Société et Solidarité*. 2: 53–61.

Sandrin-Berthon, B. 2008. Qui éduque l'autre? *Contact santé* 225: 43–45.

Schwab, K. 2017. *La quatrième révolution industrielle*. Paris: Dunod.

Suàrez-Herrera, J.C. 2010. *L'intégration organisationnelle de la participation: Des enjeux locaux pour une santé publique globale, Thèse de doctorat en santé publique, option organisation de soins*. Faculté de médecine de l'Université de Montréal.

9

Expert by Experience: Valuing Patient Engagement in Healthcare

Yann Le Cam and Matthew Bolz-Johnson

Introduction

The movement of people living with a rare disease in Europe is at the root of several innovative approaches to shaping health policies, participating in health organizations and transforming healthcare.

The involvement of rare disease patient representatives in policy, scientific assessments, ethical reviews, management of healthcare provision services, and health agencies is growing at both the national and European level. The most unique feature of the rare disease movement (compared to the dynamic of patient involvement in HIV/AIDS or cancer, which involved patient representatives first at national level and then later at European level) is that it was initiated as a bottom-up approach by patient organizations to create a legitimate and credible umbrella movement at the European level. This helped them to grow their voice first at the EU level, where patients advocate created EU legislation and policies to address their needs. They are then involved in the implementation of

Y. Le Cam (✉) • M. Bolz-Johnson
Eurordis, Paris, France
e-mail: yann.lecam@eurordis.org; matt.johnson@eurordis.org

M.-P. Pomey et al. (eds.), *Patient Engagement*, Organizational Behaviour in Healthcare,
https://doi.org/10.1007/978-3-030-14101-1_9

these policies through their engagement in EU agencies, scientific committees, EU joint actions with public agencies, or joint actions with Member States, thereafter trickling down to the national level. This double constant flow is what enables the rare disease patient advocacy movement to work at European level with a 360° approach to research, healthcare, treatments and social inclusion, while also integrating progress on the national level.

This chapter will focus on the European level, while still indicating implications of EU action at the national level.

What Is a Rare Disease? How Many People Are Affected?

A rare disease, also referred to as an orphan disease, is any disease that affects a small percentage of the population. Eighty per cent of rare diseases are of genetic origin. Rare diseases include rare cancers, and thus all paediatric cancers and most adult cancers, as well as rare infections. Rare diseases are often chronic, debilitating and life-threatening. They are characterized by a wide diversity of symptoms and signs that vary not only from disease to disease but even from patient to patient living with the same disease. Relatively common symptoms can hide underlying rare diseases, often resulting in misdiagnosis. When the rare disease is genetic, it is present throughout a person's entire life, even if symptoms do not immediately appear. Rare diseases do not only affect the person diagnosed—they also impact families, friends, care takers and society as a whole.

A disease or disorder is defined as rare in Europe when it affects less than one in 2000 people. At the EU level this means a disease affecting less than 250,000 persons. One rare disease may affect only a handful of patients in the Europe or in the world, and another touch as many as 250,000. The vast majority of rare diseases are far rarer, affecting less than 1/10,000, and hundreds of rare diseases affect only a few thousand or hundred or only a few families. In total, about 6000 diseases are defined as rare. An individual rare disease may affect only one person in a million, but all together, rare disease patients comprise 6 to 8 per cent of the population, an estimated 30 million EU citizens overall. In the absence of sufficient epidemiological knowledge, using the more conservative number of 4 per cent of the population, over 300 million people worldwide are affected (Council recommendation of 8 June 2009 on an action in the field of rare diseases, eur-lex.europa.eu/LexUriServ/LexUriServ.do?uri=OJ:C:2009:151:0007:0010:EN:PDF).

How Do Rare Diseases Collectively Create Opportunities to Improve Care and Structure New Healthcare Offerings?

Each rare disease is highly heterogeneous, with a wide diversity of expression of the disease from one patient to another, according to subtype, age, advancement of the disease, co-morbidities and previous care. Rare diseases are a wide range of metabolic, neurological, neuro-muscular, lung, kidney, eye, lung, skin and bone diseases, as well as the majority of other organs or systems, affecting both children and adults, often multi-systemic syndrome, often generating a spectrum of impairments affecting the person's functionalities. Still, and this is the whole concept of rare diseases, across these wide varieties, and when you take, at the right level, the critical mass of persons, we can identify the common issues faced by the people affected and their families: the lack of awareness, information, research and investment in R&D, as well as a lack of treatments approved for licensing in rare indications, specialized centres of care with a multidisciplinary approach, holistic approaches to bridging medical and social care, and training of healthcare and social care professionals.

It is not possible to develop specific policies or to adapt healthcare organization to each rare disease, not even to a few hundred rare diseases. But it is possible to develop public policies addressing the identified common needs of people living with rare diseases: awareness campaigns, for example the annual Rare Diseases Day campaign that takes place the last day of February each year; information, for example the multi-lingual online portal of rare diseases, Orphanet, covering over 32 countries in the world, or the national rare diseases help lines; the education of professionals, for example medical university and continuing education, to change the behaviour and method of diagnostics to better tackle rarity; research, for example research infrastructures, research calls based on excellence, or common strategies on bio banks and registries; investment, for example specific incentives through EU legislation or national tax advantages; and healthcare, for example national designated centres of expertise.

Presentation of EURORDIS

How Has EURORDIS-Rare Diseases Europe Enabled the Emergence of a Rare Disease Movement?

The backbone of this movement is EURORDIS-Rare Diseases Europe (www.eurordis.org). Before EURORDIS was created, every patient organization representing a disease such as cystic fibrosis, Duchenne muscular dystrophy, haemophilia, epidermolysis bullosa, X-Fragile, Prader Willi Syndrome, Gaucher, San Filippo, retinis pigmentosa, spina bifida, neurofibromatosis, or osteogenesis or osteosarcoma was isolated in their action, as support group or advocacy group as well as funders of research or centres of expertise. At best, a few had a European Federation for their disease. In fact, the vast majority of the 6000 rare diseases did not even have a patient group and therefore no collective voice.

The disruptive idea was to gather all rare diseases at the European level so as to gain visibility and create a new social space, going from dark to light, and emerge as a civil society community able to voice the needs and expectations of 30 million people living with a rare disease in Europe. This in turn would create a critical mass of patients and families that could no longer be ignored by society and decision makers. In the early 1990s, the only exceptions were the UK (Contact a Family, Genetic Alliance UK) and Denmark (Organisation for Rare Disorders Denmark), where forms of collaborations across patient groups did already exist.

The vision behind this movement is that the construction of Europe, as a more unified political and economic space, particularly with the EU, offers new opportunities to address rarity at this continental scale; and that the emergence of this critical mass of people living with a rare disease and their families enables collective common action, in turn catalysing a critical mass of doctors, experts, researchers, policy makers, knowledge and resources to address the needs shared across this multi-stakeholder cross-border community.

How Has the Empowerment and Engagement of Experts Gone from Vision into Sustainable Action?

The European Organisation for Rare Diseases (EURORDIS) was established in 1997. Twenty years later, it is now named EURORDIS-Rare Diseases Europe (EURORDIS Activity Report 2017, www.eurordis.org/publication/eurordis-activity-report-2017).

The vision is to enable better lives and cures for people living with a rare disease. The mission is to work across borders and diseases to improve the lives of people living with a rare disease.

The common language is English but the organization uses seven languages in total (English, Spanish, French, German, Italian, Portuguese and Russian) for its communication (website, newsletter, Member News). The multi-cultural and multi-lingual nature of Europe is a constant challenge when trying to create a community of patient experts sharing the same vision, strategy and practices.

The strategy has evolved over time. Initially it was to create the rare disease community and speak with one voice. In time, it became to provide information to patients as well as networking capacity-building opportunities, and also to advocate on behalf of and with patients. Now the strategy is a triptych: (1) Patient Empowerment; (2) Patient Engagement and (3) Patient Advocacy (see Fig. 9.1). Patients come first; everything is done for, and with, the patients. Everything EURORDIS-Rare Diseases Europe do is in partnership with patients. It aims to create value first for the people living with a rare disease, and as much as possible for all stakeholders and society.

EURORDIS-Rare Diseases Europe gathers over 862 member patient organizations from all 48 countries in Europe and beyond (over 70 countries in total). It represents the voice of an estimated 30 million patients, including all rare diseases, with or without a patient group. Thirty-two

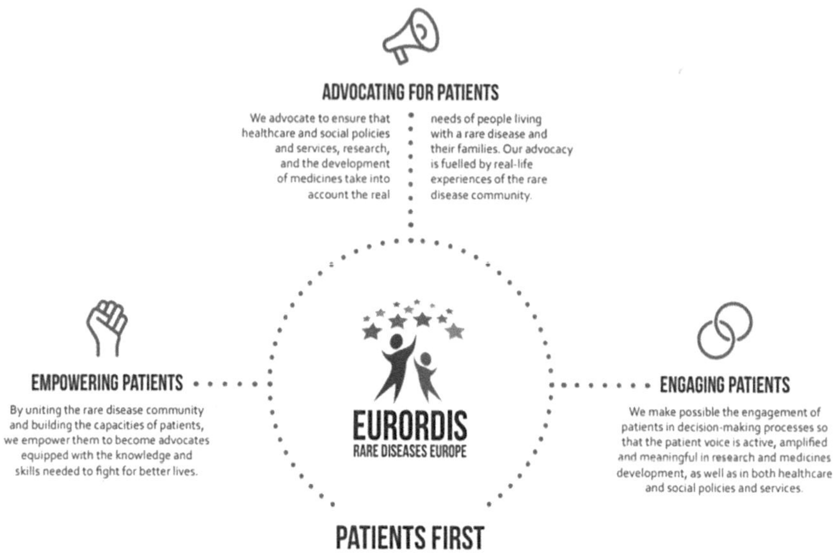

Fig. 9.1 EURORDIS' strategy[1]

national alliances for rare diseases have progressively been established or repositioned in Europe in the dynamic of EURORDIS development, in all 28 EU countries and elsewhere in Europe such as Serbia, TFYR Macedonia, Georgia, Ukraine and Russia. The organization has helped establish most of the 67 disease-specific European Federations or Informal networks. Over the years, it has created a network which is open, inclusive and structured with the European Network of National Alliances for Rare Diseases animated by a Council, a European Network of European Federations animated by a Council, and a European Patient Advocacy Committee which supports about 30 advocates having a permanent mandate of representation as authorized spokesperson empowered to act with autonomy on behalf of the organization.

How to Link Patient Advocacy, Patient Empowerment and Patient Engagement?

The organization believes that democracy, good governance and strategies based on evidence provided by patients, and then developed with patients and for patients, are essential to enable patients to justly speak on behalf of such a wide and diverse community. It therefore pays a lot of attention to clearly defining the three—patient advocacy, patient empowerment and patient engagement. Patient empowerment and engagement do not happen in a vacuum; they have to be encouraged, organized and supported.

EURORDIS, a unique, international non-governmental organization (INGO), is a not-for-profit alliance of rare disease patient organizations that work together to improve the lives of the 30 million people living with a rare disease in Europe. The organization is incorporated in France as an *Association Loi 1901*, with this status setting the legal elements and by-laws which shape the organization's governance and functional rules.

Full members are all rare disease patient organizations that are based in one of the 48 European countries; incorporated with more than two years of existence; have a track record of advocacy and support activities; have a majority of constituencies and governing board composed of people affected by a rare disease as patient or parent or relative; and have funding that ensures their independence (pharma funding cannot represent more than 50 per cent and has to come from several sources). Associate members are organizations not fulfilling one of these criteria but still dedicated to rare diseases, for example, recently created patient groups, groups from outside Europe (from 70 countries in total) or relevant research foundations. Each full member carries one vote—at the Annual General Assembly, they vote on the activity report, financial report and auditor's report of the previous year, and on the action plan, budget, governance organization and team chart of the next year. They also vote to elect the Board members. The Board is composed exclusively of patient advocates; their candidacy is presented by their affiliation member organization, but when elected they represent only themselves and act as a board of trustees, not on behalf of specific disease or country interests. The Board meets four times a year over two days of intense meetings dedicated to review and evaluation of activities and strategic orientations. The governance structure includes a set of Councils, Committees for Advocacy, Editorial or Conference Programming, Task Forces for Access to Medicines or for health technology assessment (HTA), and Steering Groups for each project or programme.

The objectives of the organization are achieved by connecting patients, families and patient groups, as well as by bringing together all stakeholders and mobilizing the rare disease community. Partnership with stakeholders is one of the key ways that EURORDIS strengthens the patient voice and shapes research, policies and patient services; the expertise of experience, the patient knowledge and contribution to healthcare would not be recognized and accepted without this tight fabric of inter-relations. This translates into a large set of partnerships established through a variety of instruments:

- Memorandums of Understandings with major rare disease national organizations, for example, the USA, Canada, Japan, Russia, China and Iran, or with learned societies such as the European Society of Human Genetics, Health Technology Assessment International and The Professional Society for Health Economics and Outcomes Research (ISPOR);
- Partnering through Consortiums, for example, Accreditation Canada for Partnership for the Assessment of Clinical Excellence in European Reference Networks (PACE-ERN), DOLON Consulting for Rare Impact on gene and cell therapy, university biomedical or social research academic teams for projects funded by Innovative Medicines Initiatives or EC Horizon 2020 Research programme;
- Partnering through projects with ministries, hospitals, university and research institutions, for example, Sick Kids Hospital Toronto, French National Institute for Health and Medical Research (INSERM), universities in Barcelona or Tubingen or Newcastle, Ministry of Social Affairs in Spain, ministries of health in 18 countries within Joint Actions;
- Partnering for conferences, for example, European Medicines Agency (EMA), FDA, National Institutes of Health (NIH), ministries and national institutions, and learned societies;
- Corporate partnership through membership of the EURORDIS Round Table of Companies for pharmaceutical companies, CRO (contract research organizations) and specialists in rare disease therapy development.

Each partnership is formalized through a letter of agreement, MoU, Consortium agreement or other form of contract. Each partnership is managed by a specific member of staff. This translates into a complex governance chart.

EURORDIS human resources include staff and volunteers who function within a multi-cultural, multi-lingual, multi-skilled and decentralized network.

The staff is composed of 45 full-time or part-time employees. They are all highly qualified, representing over 17 nationalities and speaking over ten languages. English is the common language. They operate from offices in Paris, Brussels and Barcelona. Part of the staff is working remotely from London, Geneva, Cologne and Belgrade. Professional nomadism, working on the road, is the work style for half of the team. EURORDIS value building capacities, autonomy, self-drive, team work, agility and learning from mistakes. Internal rules for staff set out the values and agreed common rules. These characteristics are influencing the culture of the patient advocates engaging in European research, treatments or healthcare activities.

- The main functions in the team are:
- Governance and strategic planning;
- Finance and support services;
- Relations with patient organizations and relations with volunteers;
- European advocacy (including the Rare Barometer survey programme) and international advocacy (including Rare Diseases International and the UN and NGO Committee for Rare Diseases);
- Communication and information (including Rare Disease Day), events (including the European Conference on Rare Diseases) and resource development and corporate relations (including the EURORDIS Round Table of Companies);
- Research and infrastructure;
- Therapeutic development (including regulatory work at the European Medicines Agency) and information and access to medicines (including HTA);
- Healthcare and European Reference Networks (ERNs) and social policy and services, including the RareConnect online patient communities.

EURORDIS had around 500 volunteers in 2018. The organization is unique in Europe in having such a strong volunteer community and this is a strong unique asset. They have been able to progressively grow the engagement of volunteers over the last ten years.

All volunteers are patient advocates—patients themselves or parents, relatives or staff from a patient group—who keep a link with their patient group of origin but who decide to give from 5 or 10 days per year to 100 days or more per year. The base of engagement is the Charter of Volunteers (EURORDIS Volunteer Charter, www.eurordis.org/volunteering#tabs-2). Each volunteer has a clear written description of their mission and role and a clear duration of the mission or mandate. Each volunteer is referred to and supported by a specific member of the staff. The vast majority of volunteers are selected based on a call for expression of interest customized to the activity planned. The time spent on activities by a volunteer throughout the year is recorded and valued for its economic worth. This assessment is validated by external auditors Deloitte as part of their annual financial review.

The main functions of volunteers are to be patient representatives in EU institutional committees or expert groups, patient representatives in the ERNs, and active participants in internal task forces or committees, and to take on an advisory capacity in projects, and as online community managers.

Volunteers create a huge additional value as they are themselves patients and family members—they constitute the real life shape of the European rare disease patient voice, bringing a broad diversity of personal and group experiences, as well as expertise in different domains. These volunteers also represent the diversity of rare diseases, countries and cultures, as well as beliefs or values and professional backgrounds. The critical mass of over 500 volunteers has helped to increase individual empowerment and the capacity to engage as experts based on their experience.

What Is the EURORDIS Advocacy Strategy and What Has It Helped to Achieve So Far?

The advocacy strategy focused first on EU pharmaceutical legislation, and thereafter on health and research policy. Over the last 15 years, the rare disease community has shaped and advocated for a total of seven pieces of European legislation.

The main construct of the EU is the unique market; legislation on pharmaceuticals result in 'hard' laws (otherwise known as EU Regulations), which when adopted immediately become laws in all EU Member States. EURORDIS saw the success of the US Orphan Drug Act and wanted to bring this to Europe. It has been the patient advocates on the frontline pushing for three pieces of EU legislation that have had a major impact on the lives of people living with a rare disease in Europe:

1. The EU Regulation on Orphan Medicinal Products in 1999;
2. The EU Regulation on Paediatric Use of Medicines in 2006 and
3. The EU Regulation on Advanced Therapies in 2007 (gene and cell therapies, tissue engineering).

Each of these pieces of legislation resulted in the creation of new scientific committees at the EMA. Two or three patient representative positions were created in each of these Committees, holding the same powers as the representatives of regulatory agencies of the EU Member States. This innovative step to involve patients in this way was a world first, opening the door to patients' participation in national regulatory agencies. EURORDIS also introduced special provisions in the EU pharmaceutical legislation during the review of 2003, including the EU centralized procedure for the marketing approval of orphan medicines and the participation of patients in the Management Board of the EMA, as well as the establishment of a structured dialogue with all stakeholders.

Building on the milestones of these three pieces of EU pharma legislation, EURORDIS was able to gain credibility while building up the legitimacy of their membership and the competences of patient representatives to become patient advocates. Based on this progress, EURORDIS also advocated for two soft laws:

1. A European Commission Communication on Rare Diseases in 2008, which crucially established rare diseases as a health and research priority within the European Commission's policy and programmes; and
2. The European Recommendation on an Action in the field of Rare Diseases in 2009, based on which all EU Member States committed to establishing a national plan for rare diseases by the end of 2013.

The Council Recommendation also led to the creation of a European Commission Expert Group on Rare Diseases (EUCERD) composed of all 28 EU Member States, including four patient representatives, four industry and insurance representatives, and several academic representatives from leading EU-wide infrastructure projects in rare diseases. This multi-stakeholder approach and the recognition of the crucial role of patient representatives have opened the door to the engagement of patient representatives in policies and projects in most EU Member States. However, that is not to say that the seat at the table is ever guaranteed, and the organization continues to have to justify their role.

It was only in 2010 that the EU Directive on Patients' Rights to Cross-Border Healthcare was adopted. In the European legislative system an EU Directive is a hard law, that is, stronger than a Recommendation or Communication but weaker than a Regulation. An EU Regulation immediately becomes law in each EU Member State and needs to be transposed in each EU Member State, leaving room for a significant margin of interpretation and customization.

The EU Directive on Patients' Rights to Cross-Border Healthcare provides the legal basis for the EU to establish ERNs for low-prevalence and complex diseases. This is the first time ever that healthcare provision has been organized at an EU level, and this is extremely meaningful politically. The Directive also opens the door to stronger EU collaboration on HTA, setting the foundations to move towards EU legislation on HTA, which will enable the integration of some HTA activities at the European level. In addition, the Directive sets out in stone that rare diseases are a top priority in European cross-border healthcare. However, this Directive does not specifically set out the need for participation of patients, neither in the ERNs nor in the EU-level HTA cooperation.

Indeed, the role of patient representatives in institutional scientific committees was not gained because policy makers were convinced of the credibility of the expertise brought by patients, but rather was accepted by policy makers as a political added value to showcase active citizen participation and social democracy. EURORDIS only managed to achieve progress at the EMA as patients' participation was seen as a way to consolidate the perception of transparency and public trust in this new powerful European institution. However, over time, the participation of patients at the EMA, in HTA processes, at payer bodies, at the European Commission, within ERNs, and also within research projects has now come to be properly recognized for its intrinsic value, even if it is still always organized in an ad hoc fashion.

Since the beginning, the strategy to advocate for legislation and policies AND to take an active part in their implementation has been embedded at the core of the organization's ethos, to ensure that the experience of patients and families is taken into account as much as the experience of institutions, researchers and clinicians. This creates a two-way flow of knowledge and exchange of experience that goes towards co-building policies, best practices and common cultures. EURORDIS often ends up playing the role of mediator, while always putting patients at the centre.

EURORDIS' current advocacy focus is on the future EU Regulation on HTA, the legislative proposal for which is in process in 2018 and 2019. In parallel, the organization is preparing for a potential in-depth review of the EU Pharmaceutical legislation as well as of the EU Regulations on Orphan Products, Paediatric Regulations and Advanced Therapies.

Advocacy priorities for international legislation or policies focus on ensuring the inclusion of rare diseases in the UN's Sustainable Development Goals, the ongoing preparation of a Collaborative Framework with the WHO, and the inclusion of rare diseases in the UN Declaration on Universal Health Coverage, and working towards a future UN Resolution on Rare Diseases for the world.

Over the years, the acceptance that patients are stronger together has grown. There is increasing confidence that common action is really shaping policy, which in turn results in action to address patients' needs. The authenticity, the boldness and the co-constructive approach with all stakeholders that EURORDIS and its community take enables the voice of people living with rare diseases to be heard. They do not wait to be asked; they ask. The 360° view, the knowledge they have at the local, national, European and international levels, the continuity of their progressive action over time—these aspects are all characteristics of the movement of expert patients, one which is authentic and acts as an authoritative reference for all stakeholders and policy makers.

Patient Involvement in Europe for Rare Diseases

What Is the Actual Experience of Engaging Patients as Experts in the Activities of the European Medicines Agency, Health Technology Assessment Bodies and Payers?

The European AIDS Treatment Group (EATG) and EURORDIS pioneered active patient representative participation at the EMA. The first patient representative, who was invited by the EMA to participate in a discussion of the Committee for Human Medicinal Products (CHMP) on assessing risk benefit for licensing, was an EATG representative. In 2000, the first three patient representatives appointed by the European Commission to the scientific committee, the Committee of Orphan Medicinal Products, were all members of EURORDIS. One of them was elected vice president of the committee by the Member State representatives.

In 2018, EURORDIS had patient representatives on the EMA Management Board, the Committee for Orphan Medicinal Products, the Paediatric Committee, the Committee on Advanced Therapies, and the Patients' and Consumers' Working Party. In these committees, the patient representatives participate fully in the development of internal rules of procedures, work programmes, guidelines for assessors or applicants, design of clinical development, regulatory discussions and their impact for patients. Sometimes they also chair working groups or meetings between some of the drafters. For these Committees, EURORDIS supports the patients appointed by the Commission, whatever their affiliation group; the priority is to ensure that patients are involved and are supported so they can contribute in a meaningful way. All these patient advocates form the EURORDIS Therapeutic Action Group, which also gathers EURORDIS members of staff supporting the patients.

In addition, EURORDIS also brings patients as experts for scientific discussions on specific products in each of the EMA's relevant procedures (advice, risk benefit, pharmacovigilance). Every month, the organization supports the participation of patient representatives as experts in scientific advice and protocol assistance procedures. A study performed by the EMA shows that the scientific opinions are modified or significantly impacted by this participation of patients in over 50 per cent of the cases (https://www.ema.europa.eu/documents/report/stakeholder-engagement-report-2017_en.pdf). EURORDIS also support patient representative participation in innovative procedures such as Adaptive Pathways for Medicines and PRIME (priority medicines). In the last two years, they have begun to facilitate patients' participation in discussions on benefit risk, during which patient advocates can express their preferred treatment options, therefore providing an additional perspective and expertise to the one provided by the clinical and regulatory community.

In parallel, EURORDIS has supported all pilots for the participation of patients in the HTA European Early Dialogue, 24 pilots for rare and non-rare diseases, necessary for the patients as much as for HTA managers and assessors or industry. The organization has now developed the function of patient engagement in HTA, ready for when these activities will be scaled up in the context of the new EU HTA legislation.

Since 2013, EURORDIS has initiated the first platform in Europe enabling a dialogue between national public payers and companies (drug developers or marketing holders), called the Mechanism of Coordination on Orphan Medicinal Products (www.eurordis.org/en/content/moca). This group of 14 payers involves a patient representative in the steering group and associates one or more patient experts for each discussion on a product. This dialogue can take place at any time in the life cycle of the product and is usually an early dialogue during phase 1 or 2.

Creating opportunities for patient engagement through EU legislation and EMA policies is not sufficient. The organization then needs the right people who are able to engage in a meaningful way, and needs them in growing numbers. It has been a priority to invest in capacity building to raise the competences and skills of the patient community.

In 2006, the organization started the EURORDIS Summer School on Medicines Research & Development (https://openacademy.eurordis.org/summerschool/), which focuses on training on drug development, clinical trials, and EU regulatory and HTA affairs. All participants are selected based on an expression of interest, come from all over Europe, and are supported with fellowships. Summer School participants include young PhDs in biomedical or social research and patient advocates from Europe and beyond. Today, the Summer School has become a blend of online modules with concepts, terminology, reference articles, case studies and tutorials; a six-month pre-training with monthly webinars; and one week of face-to-face Master Classes and case studies. Over 12 years, over 400 alumni from 40 countries representing 75 diseases have been trained through the Summer School. The Summer School is in fact now part of a larger training programme, the EURORDIS Open Academy, which includes similar capacity building on translational research, bio bank and registries, exome and genome sequencing, gene editing, and the EURORDIS Winter School, which is also made up of a blend of online and in-person learning. After completing one of these trainings, the alumni continue their education with a mix of information provided by email, such as the monthly Therapeutic Report on activities of patient advocates at the EMA, through new tutorials and information resources online, and through regular webinars on specific topics open to all alumni. The alumni are empowered to act by themselves in their respective groups of affiliation at the national or European level. They are also a pool of experts who can be put forward to participate in protocol assistance at the EMA, in scientific advice on HTA, or on a disease-specific community advisory board. The major challenge for the coming years is to encourage and support learning from the experience of each other, working collaboratively across the alumni in topic groups to share good practices and useful tips, moving towards a structured knowledge management approach. Another challenge will be to maintain the commitment of the high-level and pro-bono faculty experts who provide the trainings.

The goal of these capacity-building programmes is to promote a generation of patient advocates who dare to take action and feel equipped to do so, to create a common culture across rare diseases and countries, and to develop a structure for how patients are involved in treatment development with academia, industry, regulators, HTA bodies and payers. Beyond the acquisition of knowledge and concrete practices, through these programmes EURORDIS aims to change behaviour, to empower patient representatives to take action and to feel legitimate and credible in doing so.

How Have Patient Advocates Shaped Policy on Healthcare in Europe for Rare Diseases? How Have Patient Advocates Established a Basis for Their Future Engagement in Care and Healthcare Organization?

Steps to launch the ERN in 2017 started in 2006. EURORDIS had been invited as observers to the EU High Level Group on Healthcare; this status was sufficient to enable them to play an active role. The organization also co-initiated a Task Force on Rare Diseases with Orphanet and the European Commission to start discussing national and European strategies on healthcare.

From 2003 to 2006, EURORDIS carried out two major quantitative surveys (https://www.eurordis.org/IMG/pdf/voice_12000_patients/EURORDISCARE_FULLBOOKr.pdf), each with 6000 patients and families across Europe for around 15 rare diseases. The first survey was on experiences of access to diagnosis and the second on experiences and expectations in accessing healthcare services for rare diseases. The results were published in the EURORDIS book *The Voice of 12,000 Patients*, bringing to light a huge mass of new knowledge showing and illustrating the reality for patients and what is expected.

From these data and from a series of workshops at the national and European level (www.eurordis.org/IMG/pdf/AMM-2008-Copenhagen-programme_old.pdf), EURORDIS was able to develop and adapt position papers on centres of expertise, European networking, registries and data collection.

In parallel and as early as the end of the 1990s, some countries were gaining experience in establishing and supporting centres of expertise for rare diseases, including the UK, Denmark and France, in the context of its national plan adopted in 2003.

These progressions by the patient movement and national policy experiences were brought to the Task Force on Rare Diseases and the High Level Group on Healthcare to shape the discussions and their outcomes. These two expert groups shaped what became part of the EU Directive on Patients' Rights to Cross-Border Healthcare regarding ERNs and rare diseases.

After the adoption of the Council Recommendation on an Action in the field of Rare Diseases in 2009, and the establishment of European Union Committee of Experts on Rare Diseases (EUCERD) 2010–2013, EURORDIS was also able to bring the patient experience and proposals to discussions. This Committee produced policy recommendations to be implemented by Member States, such as quality criteria for centres of expertise, quality criteria for the networking of these centres of expertise, data collection and registries, and social policy. This work was continued through the Commission Expert Group on Rare Diseases 2013–2016, and the Commission Expert Group on Cancer Control 2014–2017.

To support these policy activities and embed them at the national and European levels, the European Commission has supported four major projects:

1. EuroPlan 2007–2010 (led by ISS—Istituto Superiore di Sanità, Italy)
2. The Joint Action on Rare Diseases (JARD) 2010–2013 (led by Newcastle University, UK)
3. The Joint Action RD-Action 2014–2017 (led by INSERM, France), and
4. The Joint Action Rare Cancers (JARC) 2015–2018 (led by ESMO, Italy)

These Joint Actions brought together most EU Member States, some academic partners and EURORDIS—it was the first time an NGO was involved in Joint Actions with EU Member States (https://www.eurordis.org/content/joint-action-rd). These committees and joint community projects shaped the implementation of the Directive on Cross-Border Healthcare and provided the financial resources and framework for policy shaping and adoption.

Under the Joint Action RD-Action, the partners (EURORDIS, Newcastle University and Orphanet) were able to use the available collaborative resources to structure the approach, not only to create EU recommendations and guidelines under the Commission Expert Group for Rare Diseases, but also to support their implementation. For example, the development of the thematic grouping structure for the future rare disease ERNs specifically: engaging with the clinical community to form the networks according to these thematic groupings; building interoperability between the 24 ERNs; and leading on the organization of the patient community, led by EURORDIS, to structure patient involvement in all ERNs.

With the Evolution of Healthcare in Europe Came the Evolution of Patient Involvement

Knowledge is finite, but the thirst for knowledge is not. The rare disease community lives with the realities of the limitations of current clinical knowledge, and many within this community spend significant time searching for an expert who has appropriate knowledge and who can help. Rare diseases are rare, but experts are even rarer. Many members of the community spend a lifetime searching for an accurate diagnosis and enduring a never-ending cycle of ineffective, and often expensive, tests and treatments. Studies have shown that an accurate diagnosis for a rare condition is the direct result of a doctor considering the possibility of a rare disease or that the condition is as yet an undiagnosed disease, trigging an onward referral to an Expert Centre (Bhattacharya et al. 2014; Blöß et al. 2017; Coren et al. 2002; Hallal et al. 2012).

For patients and doctors alike, many do not know who the experts are, as this information sits outside their knowledge and that of their healthcare system. Fewer than 10 of the 28 EU Member States have a national accreditation system in place to identify and recognize their own experts. Through living every day with a rare disease, patients acquire a lifetime of knowledge and become 'experts by experience'. They hold valuable insights into disease burden, natural history, symptomology and what is effective to improve their quality of life. The opportunity to harness together the collective knowledge of the clinical community and the insights of 30 million experts by experience patients is here now and possible on a scale never before undertaken. EURORDIS has created a platform for these 'experts by experience' to come together and build their competencies in medicine, research and healthcare. All that was needed was the formal networking structures that connect experts, hospitals and countries, to be developed under European networks of experts who can share their knowledge, giving expert advice, collaborating together to acquire new knowledge and push the pace of research. And so the idea of the European Reference Networks (ERN) was born.

The public health needs of rare diseases are well documented, and it is recognized that no single country can meet the needs of all rare diseases alone (Hanna et al. 2017; Rath et al. 2017). Healthcare is best managed and coordinated locally, to best meet the needs of the local population. A minimum population size is needed to effectively organize services that are able to adequately address their population needs. The low incidence rates of many rare diseases mean healthcare services need to be organized on the basis of national populations. But still, for some rarer diseases this is not enough and they require cross-border collaboration, which traditionally had been undertaken on an informal basis, relying on personal networks and relationships. Individually each of the clinicians is each brilliant in their field of expertise, but together they know even more. The bold vision and far-reaching ambition of ERNs was to create a central platform for knowledge sharing, for expertise to travel and not the patient, formalizing these once informal exchanges of personal relationships. ERNs have the potential to revolutionize how healthcare is delivered and offer hope to improve the lives of 30 million people living with a rare disease in Europe, to have improved access to high-quality diagnosis, care and treatment, to share, care and one day even find the possibility of cures.

What Are the European Reference Networks in Reality?

ERNs are first and foremost healthcare networks. ERNs are inclusive, not exclusive; multi-disciplinary, not single professional 'members clubs', currently connecting 900 experts and 300 hospitals across the 26 Member States in the EU with the aim that all EU Member States are represented in all 24 ERNs. These networks span Europe, complementing national health systems, to create a new healthcare ecosystem, that extends the care chain from multi-disciplinary care in individual clinics to networked care (Rath et al. 2017) that reaches beyond traditional hospitals and their geographical catchment areas, across Europe and beyond, connecting

Europe's brightest and best experts. ERNs are harnessing the collective intellectual acumen and experiences of our leading lights, to guide care delivery locally to the patient.

Necessity Is the Mother of Innovation

ERNs were born out of the necessity to address the unmet needs of rare and complex diseases and highly specialized healthcare, where the patient population and experts are scattered. The needs of each rare disease patient are unique and push how care is delivered beyond the clinic and into the realm of extended healthcare networks. As this new model for healthcare takes root in national healthcare systems, extending the care chain from multidisciplinary team (MDT) to networked care, so too does the role and contribution of patients need to evolve. In MDT care, patients are a partner in their own care and invest their experiences, as experts by experience and their needs and experiences are the foundations on which a national health system should be built. Now with care extended above and beyond any single population or country, networked care requires the evolution of patients as leaders, developing their authority to represent the wider patient community globally (Rath et al. 2017; Sharma et al. 2017). This evolution in patient involvement sees a shift from where patient representatives draw their legitimacy, from being 'experts by experience' to being confident and competent in their authority to act and represent wider populations and the needs of groups of rare diseases beyond their own.

Is Patient Involvement Alive and Well in Healthcare?

Healthcare services are built from the grass roots of local populations, whether in big capitals—Berlin, Paris, Rome, Stockholm or Warsaw—or in rural communities or regional towns, from the north of Finland to the east of Romania and the south of Greece. Healthcare systems across this diverse EU landscape are all unique and each stands alone, with tailored legislation, structures and processes to meet the needs of their populations. One common unifying aspect to all healthcare systems is a patient-centred approach to the delivery of multi-disciplinary care, but this is not the case for patients involved in healthcare design and development. The degree to which this central and unifying concept has been developed fluctuates between clinicians, hospitals, regions and countries. Whilst the political and policy climate for patient involvement in the EU Regulation on Orphan Medicinal Products had been primed over the past 20 years, this has not yet been translated into healthcare, where patient involvement remains in its infancy. Experience and appreciation of patients as valued partners in a healthcare organization and their operational delivery varies from clinician to clinician, from hospital to hospital, from country to country. Patients in healthcare are the subject of discussion and treatment given, and not necessarily included in the design and delivery of healthcare services.

Patient involvement remains at best limited to the role as partners in their own care, and in many countries even being a partner in their own care has experienced an arrested development, with few countries systematically involving patients in healthcare design and delivery. However, there are some shining examples of best practice and innovative approaches reported of patients involved in service design and delivery. European Professional Societies have a long history of meaningful patient involvement in the evaluation and development of clinical guidelines (e.g. the European Respiratory Society, European Association for Urologists). A European Commission study which mapped the landscape of accreditation of highly specialized healthcare (PACE-ERN consortium's *European Union's National designation and assessment practices in highly specialized healthcare: Written Consultation and Onsite visits 2015*) reported that:

- in the U.K., patients are involved at all levels of policy, from needs identification, to specification of services, care pathway and treatment guidelines (cf. Chap. 8)
- in The Netherlands, patient representatives informing and endorsing national experts in a specific field of medicine
- in Sweden, hospitals had included the patient voice in service design as it was believed to result in greater clinical efficacy and service efficiency (cf. Chap. 6).

The 'seat' for patients around the table, where discussions on the specification of healthcare services are held, may be silently there, but meaningful patient involvement is never a given and is often forgotten. Having a patient representative 'sat around the table' fundamentally changes the dynamic of the dialogue and debate, and the basis and starting point for meaningful patient involvement. This enables greater public scrutiny and confidence, as it provides transparency to the discussions and decisions, but can be perceived as threatening for some.

ERNs are formed in a new space of healthcare at an EU level, where patients have been the consistent partner round the table in EU policy development, nurturing the birth of the ERN concept in the High-Level Group (2004) through to its germination into the Cross-Border Healthcare Directive. The small step from policy and legislative preparedness to ERN implementation was an important point where the patient community could unknowingly be left behind and left out of discussions and decision making, whilst professionals and administrators honour their commitment and take charge. Patients have been valued in creating the political need for ERNs, but this value, as an integral partner in delivery, is not a given and the rationale and reasoning for being included remains a constant battle. Patient involvement in the delivery of healthcare at an EU level, inherited from EURORDIS' legacy of patient involvement in EU medicine regulation, was always ensured. However, whilst the 'gun' of patient involvement in healthcare delivery was loaded, it had yet to be fired.

Patients' Added Value

What Is the Added Value of Patient Involvement in Healthcare?

Patient experience has been demonstrated to be the single most important element in assessing the quality of healthcare services, as it has been evidenced to be a predictor of survival rates in some cancers (Gupta et al. 2013, 2014). Studies have also evidenced that patient involvement in healthcare services and their evaluation and designation improves the relevance and quality of the healthcare services and improves their ability to meet patient needs (Brett et al. 2014; Cornman and White 2017; Fønhus et al. 2018; Sharma et al. 2017; Tokhi et al. 2018). Patient representatives are the best people to say what outcomes are important to them, when making decisions about health and judgements about decisions that balance the different benefits and side effects from some treatments.

Patients can be included and provide input at each step in the commissioning process. They are the consistent stakeholders in healthcare and research, from the identification of their needs, to the creating of new policy and legalization, through to receiving care after service change has been completed. Patients are the only stakeholders to hold a vested interest in all parts of the health research and care continuum—from basic research, to clinical trials, through healthcare delivery, to the reporting of the outcome of care and living with the results of that care.

What Is the Mandate for Patients to Be Involved in European Reference Networks?

ERNs are hailed as a new dawn in healthcare, driving access to high-quality diagnosis, care and treatment for all. The European Commission (EC) ERN Delegated Acts form the legal basis for ERNs to be established. This legalization was formed from EUCERD Recommendations on ERNs and Quality of Centres of Expertise. A patient-partnership approach forms the backbone of ERNs, ensuring that they empower and involve patients. All of the EUCERD recommendations were used to form the legalization except for two recommendations as they specifically focused on rare diseases, and officially the scope of ERNs is broader than rare diseases, also covering complex conditions and highly specialized interventions.

Specifically, the two EUCERD recommendations that did not make it into the legislation were:

1. *RD ERNs must cover a group of rare diseases and not just one, to meet the need that: all 8000 rare diseases have a home under one of the networks*;

2. *Patients' involvement is more fundamental in the rare disease field due to the limited body of knowledge, experience and expertise, and a higher level of involvement of patients in the decision- and opinion-making process is essential to ensure successfully development of RD ERNs.*

Due to the importance of these two recommendations, the expert group issued an Addendum to the original EUCERD recommendations, to underscore the importance of two policy recommendations. The Addendum has been one of the most significant policy documents published for the rare disease community, as it directed the clinical community to form networks based on a thematic grouping, instead of structuring their communities under a single disease area, and, more importantly for the patient community, planted the flag of patient involvement in ERNs as experts and co-producers of knowledge, in the new space where ERNs would be established. The Addendum is the mandate for patient representatives to be included in the ERNs as equal partners. Whilst patient representatives are not 'legal members', as the legalization was formed to structure how hospitals and their clinical leads organized themselves under an ERN, patients are now also accepted as members, sitting on network boards, clinical committees and working groups. Embedding patients' representatives in the networks is a significant and hard-won achievement based on the legacy of 20 years of preparation of patients' representatives being credible partners.

The clinical community had the luxury of legal requirements set out in the EC ERN Delegated Acts that set standards for the formation of ERNs and the organization of their members. The lack of recognition of patient representatives as ERN members in the legislation required rules of procedure to be developed and to specify the role of patient representatives active in an ERN and the processes for governing recruitment, and to support their involvement in the networks. EURORDIS, its members and the patient community needed to work together to organize and ensure that patient involvement in ERNs was optimized, instead of leaving it to personal relationships or chance. Together patients are stronger as a community and united in their common needs. EURORDIS needs to maintain the political ownership of the public health unmet needs of rare diseases in the EU.

Establishing Credibility for Patients as Experts and Leaders in Healthcare

Credibility needed to be secure in the first step of ERN implementation, to give confidence in the new networks as trusted, expert networks for them to be accepted as the go-to reference point for Member States and European institutions. Following a decade of policy and legislative gestation and mounting anticipation, all eyes turned to the EC to see if the 'good idea' which is ERNs could be turned into a reality. The first step in implementation was the 2014 European Commission Call for Tender for a 'Technical proposal for an Assessment Manual and Toolbox (AMT) for European Reference Networks (ERNs)', which set out the application process and assessment framework for all ERN applications used in the first call for ERN applications. EURORDIS stepped forward, on behalf of the rare disease community, to form and lead the Consortium—PACE-ERN with the European Organisation of Hospitals (HOPE) and Accreditation Canada International that was successful in securing this contract. This is an essential element illustrating how patients as experts of experience take an operational role in shaping ERN (https://www.eurordis.org/news/eurordis-wins-call-tender-develop-ern-manual-toolbox). EURORDIS demonstrated how patient representatives are experts and have a legitimate place in the formation of ERNs and establish them as patient-centred networks.

ERNs have created a new space for clinicians and patients to work together with a common purpose and shared goal. ERNs started with a blank page which was an opportunity to put all stakeholders on the same footing, working in thematic groups and not individual rare disease. This space enabled patients to be accepted as equal partners and leaders for the first time. EURORDIS demonstrated, by example, that patient representatives are competent experts and leaders with technical knowledge; within the scope of the PACE-ERN consortium, they literally wrote the manual on ERNs and how to define the assessment framework. This manual serves as the operational criteria for networks. These operational criteria defined the standards, measures and evidence that networks must achieve in order to be in line with the legislation. EURORDIS and the PACE consortium were able to articulate these operational criteria as standards in all ERN activities and specify how they would be met and assessed, positioning the important and valued role of patients in all ERN activities, based on the published evidence-base and Member State best practice experience. The operational criteria expressed the active and meaningful involvement of patients in all ERN activities: strategic planning, prioritization and decision making; evaluation of expert centres; quality, safety and data protection assurance; patient-centred care and choice; communication and information sharing; and patient experience feedback. The operational criteria are not just a blueprint for future ERNs but influenced how clinicians would think about ERNs and started to create the culture of the future networks. The operational criteria respected and recognized patients as experts and valued their contributions, creating the dimension of patient involvement as an equal partner in designing and delivering ERNs.

How Was Patient Involvement in European Reference Networks Organized?

Networks, simply put, are groups of relationships. The quality of these relationships has a direct influence on the quality of the care delivered under the network. Brokering successful partnerships between clinicians and patients is essential to the success of ERNs. The formation of ERNs, in their scope and ambition, was orchestrated by the Joint Action RD-Action partners engaging both the clinical and patient community to develop the first ERN applications for the EC call for networks in 2016. Newcastle University, one of the Joint Action RD-Action partners, coordinated the interests of the clinical community across the EU through a matchmaker programme, where clinicians wishing to be a member of an ERN connected together to form a network application for a specific group of rare diseases; and EURORDIS set up new patient forums—European Patient Advisory Groups (ePAGs)—one for each ERN, that aligned and organized the patient community under the scope of each of the ERN applications. In this period where applications were developed, the patient community was asked in which grouping they felt their rare disease was best situated. In this early stage of the ERNs forming, patient representatives had a voice in defining the scope of each of the ERNs.

EURORDIS in collaboration with the rare disease community established 24 ePAGs forums to optimize the involvement of patients and ensure unity, solidarity and equity of patient representatives of the rare disease in the 24 ERNs. The ePAG patient representatives formed a bridge between the ERN boards and governance committees and the wider patient communities. Patient representatives took part in an election process to be the named representative of their community, but as the size and scope of ERNs become clearer, this approach was expanded to co-opt patient representatives. This was to ensure that each of the respective ERN's disease-specific core networks had sufficient parent representation, of people with experience of living with a rare disease covered in each core network. In addition, each ERN network board and working group also had a patient representative working in partnership with the clinicians in the groups. From the early days of developing network applications to the newly established 24 ERNs, patient involvement in ERNs has grown to over 300 patient representatives. Patient involvement in the clinical networks has never been undertaken on such a scale before.

The ePAG patient involvement model was built on experience and legitimacy of patient involvement gains over the past 20 years in the Orphan Medicinal Products regulations, to position and mobilize the rare disease community to be central actors in the new and emerging EU healthcare landscape. For the first time, patients and clinicians collaborated on forming the networks from the initial idea to building the networks in reality. Patient representatives are co-founders of the networks, co-authors of network applications, designated as co-chairs of working groups and clinical committees, and granted voting rights on network boards. The votes of a few patient representatives in any network will not ultimately influence or change the outcome of the voting, but it does clearly express that patient representatives in ERNs are recognized as equal partners. Credit must be given to the ERN Coordinators who unquestionably and without hesitation embrace patient involvement in the ERNs. The healthy culture of patient involvement in ERNs has been defined by the ERN Coordinators embracing active and meaningful patient involvement in the networks and is felt throughout the network governance structures and committees, helping to shape how all 900 members include patients in their discussions and activities. It is still early days and networks are still forming, but a culture of meaningful patient involvement has started to blossom. The impact of not being a legal partner but an invited one has, however, resulted in some clinicians not involving patients or involving them in a meaningful way. More needs to be done to bring on side the remaining clinicians who still see patients as subject to their actions and not as valued stakeholders who have much-needed expertise and knowledge to share. EURORDIS has the opportunity to demonstrate the value of patient involvement and now need to show proof of concept, as was successfully done in the EU regulation of medicinal products.

On the historic eve of the decision of the first ERN applications, when confidence needed to be reassured in the ERNs, EURORDIS called Member States to approve all 24 ERN applications and ensure that no patient community was left behind. All 24 ERNs together form the minimum infrastructure required to meet the multi-system needs of many rare diseases. The validation of the proposed structure of the ERNs by the patient community gave political weight to the decision to approve all ERNs based on the needs of the community. Patient representatives have been an active partner in the needs assessment of rare diseases, in defining the policy behind ERNs, in defining the blueprint for ERNs, and in co-authoring and co-leading applications defining their needs.

To drive the benefits of the ERN, the champions and leaders of the patient and clinical community now need to step forward and be involved in shaping the networks' success, to change culture and drive home the expected benefits in their respective communities. Patient representatives, clinicians and researchers share a common ambition to find answers, treatments and ultimately cures for people living with a rare disease, to enable them to lead better lives. Whilst patients share this common ambition, EURORDIS draw on different experiences, expertise and knowledge, and see the world from different perspectives. Understanding the patient representative's role in an ERN will enable the patient—clinician partnership to deliver on this shared ambition, successfully aligning these perspectives, experiences, expertise and knowledge, and optimizing the investment of resources—time, energy and funding—to fully unlock the true potential of ERNs. The successful launch of 24 ERNs was a seismic change in how healthcare is delivered in the EU and is undoubtedly due to the successful partnership and collaboration of patients and clinicians.

Supporting effective and successful partnerships between patients and clinicians now needs a sensitive hand, as there is a huge variation in the experience of clinicians in engaging patient representatives, in the perception of the scope and remit of patient involvement, and in the confidence and competency of patient representatives in formal executive committees and engaging in network board discussions. The role of patient representatives in ERNs is pivotal in presenting and representing the voice of the wider patient community in network discussions and activities and, therefore, bringing the community's experiences of living with a rare disease directly to ERN Board discussions and decisions.

Patient representatives have a dual role to play in providing the patient perspective in ERNs.

1. At a global level, as patient leaders, they need to ensure that strategic and operational discussions are patient-centred; the transparency of decisions and outcomes; the assurance of the safety and quality of patient care are delivered, as well as a two-way communication between the ERN governance and the patient community.
2. At an individual level, as experts by experience, to inform the disease-specific clinical network committees of the needs and experiences of people living with a specific rare disease; the development of clinical protocols and healthcare pathways, as well as the prioritization and development of research and educational activities.

Now, in the early stages of ERN deployment, support is needed for patient representatives to step up to the expectations and develop the competences needed to be patient leaders. To build the capacity for patient representatives to be active in the ERNs and empower them to be confident in sharing their experiences and expertise, EURORDIS is building on the experiences of the EURORDIS Summer School and EURORDIS Winter School to create a Leadership Programme for patient representatives active in the ERNs. Patient representatives must develop as leaders of their community and represent this community in the network executive committees, being confident to influence when they do not hold the authority of a legally recognized position in the ERNs, and develop the technical knowledge of ERN activities—in developing guidelines, patient pathways and research protocols, and defining patient-reported outcomes.

Patient Testimony

A patient representative involved in eUROGEN, the ERN for rare uro-genital diseases provided this testimony:

> *We find our journey as patient representatives in the eUROGEN ERN for rare uro-genital diseases and complex conditions needing highly specialised surgery, has opened many new opportunities both for patients and for clinicians. It is the first time, that as patients, we have been welcomed in clinical meetings and have been treated as peers.*
>
> *In the beginning, it was very difficult, due to our prejudice of not being listened as patient representatives by the medical audience. We started with some drawbacks: my own rare diseases has not been included in the networks scope. We did not feel initially welcome or understood by the clinical leads and every meeting was a stress. Thanks to the patience of network coordinating team and EURODIS, we learnt it was possible to share and discuss different experiences, have constructive discussions and learn from each other. This made us feel easier and made us find the best way to proceed to achieve the aims of the rare disease patient community. We both can say that ERN Coordinating Team and EURORDIS guidance has made us grow a lot both from a point of view of advocacy and in personal confidence. We both believe that the whole project of the ePAGs is quite revolutionary and goes well with the development of the ERNs. The journey that we are enjoying together with our traveling companions is very formative and is opening new perspectives, and we feel that the revolution coming up with the ERN's will go far and change the approach to the way of applying diagnosis and treatments.*
>
> *Thanks to this experience, we can now go on stage and present e-UROGEN ERN in many public events, showing how this project will change patient's quality of life and will make knowledge travel more easily. We have started to work with our Ministry of Health and with many hospitals to anchor eUROGEN ERN in our Health Care System.*

We are very proud to say the patient-professional partnership is continuously improving in the network. In the recent network annual meeting, we saw a high participation of professionals and found the meeting very constructive and harmonious, proving how important it is to work as a team putting the patient's best interest as the main objective.

Specific examples of how we have contributed to the network:

1. *Engage with the network and successfully influence the professionals to extend the scope of the network to include Interstitial Cystitis (IC) as an area of expertise in the ERN. This was a big success for our ePAG.*
2. *Contributed to identifying appropriate outcome measures for the disease areas in the network, ensuring they are directly relevant to the patients need and expectations, particularly in a sensitive area like urogenital diseases where the impact on the quality of life of the patients concerned can be devastating.*
3. *Contributing to on the development of clinical guidelines, transitional of care and updating the Orphanet coding to better reflect the needs of patients living with a rare urogenital disease.*
4. *Representing the network at international conferences and raising the awareness of the ERNs and the benefits they can offer our community.*

   We are thankful for building the competency and confidence of patient representatives to actively contribute into the ERNs and discuss with the professionals as peers.

Conclusion

The EU landscape is a rich and diverse place, one that should be valued and not taken for granted. The EU is a merging of different worlds, cultures and experiences, in which the variation in healthcare practices should be celebrated, as this variation in practices and approach is the hot bed for innovation and new emerging best practice. We should only standardize an approach to organizing healthcare where there is clear evidence of added value and evidence that it improved the outcomes to diagnosis, care and treatment. Often criticized as a world of compromise, the reality is that compromise at the EU level often results in collaboration and cooperation between countries at a national level, unified under a common goal to meet a common need. Once support has been secured in the EU, it has the potential to turn a 'good idea' into a 'game changer' for society. ERNs are one such 'good idea' that has successfully secured unprecedented support from all stakeholders—the European Commission, Member States, regulators, payers, research and clinical networks, and the rare disease community. In 2017, 24 ERNs were launched and the opportunity to revolutionize how healthcare was delivered, breaking the isolation of patients and siloed experts, and helping to reduce the current inequality in care reported between rare diseases and between Member States.

EURORDIS and the rare disease patient community can look back and see the role they played in the creation of these networks and will undoubtedly have a hand in their success. In establishing the ERNs, the rare disease movement, collaborating together with all stakeholders, has made ground in tackling the public health needs of people living with a rare disease. The mobilization of the patient voice to express the community's needs and shape EU policy and legislation has the opportunity through the ERN to improve national healthcare services for the benefit of local populations. The mature experience collected over the past 20 years of patient involvement in the EU Regulation on Orphan Medicinal Products has now been drawn on in the healthcare sphere. Together, the rare disease community can forge a new way forward, one that is built on voluntary cooperation and mutual respect, to shape healthcare and medicine development to meet the public health needs of rare diseases, which so many people face.

Note

1. Reproduced with permission from EURORDIS.

References

Bhattacharya, K., S. Balasubramaniam, Y.S. Choy, et al. 2014. Overcoming the barriers to diagnosis of Morquio A syndrome. *Orphanet Journal of Rare Diseases* 9: 192. https://doi.org/10.1186/s13023-014-0192-7.

Blöß, S., C. Klemann, A.K. Rother, et al. 2017. Diagnostic needs for rare diseases and shared prediagnostic phenomena: Results of a German-wide expert Delphi survey. *PLoS One* 12 (2): e0172532. https://doi.org/10.1371/journal.pone.0172532.

Brett, J., S. Staniszewska, C. Mockford, S. Herron-Marx, J. Hughes, C. Tysall, and R. Suleman. 2014. Mapping the impact of patient and public involvement on health and social care research: A systematic review. *Health Expectations* 17: 637–650. https://doi.org/10.1111/j.1369-7625.2012.00795.x.

Coren, M.E., M. Meeks, I. Morrison, R.M. Buchdahl, and A. Bush. 2002. Primary ciliary dyskinesia: Age at diagnosis and symptom history. *Acta Paediatrica* 91 (6): 667–669.

Cornman, D.H., and White, C.M. 2017. *Discerning the perception and impact of patients involved in evidence-based practice center key informant interviews.* Agency for Healthcare Research and Quality (US), Report No.: 17-EHC032-EF. AHRQ Methods for Effective Health Care.

European Union Council Recommendation on an action in the field of rare diseases. 2009. June 8. eur-lex.europa.eu/LexUriServ/LexUriServ.do?uri=OJ:C:2009:151:0007:0010:EN:PDF.

EURORDIS Activity Report 2017. www.eurordis.org/publication/eurordis-activity-report-2017.

——— Volunteer charter. www.eurordis.org/volunteering#tabs-2.

Fønhus, M.S., T.K. Dalsbø, M. Johansen, A. Fretheim, H. Skirbekk, and S.A. Flottorp. 2018. Patient-mediated interventions to improve professional practice. *Cochrane Database of Systematic Reviews* 11 (9): CD012472. https://doi.org/10.1002/14651858.CD012472.pub2.

Gupta, D., C.G. Lis, and M. Rodeghier. 2013. Can patient experience with service quality predict survival in colorectal cancer? *Journal for Healthcare Quality* 35: 37–43.

Gupta, D., M. Rodeghier, and C.G. Lis. 2014. Patient satisfaction with service quality as a predictor of survival outcomes in breast cancer. *Support Care Cancer* 22: 129–134.

Hallal, C., C.O. Kieling, D.L. Nunes, C.T. Ferreira, G. Peterson, S.G. Barros, C.A. Arruda, J.C. Fraga, and H.A. Goldani. 2012. Diagnosis, misdiagnosis, and associated diseases of achalasia in children and adolescents: A twelve-year single center experience. *Pediatric Surgery International* 28 (12): 1211–1217. https://doi.org/10.1007/s00383-012-3214-3. Epub 2012 Nov 8.

Hanna, E., C. Rémuzat, P. Auquier, and M. Toumi. 2017. Gene therapies development: Slow progress and promising prospect. *Journal of Market Access & Health Policy* 5 (1): 1265293. Published 2017 Jan 3. https://doi.org/10.1080/20016689.2017.1265293.

Rath, A., V. Salamon, S. Peixoto, V. Hivert, M. Laville, B. Segrestin, E.A.M. Neugebauer, M. Eikermann, V. Bertele, S. Garattini, J. Wetterslev, R. Banzi, J.C. Jakobsen, S. Djurisic, C. Kubiak, J. Demotes-Mainard, and C. Gluud. 2017. A systematic literature review of evidence-based clinical practice for rare diseases: What are the perceived and real barriers for improving the evidence and how can they be overcome? *Trials* 18 (1): 556. https://doi.org/10.1186/s13063-017-2287-7.

Sharma, A.E., M. Knox, V.L. Mleczko, and J.N. Olayiwola. 2017. The impact of patient advisors on healthcare outcomes: A systematic review. *BMC Health Services Research* 17 (1): 693. https://doi.org/10.1186/s12913-017-2630-4.

Tokhi, M., L. Comrie-Thomson, J. Davis, A. Portela, M. Chersich, and S. Luchters. 2018. Involving men to improve maternal and newborn health: A systematic review of the effectiveness of interventions. *PLoS One* 13 (1): e0191620. https://doi.org/10.1371/journal.pone.0191620. eCollection 2018.

10

Discussion and Conclusion

Marie-Pascale Pomey

Through seven different health systems and the experience of EURORDIS, we were able to highlight that patient engagement is a movement which is increasingly embedded in the DNA of health systems at clinical, organizational or strategic levels. Viewed by some as a fad, this social innovation is likely to continue and lead us to completely rethink the way our health systems operate.

Indeed, by reading these different case stories, we saw that each country has taken advantage of particular windows of opportunity, anchored in health systems with specific values, social norms, laws and regulations, leading to different and original ways of conceiving patient integration. This has also led to occasional differences in vocabulary.

Thus, in France and Quebec, part of the patient inclusion movement was initially passed through legislation, including the legal obligation to incorporate user representatives in committees (Pomey and Ghadi 2009). However, this movement, rooted in a perspective of health democracy,

M.-P. Pomey (✉)
School of Public Health, University of Montreal, Montreal, QC, Canada
e-mail: marie-pascale.pomey@umontreal.ca

M.-P. Pomey et al. (eds.), *Patient Engagement*, Organizational Behaviour in Healthcare,
https://doi.org/10.1007/978-3-030-14101-1_10

has shown its limits since user representatives, chosen from patient associations (France) or the general population (Quebec), lacked the necessary knowledge to effectively share their experiences for improving the organization of services and the quality and safety of care at organizational or clinical levels. Thus, in parallel with this model, another movement has emerged, namely that of partnership with patients and their families, based on the mobilization of knowledge acquired from living with diseases and health system experiences.

In Quebec, this movement began with an interdisciplinary course taught to future health professionals and a patient recruited by the University of Montreal Faculty of Medicine. Rooted in the academic world, a place of knowledge transfer and creation and skills acquisition *par excellence*, the recognition of patients' experiential knowledge took on a symbolic value as being complementary to professionals' scientific knowledge. This academic breakthrough provided legitimacy to the movement, which made patient inclusion more easily exportable to health care settings and research. In turn, it was only in the second phase that public authorities recognized this contribution, then gradually implemented a number of structuring initiatives to facilitate the implementation of care and services partnerships in the health system, whether in health institutions or in primary care (*Centre de pédagogie appliquée aux sciences de la santé* 2013).

In Scandinavia, Sweden is known for excellent work performed by universities in terms of patient engagement (Fredriksson et al. 2018). The movement of patient engagement in care has permeated through the clinical level, taking into consideration self-care and co-care practices. Furthermore, not only were tools developed to support the movement, but also technologies were made available to help move from the patient-centred care paradigm to one of self- and co-care.

In both the United Kingdom and the United States, the legitimacy of patient engagement was also channelled through research funding to ensure the alignment between invested sums and real patient needs. At the same time, through an applied approach, patient engagement took shape in the health system to develop evidence regarding patient oriented-practices and ensure that quality of care effectively improves patient experience.

Australia, however, particularly integrated patient engagement into the system level in order to foster patient engagement in accreditation standards. The Australian model allows patients to be engaged in Health Standard Organization (HSO) governance, quality improvement initiatives and research.

Even though these diverse experiences were not always followed up by assessment studies (to indisputably prove how this knowledge can contribute to meeting health system challenges), a growing number of publications report significant improvement thanks to the participation of patients, relatives and citizens (Brett et al. 2014; Cornman and White 2017; Sharma et al. 2017; Fønhus et al. 2018). As highlighted by Rosener (1981), in such cases, assessment is complex. Indeed, clearly defining what is meant by patient engagement (PE) is not always a simple task, since there is no consensus on evaluation criteria and measurement methods, not to mention that tools remain rare as well (Staniszewska et al. 2008; Boivin 2019). Thus, an increasing number of tools and outcome indicators are currently being developed to measure effects (Mockford et al. 2012; Sanders et al. 2013; Phillips et al. 2015) and processes (Barr et al. 2015; Abelson et al. 2016).

This book's chapters, along with the scientific literature on patient engagement, show us that this breakthrough innovation (Boudier et al. 2012; Richards et al. 2013; Vincent and Antoine 2018) substantially modifies power relations between health professionals and patients and the very way we design our health systems, despite the on-going debate on knowledge validity (Mockford et al. 2012; Sanders et al. 2013; Brett et al. 2014; Sharma et al. 2017). However, it is important to remain vigilant about the inclusive capacity of PE for less advantaged groups. Indeed, as touched upon in previous chapters, literacy problems stand in the way of including some populations in discussions. Therefore, it remains crucial to put in place mechanisms that would allow vulnerable populations to take part in partnerships with various stakeholders in the health system, universities and the research world. Ensuring diverse points of view and limiting exclusion are critical points to bear in mind in this area.

Another issue is the notion of sustainability in patient engagement. For example, Quebec explicitly decided that patient advisors were not entitled to financial compensation, but could be compensated for their travel and meals at best. This stands as a real problem to ensure the participation of people who cannot afford to spend free time on activities related to improving the health system. Ethical and equitable reflection should take place to consider different scenarios. In mental health, for instance, thanks to their participation in the health system, peer helpers are reintegrated into society and find true recognition of their knowledge which is conducive to their recovery. For financially vulnerable people, who cannot afford the luxury of taking time off work, it would be appropriate to think of citizen days—such as sick days—to allow employed people to take time off without financial loss. Such a model could yield a return on investment which has yet to be demonstrated, but seems promising.

Moreover, this movement is reinforced by the emergence of connected health and artificial intelligence. Indeed, as Topol wrote in 2016 in *The Patient Will See You Now: The Future of Medicine is in Your Hands* (Topol 2016), miniaturization and lower costs of medical technology, as well as their accessibility via the Internet, allow patients to use them without having to go through health professionals. For example, in the field of genetics, it is possible to order online genetic sequencing tests such as AccuMetrics/Viaguard, EasyDNA and 23andMe that evaluate risks associated with certain so-called genetic diseases by way of simple saliva collection. That said, because these tests do not all measure the same things and use various measurement methods, patients end up acquiring information about themselves which has not been collected in a clinical context. While current non-targeted complete genome screening is difficult to understand, access to artificial intelligence makes it possible to combine them with complementary data on the environment, lifestyle, personal and family history of patients and to analyse it according to other databases, thus making it possible to specify particular risks.

What wrote Topol is also found in interventional and therapeutic diagnostic imaging. In the example of ultrasounds, technology has miniaturized to the point where a probe connected to a smart phone makes the procedure accessible and portable. From the phone, it is possible to send data to be examined more precisely, or to be stored on a server and then analysed by machine learning algorithms. This technology can used by non-experts as diagnosis does not require the intervention of health professionals. In a relatively near future, it may even be possible for interventions to be easily performed by patients themselves. Examples include treatments for kidney or gallbladder stones, not only thanks to the miniaturization and precision of extracorporeal lithotripsy, but also the use of a thrombolytic following a stroke through access to remote diagnosis and medication acquisition within three hours.

In 2018, Uber Health was created to help the 3.6 million Americans who miss their doctor appointments due to a lack of reliable transportation and drive the 30 per cent no-show rate. The idea is to partner with health care organizations to provide reliable, comfortable transportation for patients through a dashboard and an Uber Health application program interface (API). This allows for transportation to be scheduled for appointments while still at the health care facility. Multiple rides can be scheduled and managed at the same time, all from a single dashboard. (https://www.uber.com/newsroom/uber-health/).

Drawing inspiration from the model that Uber has put in place in the field of transport (https://www.uberhealth.com), the concept could go even further. One could imagine Uber, or another company, setting up a health system parallel to the one that currently exists. Indeed, with ageing populations, the increase in the prevalence of chronic diseases and the retirement of many health professionals, one could consider that chronic disease patients and retired health professionals could offer their services to support patients in disease management through online platforms with connected objects, allowing faster, more agile and efficient virtual consultations than what is currently available. Funding for such devices could be provided by employers, as is currently the case in Quebec with Dialogue (https://dialogue.co/fr/), which offers a quick online consultation service to employees by health professionals who, after diagnosis, can prescribe and place drug orders directly with the patient in a matter of minutes.

Access to health with connected objects, intelligent electronic health records and interactive platforms will facilitate the increasingly important revolutionary movement of civil society and patient engagement in the health system. Indeed, data will no longer be exclusively held by health professionals, but by people who monitor their own health status. People will determine with whom they are willing to share their data, which may very well be entities other than those currently making up our health systems. Some health technology companies already provide feedback and advice on monitored physiological data through artificial intelligence. Again, if health systems—as they are today—do not find ways to be more agile and respond quickly to new population needs, they risk losing a major battle. This is all the more disturbing when noticing the general lack of interest currently shown by health professionals towards these new technologies (Pare et al. 2018), while citizens and patients seem to be increasingly interested in them (Pare et al. 2018).

Probably, by the time this manual is published, many new ways of designing health systems will already be implemented, and the role of patients will have grown in importance, not only through recognizing their experiential knowledge, but also integrating their ability to share their data. The web giants known as GAFAM (Google, Apple, Facebook, Amazon, Microsoft) or BATX (Baidu, Alibaba, Tencent and Xiaomi) are making no mistake about it and are already implementing strategies to access population data collected via smartphones or connected objects. The arrival of ultra-fast mobile telecommunication transmission systems such as 5G, available in all parts of the world, will only strengthen this capacity. With expert systems in place, these giants may need to know information about people before they become aware of it. The sale of its data could be of interest to insurers who, in turn, may be reluctant to cover people whose risks of becoming ill have been determined through artificial intelligence. What recourse will those people have if public health systems are no longer there to cover them? Could a citizen counter-power be created against these web giants, and would it be able to reverse this commercial trend? What protection could there be for the poorest without access to all these technologies or understanding of the new rules?

In this context, publicly funded health systems must urgently reflect on how they can evolve and become a real learning, agile and flexible system capable of competing with tech giants. Today's hospital structures are set to explode, and tomorrow's professions will also have nothing to do with those of today.

Indeed, technology may be able to overtake man in terms of diagnostic reasoning and computer- robot-assisted interventions. In this respect, the positioning of health professionals, in particular, physicians as masters of medical knowledge and reasoning is being called into question. Therefore, the place of human relations will have to be at the heart of our systems' concerns. By supporting patients through complex decisions brought about by technologies, professionals will be able to find their place. They are led to become intermediaries between intelligent and rational machines and human beings with emotional support needs. It is at this level that the partnership of care and services makes sense by positioning health professionals and experienced patients as supporters of individuals to help them prevent health problems or live with chronic health conditions that require behavioural changes.

Finally, this revolution in digital health care carries along important moral and ethical issues that are reminded by the Montreal Declaration on Artificial Intelligence (https://www.montrealdeclaration-responsibleai.com/the-declaration). We must be collectively vigilant so that technology remains at the service of human beings and not the other way around. In a world where profit comes before the well-being of individuals, there is reason to worry.

References

Abelson, J., K. Li, G. Wilson, K. Shields, C. Schneider, and S. Boesveld. 2016. Supporting quality public and patient engagement in health system organizations: Development and usability testing of the Public and Patient Engagement Evaluation Tool. *Health Expectations: An International Journal of Public Participation in Health Care and Health Policy* 19 (4): 817–827.

Barr, P.J., I. Scholl, P. Bravo, M.J. Faber, G. Elwyn, and M. McAllister. 2015. Assessment of patient empowerment—A systematic review of measures. *PLoS One* 10 (5): e0126553.

Boivin, A. 2019. From craft to reflective art and science; comment on "metrics and evaluation tools for patient engagement in healthcare organization- and system-level decision-making: A systematic review". *International Journal of Health Policy and Management* 8 (2): 124–127.

Boudier, F., F. Bensebaa, and A. Jablanczy. 2012. L'émergence du patient-expert: une perturbation innovante. *Innovations* 39 (3): 13–25.

Brett, J., S. Staniszewska, C. Mockford, S. Herron-Marx, J. Hughes, C. Tysall, and R. Suleman. 2014. A systematic review of the impact of patient and public involvement on service users, researchers and communities. *Patient* 7 (4): 387–395.

Centre de pédagogie appliquée aux sciences de la santé. 2013. *Guide d'implantation du partenariat de soins et de services, vers une collaboration optimale entre intervenants et avec le patient.* Montréal, QC: CPASS, Université de Montréal.

Cornman, D., and C. White. 2017. *Discerning the perception and impact of patients involved in evidence-based practice center key informant interviews.* Rockville, MD: Agency for Healthcare Research and Quality.

Fønhus, M.S., T.K. Dalsbø, M. Johansen, A. Fretheim, H. Skirbekk, and S.A. Flottorp. 2018. Patient-mediated interventions to improve professional practice. *Cochrane Database of Systematic Reviews* 11 (9). https://doi.org/10.1002/14651858.

Fredriksson, M., M. Eriksson, and J.Q. Tritter. 2018. Involvement that makes an impact on healthcare: Perceptions of the Swedish public. *Scandinavian Journal of Public Health* 46 (4): 471–477.

Mockford, C., S. Staniszewska, F. Griffiths, and S. Herron-Marx. 2012. The impact of patient and public involvement on UK NHS health care: A systematic review. *International Journal for Quality in Health Care* 24 (1): 28–38.

Pare, G., C. Leaver, and C. Bourget. 2018. Diffusion of the digital health self-tracking movement in Canada: Results of a national survey. *Journal of Medical Internet Research* 20 (5): e177.

Phillips, N.M., M. Street, and E. Haesler. 2015. A systematic review of reliable and valid tools for the measurement of patient participation in healthcare. *BMJ Quality & Safety* 25 (2): 110–117.

Pomey, M.-P., and V. Ghadi. 2009. La participation des usagers au fonctionnement des établissements de santé: une dynamique encore à construire. *Santé, Société et Solidarité* 2: 53–61.

Richards, T., V.M. Montori, F. Godlee, P. Lapsley, and D. Paul. 2013. Let the patient revolution begin. *BMJ* 346: f2614.

Rosener, J.B. 1981. User-oriented evaluation: A new way to view citizen participation. *The Journal of Applied Behavioral Science* 17 (4): 583–596.

Sanders, A.R.J., I. van Weeghel, M. Vogelaar, W. Verheul, R.H.M. Pieters, N.J. de Wit, and J.M. Bensing. 2013. Effects of improved patient participation in primary care on health-related outcomes: A systematic review. *Family Practice* 30 (4): 365–378.

Sharma, A.E., M. Knox, V.L. Mleczko, and J.N. Olayiwola. 2017. The impact of patient advisors on healthcare outcomes: A systematic review. *BMC Health Services Research* 17 (1): 693.

Staniszewska, S., S. Herron-Marx, and C. Mockford. 2008. Measuring the impact of patient and public involvement: The need for an evidence base. *International Journal for Quality in Health Care* 20 (6): 373–374.

Topol, E. 2016. *The Patient Will See You Now: The Future of Medicine is in Your Hands*. New York, NY: Basic Books.

Vincent, D., and B. Antoine. 2018. A Canadian take on the international patient engagement revolution. *Healthcare Quarterly* 21 (Special Issue): 1–6.

11

Future Directions for Patient Knowledge: A Citizen-Patient Reflection

Carolyn Canfield

We have now examined international examples of the gradual infusion of patient knowledge into the content and conduct of every sector of healthcare. These chapters present a remarkably rich diversity of approaches to recognizing the legitimacy of patient contributions, both as generators of information and as participants in knowledge translation. Patients and caregivers are influencing every component of healthcare systems, but not universally, and not even in similar ways across jurisdictions for a particular setting. And nor should they. All of these healthcare systems reflect their different historical origins, cultural settings, iconic events and leaders and current troubles. Patient populations also carry a legacy coloured by distinct leadership, crisis and resolution, legal heritage, organizational sponsorship, cohesion, internal conflict and influence. These factors profoundly shape health systems and their functioning.

Also in this volume, we have learned about some strategies that are newly emerging as trials, while others have evolved over decades of experimentation, adaptation and growth. The strength of this survey lies in its

C. Canfield (✉)
University of British Columbia, Vancouver, BC, Canada
e-mail: carolyn.canfield@ubc.ca

M.-P. Pomey et al. (eds.), *Patient Engagement*, Organizational Behaviour in Healthcare,
https://doi.org/10.1007/978-3-030-14101-1_11

dramatic contrasts, inviting extraordinary scope for future development. From our position in this moment, what themes might we draw from such an array of meanings for patient knowledge and how its influence might affect healthcare? Can we discern a "direction of travel"?

Perhaps rather than a "cornerstone" as in this volume's title, patient knowledge might be seen more as a metaphoric sea anchor to help healthcare navigate on course for the patient, even while buffeted by the countervailing tempests of disruptive technology, management fads, open data access, research discoveries, escalating costs, emerging informatics, demographic forecasts, regulatory demands, novel compensation schemes, guidelines revisions, workforce instability, performance penalties, new drugs, public reporting, recruiting incentives, accreditation criteria and political opportunism. Consciousness of patient needs becomes a powerful touchstone to stay on track with the fundamental principles that must drive good healthcare: What helps patients live as well as possible? How would we know?

Improvement in practice, training, research, or any other healthcare sector starts most often with the system identifying gaps and what is needed to fill them. It is often quickly apparent that patient priorities may not only be divergent, but invisible to the system itself. Finding out what matters to patients may begin with the system forming the questions, asking and then recording essential care and service characteristics, as identified by patients. In the beginning, patient knowledge may seem to be an entity to be tapped in morsels when professionals feel the need to ornament a project with patient-centricity. Looking over the trajectory in these chapters, where patient knowledge is increasingly embedded in facets of various healthcare sectors, token gestures do not last long. It seems that more genuine patient-centredness is slowly but inexorably taking hold when patients begin to participate in person in a more dynamic and integrated collaboration throughout the lifecycle of a project.

Patient knowledge and patient participation are not synonymous. Perhaps they should be? That is, there can be little true patient knowledge without authentic participation. A nuanced knowledge of the invisible world of "patienthood" may only be revealed through trusted partnerships where patients and caregivers gain credibility, responsibility and even leadership. It is often noted that the patient and family's lived experience bridges all the siloes of settings and specialties, drawing healthcare workers together, sometimes for the first time. Only then is it possible to make real sense of the full health system. This revelation can powerfully impress health professionals on the team, as they realize how an isolated activity on the assembly line of the "medical industrial complex" may profoundly impact real human lives, far beyond the horizon of individual clinicians.

We have many examples of how transformative it may be to bring active participation of patients into service design and improvement, health professional training, governance and regulation, priority setting for research and improvement, and more. I have often heard health professionals say, "I'll never again assemble a team without patients on it". It seems no exaggeration to say that close collaboration throughout a project always produces unexpected and often profound personal learning and growth, quite beyond the intended patient knowledge. This discovery of such surprising meaning can powerfully counteract burnout and drudgery. Imagine the transformative power for either a new or a seasoned team member to hear revealed "what matters" when patients propose revealing outcome measures for a trial that otherwise would rely on conventional metrics. Simply engaging in such a discussion with patients can revitalize a researcher's or improvement leader's ambition, creativity, drive and satisfaction. Of course, the patients also feel encouraged and energized to learn about the health system and how change happens.

Gaining knowledge, then, will also be collaborative and shared. As professionals and patients work together, everyone learns how to listen actively, how to probe the unknown with sensitivity to clarify what is confusing and how to encourage acceptance of new perspectives to engender the necessary courage to take action for better care. This iterative process of building trust through collaboration not only amplifies the relevance and effectiveness of the work, but it can replenish energy and renew commitment and reward. Why would we not choose to work together in mutual exploration, when such profound results are at hand?

Another theme flowing from the growing experience with mobilizing patient knowledge addresses the moving target of "what matters to patients and carers". Conventional system-sourced terminology is crumbling before shifting redefinitions and refinement by patients. Patient knowledge alters and expands concepts like harm, risk, reward, values, costs, health versus unwellness, the burden of treatment and factors within quality of life. Lines become blurred between medical care and social care when patients describe their experiences of coordination failure. Already we see examples of administrative merging of healthcare and social welfare (e.g. Scotland, Finland). "Social prescribing" by physicians for non-medical help has begun with care teams expanding to include specialized community navigators to access housing, employment, transportation and education as components of healthy living.

To ask "what matters to the patient" invites the proliferation of individual definitions of wellness as care goals. No longer can the clinician determine the endpoints in an episode of care, as diagnosis and care planning rely on shared decision-making to achieve personal quality of life goals. With a demographically-driven shift from acute treatment to chronic condition management, health system services are no longer so hospital-centric, but more likely identified in the community by patients. As we look for opportunities to integrate individualized patient knowledge into healthcare systems, the idea of a patient or carer "representative" loses meaning. It is difficult to conceive of who might be "typical", much less what accountability might mean for similarly situated patients. Great value can be gained from individual patient knowledge without ascribing a generalized patient experience.

Engaging patients in co-design and co-production develops its potential best with a broad diversity of perspectives and a depth of collaboration. This relies in part on creating opportunities where patients actually live. Too often, it is the patients who must relocate and adapt to meet the narrow requirements, convenience and purposes of researchers, teachers, improvement specialists, governance councils and professional learners, wherever and whenever system institutions dictate. By contrast, sincere collaborations will also invest in developing the skills and orientation needed by patient partners, not just for a single task, but also for expanding patient-informed analysis and insight.

We have seen hierarchical models of care giving way to shared decision-making. We may not be far from the emergence of "patient-led" care as the next popular model. Individualized care finds resonance in new molecular and genetic science where our 'omics mediate our most effective meds and recommended care. The notion of an evidence-base for individualized care will rely on informatics tools that continuously tap into vast secure stores of personally-generated Big Data. We may come to see patient generated knowledge as present in many datasets, self-management aids and novel care settings, but selected and controlled by the patient.

In such a future, health literacy equips patients to pursue their personal evolving concepts of well-being over a lifetime. Such patient control would drive more care into the community. For systems to succeed in equitably offering self-directed care to individuals across whole populations seems daunting. Seamless continuity through closely-connected care teams joined up by this data river could support long and close relationships with the patient and community. In return, in fact, I can imagine no more gratifying and sustaining practice for health workers. Even when mediated by artificial intelligence and who knows what else, the core of good care will always aim to strengthen shared trust, as the truest practice for honouring patient knowledge.

Index

M.-P. Pomey et al. (eds.), *Patient Engagement*, Organizational Behaviour in Healthcare,
https://doi.org/10.1007/978-3-030-14101-1

Kolibri 360 GmbH
Ferdinand-Jühlke-Straße 7
99095 Erfurt, Deutschland
produktsicherheit@kolibri360.de